R-14

TWELVE ORIGINAL ESSAYS

is a collection of critical essays on important American novels, including The Scarlet Letter, Moby Dick, Huckleberry Finn, The Ambassadors, The Great Gatsby *and* Light in August. *Among the contributors are such important contemporary critics as Malcolm Cowley, Granville Hicks, George P. Elliott, John Aldridge, Mark Spilka and Alfred Kazin. Each essayist had complete freedom in discussing his chosen novel, and the result is an eclectic volume of criticism characterized by the writers' enthusiasm for their subjects.*

Charles Shapiro, the editor, is a well known writer on the contemporary American scene. His articles have appeared in the New Republic *and* The Nation.

This is a reprint of the original hardcover edition also published by Wayne State University Press.

LIBRARY
BRYAN COLLEGE
DAYTON, TN. 37321

TWELVE ORIGINAL ESSAYS

ON

GREAT AMERICAN NOVELS

EDITED BY CHARLES SHAPIRO

DETROIT • WAYNE STATE UNIVERSITY PRESS • 1958

45916

LIBRARY OF CONGRESS
CATALOG CARD NUMBER 57–13316

First printing, clothbound edition, January 1958
Second printing, paperbound edition, March 1959

COPYRIGHT 1958
WAYNE STATE UNIVERSITY PRESS
DETROIT 2, MICHIGAN

CONTENTS

v

INTRODUCTION

This collection of critical essays on twelve important American novels is a tribute to the variety and intensity of our contemporary critics. Each contributor has been given complete freedom to discuss his chosen book in any way he saw fit. As a result we have an eclectic approach, bound together only by each essayist's enthusiasm for his subject. These careful and often exciting studies should prove of value to those to whom literature is a vital part of life, offering new insights and, most important of all, stimulating a reading or rereading of the novels.

The American novel has survived being ignored, scorned, and cubbyholed. Communists, Neo-Humanists, super New Critics, scholars—all have been at work taking from the books only that material which fitted their purposes. Yet, despite the nibblings of the special pleaders and the PhD candidates, the novels remain as part of our American experience—to be studied, discussed, and loved. For as George P. Elliott remarks in his essay on *Huckleberry Finn*, "a novel is not just a work of art: it is, somehow, a work of life as well."

Art, according to Edmund Wilson, "is that which gives meaning to experience," and as I hope to point out in my piece on *Jennie Gerhardt*, our experiences and their translation into fiction are many and diverse. A book such as *The Deerslayer*, for example, may seem oddly remote from us, yet David Brion Davis shows how some of our modern problems are boldly outlined in Cooper's novel. The avaricious trapper, the saintly, heroic Leatherstocking, symbolize "possible meanings of the American democracy." The trapper becomes "one of the unhappy concomitants to continental expansion," while Leatherstocking, crude and naive, demonstrates the potentialities of our frontier society.

Later on, the American hero would become more cunning, less innocent. An admirable contrast to Leatherstocking is found in F. Scott Fitzgerald's Gatsby, described by John Aldridge as "a major figure in the legend created by the complex fate of being American." Gatsby, a self-appointed modern agent for the American Dream, is "the hero of the tragic limitations of that fate in the modern, materialistic world." And Aldridge finds dramatic justification for a scene at the close of the novel where Nick tells of Gatsby's aspiration "to the feelings aroused in the early Dutch voyagers to America by their first glimpse of the 'fresh green breast of the new world.'"

We learn about America, but we also learn about our-

volume was in the daydream stage. I would especially like to thank Dr. Richard Ellmann of Northwestern University, Dr. Newton P. Stallknecht of Indiana University, Professor Alexander Brede, Editor, and Dr. Harold Basilius, Director, of Wayne State University Press. Above all, I am indebted to the contributors who gave of their time, energy, and wisdom.

I am dedicating this book to the memory of Dr. Richard Hudson.

C. S.

THE DEERSLAYER, A DEMOCRATIC KNIGHT OF THE WILDERNESS

COOPER, 1841

by **DAVID BRION DAVIS**

In the Leatherstocking series Fenimore Cooper hoped to create the Great American Epic. Like Cotton Mather and Joel Barlow in earlier generations, he was convinced that American history offered a theme equal, if not superior, to the themes of Homer and Virgil. For Cooper, as for many of his countrymen, there was no subject with greater drama and significance than the destiny of Christian morality in the American wilderness. More explicitly, he was concerned with the relation between Christian morality and the skills necessary in America for survival and exploitation, the skills esteemed and cultivated by the self-sufficient and individualistic woodsman hero. An attempt to combine Homeric heroism and Christian sainthood in the figure of the American pioneer was doomed to certain failure, but it was a magnificent failure, and, in a larger sense, America's failure. In spite of his serious faults as a convincing character, Leatherstocking stands as not only the greatest, but as the prototype, of American fictional heroes. With all his shortcomings as an artist Cooper must be taken as one of the few writers whose imagination gave form to American ideals, and whose plots, however juvenile, dealt directly with problems basic to the American experience.

Although *The Deerslayer* was the last of the Leatherstocking tales to be published (appearing in 1841, nineteen years after *The Pioneers*), chronologically it is the first of the five romances which trace the history of Leatherstocking from the first test of manhood to the noble exploits of an aged Odysseus on the American prairies. Thus Cooper concluded the saga by returning to his hero's youth, to " the first war-path " (the subtitle of the romance), and we must not forget that the callow hunter who exclaims in wonder at the shimmering expanse of Lake Otsego was conceived in the light of a mature Leatherstocking, whose character had been fully developed in previous tales. As a result, *The Deerslayer* is not the story of a youth showing promise of future heroism, but is rather a portrayal of the fresh innocence, spontaneous honesty, and supreme courage of a famous hero's early manhood.

It is impossible to understand Cooper, or for that matter the mass of popular adventure fiction indebted to him, unless we recognize that his narratives were intended to reveal ideal modes of action. Cooper was primarily a moralist, that is to say, an expounder of a particular code of morality, not a philosopher seeking moral truth in the ambiguities of human experience. While he strove to arouse interest and suspense, his contrived episodes were but devices for conveying moral values in specific terms. The rather monotonous rhythm of capture and escape does not represent a genuine and unpredictable struggle between human beings. On the contrary, the intense concentration on physical action illustrates fixed differences in individual skill and morality. Cooper's characters are essentially unchanging, ideal types, and he was more interested in showing facets of each character as revealed by varieties of physical experience than in tracing the development or fulfillment of a given person. If his tales sacrifice psychological reality, they succeed in portraying the social significance of contrasting states of morality.

Before turning to the moral implications of the romance, however, we must first briefly summarize the action, for it is only in action that Cooper's characters reveal their fundamental differences. In his tale of the first war path Cooper's narrative covers only six days and the action is limited to the shores and surface of Lake Otsego, or the Glimmerglass. It is a summer in the early 1740's, and war has just broken out between the English and the French, leaving the Otsego country, though nominally British, a kind of no-man's land between hostile forces. Cooper incorrectly places the Hurons on the side of the French, while making the Delawares, who are supposed to be morally superior to the Iroquois, loyal to England. Deerslayer has been reared by the Delawares, but his Indian training in hunting and warfare has been softened somewhat by the Christian pietism of Moravian missionaries. Before the story opens, Deerslayer has set out alone through the forest for the Glimmerglass, where he plans a rendezvous with Chingachgook, an

Indian friend. The purpose of the expedition is to help Chingachgook rescue his betrothed, the beautiful Delaware maiden, Wah-ta!-Wah (the Wild Rose), who has been kidnapped by a Delaware traitor and taken to a Huron camp.

Traveling toward the Glimmerglass, which he has never seen before, Deerslayer meets and accompanies Hurry Harry, a gigantic young hunter bound for the same country. Harry is returning to the lake to woo Judith Hutter, a coquettish, beautiful, and high-spirited girl who is visited frequently by hunters and English officers from the settlements, and who lives at the lake with her father and half-witted sister Hetty. Tom Hutter is not, however, the real father of Judith and Hetty, but a former pirate who took the girls, their mother, and a chest of booty to the Glimmerglass, where he traps muskrat and lives securely beyond the reach of the law. The three Hutters (for the mother died) live in a "castle" built on a shoal in the lake, but spend part of their time in a houseboat or "ark" which is used for trapping and which in war-time gives the family command of the Glimmerglass.

On the first day of the narrative Deerslayer and Harry arrive at the lake, Deerslayer is introduced to the Hutters, and a band of Hurons makes a surprise attack on the ark. The Hurons, who are returning to the Canadas from a hunting trip, have just learned of the war and hope to take scalps to the French for bounties. If the Hutters and their friends can protect themselves for a few days, and keep the Hurons from capturing a canoe and gaining access to the castle, they are sure to be saved by British soldiers from the settlements. But while the men succeed in securing all available canoes, Tom Hutter and Hurry Harry are captured by the Hurons when they foolishly launch a night

man, but Davy Crockett and Mike Fink were more like the boastful and swaggering Hurry Harry than like Roland or Galahad. Could the illiterate woodsman, whose distinction lay in his acute senses, his highly developed forest skills, and his astonishing marksmanship, become an appropriate hero for a Christian society? To understand Cooper's answer we must examine the hero's relationship to nature, his participation in war, and his response to the opposite sex.

We have said that Cooper, like the Puritans, was concerned with the destiny of Christian morality in the wilderness. We should add, however, that Cooper found the source of morality in the wilderness itself and not in the protection and preservation of European civil society. To give religious sanction to his American hero, Cooper was forced to convert the uncouth and desolate backwoods into the unspoiled and shimmering world of God's original creation. In *The Deerslayer* trees and lakes and hills are not simply objects to be perceived, or obstacles to be overcome by civilization; they are, Cooper emphasizes, the essentially unchanged creations of God, and behind their serenity and natural harmony lies the divine law of the universe. The American wilderness is the world of Genesis, fresh, dazzling, still emanating the divine spirit of its origin. Though Deerslayer's first war path takes place in a small area of New York, the timeless quality of the virgin forest, which stretches from the Hudson to the prairie, gives it a representative, even a cosmic, significance. The six days of action seem to echo the cycle of creation, and Cooper stresses the movement of the sun, earth, and heavens when describing the dawning and fading of light on the basin of the Glimmerglass. When Deerslayer first beholds the sparkling sheet of water, he is glad it has not yet been named. In

11

the American wilderness man is free from rigid and meaningless conventions of traditional speech, from sterile logic and dry classification, and when lakes or warriors receive a name, it corresponds exactly with the thing. Cooper succeeds admirably in conveying the delight of man in intimate harmony with nature, beholding and naming creation for the first time.

If man is closest to the divine spirit in a virgin forest, it is because civilization distracts him from nature by accentuating his greed and selfishness. According to Deerslayer, people in the settlements think always of their own ends, and decay comes not as the natural cycle of life, but as the untimely consequence of waste and violence. Cooper makes it clear that previous contact with civilization is responsible for Hutter's avarice, for Harry's blind prejudice, and for Judith's vanity. Muskrat castle is a tiny point of civilization, a dissonance on the tranquil sheet of the Glimmerglass, and it is this single discordant note which breaks the peaceful harmony of nature. Throughout the tale violence revolves around this isolated and fortified castle which suggests the abrupt intrusion of civilization and the imminent corruption of natural creation.

Yet Hutter's residence is only partly a castle, for in the owner's absence on the first day, Deerslayer and Hurry Harry enter it as freely as if it were part of the landscape. A house in the American forest is never a permanent nor a truly private castle. It is always possible that such a dwelling will eventually be reclaimed by nature. On the other hand, the pirate chest is securely private and totally alien to nature. Even in an emergency Deerslayer will not touch it without Judith's permission. The buried sins and mysteries of the chest emphasize the contrast between civilization and the American forest. Moreover, the contents of the chest, unlike the castle, can never be adapted for use in the wilderness. Deerslayer's reaction to the chest and its contents suggests both his identity with the forest and his freedom from contamination by society. He first denounces the chess men as idols, which they in fact become in the eyes of the Hurons. Both the chess pieces and the brocaded gown fail to bring peace, as Judith hopes they will, and Deerslayer warns the beautiful maiden that the dress was not meant for her, that it is an unnatural and even immoral garment in the American forest. We remember the warning when, at the end of the tale, Captain Warley's desire is reawakened by the sight of Judith in the magnificent dress. Even a pistol which Deerslayer takes from the chest explodes in his hand, a final symbol of the evil and decay resulting from a misuse of these articles of civilized life. Gowns, pistols, and chess pieces did not inherently embody an evil principle, but they easily distracted man's attention, and in the wilderness they were totally out of place.

At the core of Cooper's romanticism was the belief that human character is pure or corrupt according to its degree of harmony with nature. Nature in its true glory and divinity was a kind of Holy Grail which could be seen only by the purest of heart. But if harmony with nature was limited to the morally elect, it also sanctified the martial skills of the American knight. Cooper noted that European poets chose sunset as the hour of revery, when man reached a sad and ephemeral union with nature; yet in the American wilderness sunrise was a holier moment, for then the increasing clarity of light led the mind to sublime and far-reaching thoughts. In *The Deerslayer* the most dramatic episodes occur at sunrise, when, according to Cooper, the

13

senses recover their original powers of accurate and undistracted perception. In the almost liquid lucidity of morning air, certain men acquire an acuteness of sight and smell and perceive the true nature of physical objects, as well as the simplicity and beauty of moral truths. At dawn the sparkling and bewitching clarity of atmosphere brings a sharpening of aesthetic, moral, and physical senses, since man is at such moments in subtle harmony with the inner rhythms of nature. Yet Hurry Harry and Tom Hutter, whose *moral* senses have been stunted by civilization, are blind both to beauties and hidden dangers in the morning hours. Only Deerslayer and Chingachgook perform extraordinary feats at sunrise. By uniting the physical, moral, and aesthetic senses with nature, Cooper succeeded in relating physical prowess to moral perfection and an appreciation for beauty.

Images of the lake and forest dominate Cooper's descriptions. The forest is irregular, mysterious, and physical in an almost sexual sense (Cooper frequently dwells on the "matted and wild luxuriance of a virgin American forest"). Throughout the tale the forest is a place of danger and surprise, at one moment deathly silent and at the next moment swarming with murderous Indians. Cooper likened forest scenes to the tenebrous paintings of Salvator Rosa, and even the illiterate Deerslayer is sensitive to the fascinating contrasts of "the picturesque."

But despite his love for the dense and tangled forest, Deerslayer is truly inspired only at an open spot where an expansive view conveys the idea of God's majesty and man's creaturehood. It is the wide expansiveness of the Glimmerglass that evokes in Deerslayer a sentiment half-poetic, half-religious, which is something more than response to the

14

picturesque. For example, when observing the picturesque and barbaric scene of Indians in the flickering light of campfires, Deerslayer is tensely fascinated, his excited senses alert for instant action; but suspended in a canoe on the calm sheet of the Glimmerglass, he experiences the repose and spiritual uplift of one in the presence of the sublime. The contrast of forest and lake, of picturesque and sublime, of sudden violence and peaceful solitude, tends to harmonize the hero's feats of physical skill and bravery with his Christian selflessness and humility before God's works. Thus nature insulates Deerslayer from the corruptions of civilization, and at the same time purifies his acts of violence by relating them to the natural rhythms and contrasts of the wilderness. Just as lake and forest merge into a harmonious unity when seen from a distance, so serenity and martial skills finally combine in the figure of the woodsman hero.

When we turn from Deerslayer's relationship with nature to his participation in war, we should perhaps remind ourselves that the Leatherstocking tales are dominated by the theme of killing Indians. In *The Deerslayer* Cooper was concerned with racial war beyond the boundaries of human justice, and with the circumstances and morality of a young American's first homicide. More than forty years before Cooper wrote, Charles Brockden Brown had described the ritual of a young man killing his first Indian victim, but in Brown's novel the act was a "loathsome obligation" followed by anguish and remorse. In the frontier tales of the 1830's and 1840's, however, it was almost necessary for the heroic youth to establish himself as a free American citizen by "killing his brute," as it was termed by Robert Montgomery Bird. Certainly many Americans had actually experienced the killing of an Indian as part of the process of maturity. Writers had a certain justification for dwelling upon the ritual, since it signified the free white man's possession of the rights and privileges of his civilization, a racial eucharist, granting secular freedom and wealth after the sacrifice of a red man's flesh and blood. But even a ritualistic slaying may involve guilt, especially when the victim represents a persecuted and dispossessed race.

In the opening pages of *The Deerslayer* we learn that the hero has never shed human blood, his unusual fame as a hunter notwithstanding, and that the loss of this innocence is to be one of the themes of the tale. Hurry Harry, the crude but experienced braggart, chides Deerslayer the same way an older soldier might tease an obviously virginal recruit. According to Harry, a man is not a man until he has killed and scalped an Indian. As a test of skill and training, Deerslayer looks forward modestly to his first combat, but he condones neither scalping nor wanton killing. As we have seen, Harry's lust for scalps nearly brings destruction to the company of white characters. Although he feels guilt after needlessly taking human life, he projects this guilt on the victims themselves, arguing that Indians are subhuman monsters who do not deserve to live. Blind to the glories of nature, Harry is consequently inferior to Deerslayer in both skill and morality. Living beyond the reach of human law, his brutal aggressiveness condoned by a government which offers bounties for scalps, Hurry Harry leaves a wake of evil and suffering behind him.

In contrast, Deerslayer approaches his first combat in the solitude and tranquility of daybreak. Drifting softly in a canoe toward a seemingly deserted point of land, he is in perfect harmony with the sublime rhythms of light, air, and mirror-like water. The combat itself is a lyrical movement of graceful and faultless skill against a background of singing birds and the shining sky of sunrise. Deerslayer is calm and gracious, yet his muscles and animal senses are prepared for instantaneous and deadly action. He is like a champion bullfighter who shows profound respect for his antagonist, but who gracefully and deliberately risks his life, in every way maximizing the danger to himself, while at the same times maintaining exquisite control over his dangerous enemy. Refusing to take advantage of the Huron, Deerslayer shoots only in self-defense, after the Indian has attacked him. The Huron dies in his conqueror's arms, rewarding Deerslayer with a new name, Hawkeye, and the hunter concludes in a melancholy mood that the brave's treachery, like his own marksmanship, is a racial gift. Deerslayer had not desired the Indian's death, and doubted the virtue of any killing, yet he reflects that he had acted only according to his training and his God-given nature.

In his sympathy and respect for the hostile savage, Deerslayer redeemed his less sensitive brothers. Even the Huron mistook him for a missionary at first, when the hunter observed that the world was large enough for both of them. But in spite of his Moravian ideals, Deerslayer had the power and skill to shoot a human being, and in one sense, this soft-hearted, musing hero was but America's gesture of apology to a vanquished foe. A sordid fact of American history was purified when the woodsman killed the noble savage in this idyll of death in the midst of unspoiled nature.

However, Deerslayer's aggression is justified not only by his intimacy with nature, but also by his relation to woman. On the second night, when Deerslayer and Chingachgook are alone for the first time, the Indian gazes in-

17

tently at his young friend, obviously aware that the hunter is no longer the callow youth he had once known. Deerslayer finally confirms Chingachgook's suspicions, and admits that he has killed a brave. Previously, he had hoped for a chance to tell Chingachgook that he had not disgraced his Delaware training, and now Deerslayer is obviously pleased by the Indian's delight. Like one youth telling another of his first sexual conquest, Deerslayer is proud of his newly-won manhood. But the hunter's pride in physical combat can be excused, for Cooper at least, only by a negation of true sexuality. If Deerslayer is partly a Homeric warrior, he is also a Christian saint whose sanctity requires an ascetic life.

Soon after the first combat Deerslayer is alone with Judith and Hetty, since the other male characters are still captives of the Hurons. When Judith asks him about the shots she has heard, he modestly admits that he has been true to his gifts and has fought and killed an Indian while defending the canoes. Judith, who has known Deerslayer for less than a day, caresses his hand and admires his bravery. After her bitter experiences with the flattery of smooth-voiced officers and predatory frontiersmen like Hurry Harry, she is much attracted by the unassuming bravery and soft-spoken honesty of Deerslayer. His tale of Chingachgook's pursuit of the kidnapped Wah-ta!-Wah gives Judith a chance to talk of love. But when asked about his own sweetheart, Deerslayer replies that he loves only the soft rain in the forest, clouds floating in a blue sky, the dew of the morning, or the sweet water of natural springs. The wilderness he describes is a succession of water images, culminating in the sublime Glimmerglass itself. Despite Judith's free glances and forward manner, Deerslayer is un-

18

DATE DUE

Perhaps the most tender contact between the two lovers was when Judith gave Deerslayer her father's magnificent rifle, Killdeer. Unlike the pistol which nearly wounded Judith when it exploded, Killdeer is a safe and appropriate weapon for Leatherstocking, though after needlessly shooting an eagle he questions his right to possess so fine a rifle. Only after Deerslayer has proved his asceticism, his innocent purity, and his unity with nature, does he feel truly justified in carrying this symbol of masculine destructiveness.

Fifteen years after the end of the tale, Deerslayer and Chingachgook returned to the Glimmerglass, now deserted and hushed by the stillness of the primeval forest. On the eastern shore the Hutters' ark lay stranded, weather-beaten, and filled with water. We are told that Deerslayer's heart quickened when he found one of Judith's ribbons fluttering from a log. He had not loved her, Cooper adds, but he "still retained a kind and sincere interest in her welfare." The ribbon recalled both her beauty and her failings, and Deerslayer knotted it to the stock of Killdeer as a souvenir. His triumph was now complete. He flew a lady's colors from his weapon as a sign of his tenderness and warmth of heart, but the American knight's strange purity was untainted by love.

In *The Deerslayer* the young Leatherstocking kills his first Indian, wins his reputation as a hero, and protects his chastity. The tale has about it the peculiar freshness and melancholy of a youth entering manhood, which in the American wilderness was signified by the first war path. Rejection of woman and unity with nature are fused in a heroic ideal which distinguishes Deerslayer from Hurry Harry, whose violence is unsanctified by either asceticism or the touch of sublime nature. Deerslayer's aggressive

21

actions acquire moral sanction when he negates his sexuality and dedicates himself to a life in the maternal forest. If Cooper failed to convert the crude American hunter into a Homeric hero and Christian saint, he did invent a beautiful myth which embodied American fears, ideals, and values. In subsequent literature the American hero was, above all, a figure combining deadly skills with social innocence. Only harmony with the divine rhythms of uncorrupted nature could soften his terrifying efficiency at destruction and exploitation.

FIVE ACTS OF *THE SCARLET LETTER*

HAWTHORNE, 1850

by MALCOLM COWLEY

When he finished *The Scarlet Letter* in 1850, at the age of forty-five, Nathaniel Hawthorne had accomplished something new in his own career and something new in the craft of fiction. By accident or design he had invented a form that was closer to stage drama than it was to ordinary novels. That was perhaps the greatest of his technical achievements, and I plan to discuss it at some length, but it was not the last of them. In the first of his four romances, as he called them, he had also applied to a longer work the exacting standards that he and Edgar Poe, working separately, had developed in writing their tales or short stories.

Poe had defined the standards eight years before, when he reviewed and praised the second edition of *Twice-Told*

Tales. The skillful writer of tales, he said, does not fashion his thoughts to accommodate his incidents. No, "having conceived, with deliberate care, a certain unique or single *effect* to be wrought out, he then invents such incidents— he then combines such events as may best aid him in establishing this preconceived effect. If his very initial sentence tend not to the outbringing of this effect, then he has failed in his first step. In the whole composition there should be no word written of which the tendency, direct or indirect, is not to the one pre-established design." Thus, unity of effect and economy of means were two of the principal standards by which Poe judged the short story. He did not think that the two could be enforced in a novel or in any other work too long to be finished at a single reading. In his one book-length story, *The Narrative of Arthur Gordon Pym*, he did not even try to enforce them; after starting with a realistic story of boys on the waterfront, he launched into a grotesque recital of horrors at sea and ended with a Freudian nightmare of returning to the womb. It remained for Hawthorne to make the attempt in *The Scarlet Letter*— that is, to conceive "a certain unique or single effect" and then to invent such incidents, but only such, as would help him to re-establish the effect in a reader's mind.

He was thereby disregarding another standard, one that was accepted by the leading critics of the time and even by Hawthorne himself when he thought in critical terms. The critics were imbued with what they called the Shakespearian principle that the tragic should be mingled with the comic in any longer work; their ideal was the drunken porter grumbling while fate knocked at the gate. Although most of them praised Hawthorne's novel, they complained about the lack of comic relief. "In his next work," said E. P.

24

Whipple, who was Hawthorne's favorite among them, " we hope to have a romance equal to *The Scarlet Letter* in pathos and power, but more relieved by touches of that beautiful and peculiar humor, so serene and searching, in which he excels almost all living writers." Hawthorne agreed with the criticism, as he showed when writing his next novel, *The House of the Seven Gables*, which presented a mixture of moods, somber and humorous, romantic and realistic; it was " a work," he said a little less self-perceptively than was his custom, " more characteristic of my mind." But he also reported, in a letter to his publisher, that the writing of it went more slowly and seemed more laborious than that of *The Scarlet Letter*.

His first romance was written by a sort of inner compulsion that would be reawakened at moments in his later career, but never with quite the same driving power. The theme of secret guilt and public confession was one that had haunted him all his life. The controlling symbol of the scarlet A was one over which he had been brooding for many years. When he finally started writing the book, after a series of personal disasters—the loss of his position in the custom house, the death of his mother, illness in the family, and the threat of destitution—he worked on it like a man possessed by Satan. " *The Scarlet Letter*," he told his friend Horatio Bridge, " is positively a hell-fired story into which I found it almost impossible to throw any cheering light." But writing it seemed easy, so long as he followed the bent and inclination of his mind. " I had only to get my pitch," he told his publisher, " and then could go on interminably." Written all in one pitch, *The Scarlet Letter* was the first novel in English—perhaps in any language, considering that the book appeared six years before *Madame Bovary*—that

had the unity of effect and the strict economy of means of a perfect tale.

The symbol of the scarlet A had first appeared as a detail in one of Hawthorne's New England legends, "Endicott and the Red Cross," published in 1838. There, in describing the colonists who watched a muster of Endicott's trainband, he had mentioned "likewise a young woman, with no mean share of beauty, whose doom it was to wear the letter A on the breast of her gown, in the eyes of all the world and her own children." Six years later the detail reappeared in one of his notebooks, this time as the plot of a new story he planned to write. Here are a few of the other notebook entries that, as he brooded over the symbol, eventually grouped themselves around the central theme of Hester's public atonement:

1838.   A perception, for a moment, of one's eventual and moral self, as if it were another person,—the observant faculty being separated, and looking intently at the qualities of the character. There is a surprise when this happens,—this getting out of one's self,—and then the observer sees how queer a fellow he is.

In Chapter XIV of *The Scarlet Letter* we read that poor Chillingworth "lifted his hands with a look of horror, as if he had beheld some frightful shape, which he could not recognize, usurping the place of his own image in the glass. It was one of those moments—which sometimes occur only at the interval of years—when a man's moral aspect is faithfully revealed to his mind's eye."

1838.   Character of a man who, in himself and his external circumstances, shall be equally and totally

false: his fortune resting on baseless credit,—his patriotism assumed,—his domestic affections, his honor and honesty, all a sham. His own misery in the midst of it,—making the whole universe, heaven and earth alike, an unsubstantial mockery to him.

Hawthorne would say of the Reverend Mr. Dimmesdale, at the end of Chapter XI, "It is the unspeakable misery of a life so false as his, that it steals the pith and substance out of whatever realities there are around us, and which were meant by Heaven to be the spirit's joy and nutriment. To the untrue man, the whole universe is false, —it is impalpable,—it shrinks to nothing within his grasp. And he himself, in so far as he shows himself in a false light, becomes a shadow, or, indeed, ceases to exist."

1838.   Dr. Johnson's penance in Uttoxeter Market. A man who does penance in what might appear to lookers-on the most glorious and triumphal circumstance of his life. Each circumstance of the career of an apparently successful man to be a penance and torture to him on account of some fundamental error in early life.

Arthur Dimmesdale's career is a torture and a penance, merely intensified by his outward success; and at the moment when he rises to "the very proudest eminence of superiority, to which the gifts of intellect, rich lore, prevailing eloquence, and a reputation of whitest sanctity, could exalt a clergyman in New England's earliest days," he leaves the triumphal procession to stand with his former mistress on the scaffold of the pillory.

27

1841.   To symbolize moral or spiritual disease by a disease of the body;—thus, when a person committed any sin, it might cause a sore to appear on the body; this to be wrought out.

There is a scarlet A imprinted on Dimmesdale's flesh; "and those best able to appreciate the minister's peculiar sensibility, and the wonderful operation of his spirit upon the body . . . whispered their belief, that the awful symbol was the effect of the ever-active tooth of remorse, gnawing from the inmost heart outwardly, and at last manifesting Heaven's dreadful judgment by the visible presence of the letter."

1842.   A physician for the cure of moral diseases.

This is one of several notebook entries in which Hawthorne seems to be thinking in terms of what would afterward be called psychoanalysis and psychosomatic therapy. In Chapter X, "The Leech and His Patient," Chillingworth assumes the role of analyst. "You, Sir," he says to Dimmesdale, "of all the men whom I have known, are he whose body is the closest conjoined, and imbued, and identified, so to speak, with the spirit whereof it is the instrument. . . . Thus, a sickness . . . a sore place, if we may so call it, in your spirit, hath immediately its appropriate manifestation in your bodily frame. Would you, therefore, that your physician heal the bodily evil? How may this be, unless you first lay open to him the wound or trouble in your soul? "

1842.   Pearl—the English of Margaret—a pretty name for a girl in a story.

1842.   In moods of heavy despondency, one feels as if it would be delightful to sink down in some quiet spot, and lie there forever, letting the soil gradually accumulate and form a little hillock over us, and the grass and perhaps flowers gather over it. At such times, death is too much of an event to be wished for;—we have not spirits to encounter it;

but choose to pass out of existence in this sluggish way.

At the end of Chapter XVI, before his meeting with Hester and little Pearl, Dimmesdale walks through the forest with a listlessness in his gait, " as if he saw no reason for taking one step farther, nor felt any desire to do so, but would have been glad, could he be glad of anything, to fling himself down at the root of the nearest tree, and lie there passive, for evermore. The leaves might bestrew him, and the soil gradually accumulate and form a little hillock over his frame, no matter whether there were life in it or no. Death was too definite an object to be wished for or avoided." This is a passage that Hawthorne seems to have written with the notebook open in front of him. He had started that practice in " Ethan Brand," which was written, probably, a year before *The Scarlet Letter*. In his last years the practice would become an obsessive habit, with the result that more than two-thirds of *The Marble Faun* would be copied directly from his Roman notebooks.

1844.   The Unpardonable Sin might consist in a want of love and reverence for the Human Soul; in consequence of which the investigator pried into its dark depths, not with a hope or purpose of making it better, but from a cold philosophical curiosity,— content that it should be wicked in whatever kind or degree, and only desiring to study it out. Would not this, in other words, be the separation of the intellect from the heart?

1844.   The life of a woman, who, by the old colony law, was condemned always to wear the letter A, sewed on her garment, in token of her having committed adultery.

There is no indication in the notebooks that Hawthorne

29

was immediately conscious of having found a theme for the novel he had long been planning to write. But he had the habit of patient meditation, and many of his ideas gradually rearranged themselves around this new center. The idea of the Unpardonable Sin was of course to be used in "Ethan Brand," but it would reappear in the novel—with other ideas from some of his earlier stories, notably "Young Goodman Brown" and "The Minister's Black Veil." Chillingworth commits the Unpardonable Sin as a means of wreaking his revenge on Dimmesdale. The minister says of him in Chapter XVII, "We are not, Hester, the worst sinners in the world. There is one worse than even the polluted priest! That old man's revenge has been blacker than my sin. He has violated, in cold blood, the sanctity of a human heart."

1845.   In the eyes of a young child, or other innocent
        person, the image of a cherub or an angel to be seen
        peeping out;—in those of a vicious person, a devil.

Sometimes an angel can be seen peeping from the eyes of little Pearl; but once, in Chapter VI, when Hester looks into them she sees "a face, fiend-like, full of smiling malice . . . as if an evil spirit possessed the child, and had just then peeped forth in mockery." A diabolical light often glimmers out of Chillingworth's eyes; in Chapter X it is "burning blue and ominous, like the reflection of a furnace, or, let us say, like one of those gleams of ghastly fire that darted from Bunyan's awful doorway in the hillside."

1845.   It was believed by the Catholics that children
        might be begotten by intercourse between demons
        and witches. Luther was said to be a bastard of this
        hellish breed.

At the end of Chapter VI, some of the townspeople

assert "that poor little Pearl was a demon offspring; such as, ever since old Catholic times, had occasionally been seen on earth, through the agency of their mother's sin, and to promote some foul and wicked purpose. Luther, according to the scandal of his monkish enemies, was a brat of that hellish breed."

1847.   A story of the effects of revenge, in diaboling him who indulges in it.

In Chapter XIV Chillingworth is offered as "a striking evidence of man's faculty of transforming himself into a devil, if he will only, for a reasonable space of time, undertake a devil's office." The old physician says of Dimmesdale that he fancied himself given over to a fiend. "But it was the constant shadow of my presence!" he continues, "—the closest propinquity of the man whom he had most vilely wronged!—and who had grown to exist only by this perpetual poison of the direst revenge! Yea, indeed!—he did not err!—there was a field at his elbow! A mortal man, with once a human heart, has become a fiend for his especial torment!"

During the spring and summer of 1849, Hawthorne was occupied with family and business worries—his mother's illness and the political intrigues against him that did not end when he lost his post in the custom house—with the result that he scarcely tried to do any serious work. He had time, however, for some unusually long entries in his notebooks, most of them concerned with the behavior of his children: Julian, aged three, and Una, aged five. He looked at them with a father's eye, but also with the capacity for absolutely detached observation that he retained even at his mother's deathbed, in "the darkest hour I ever lived."

31

Part of one entry, written on July 30, the day before his mother died, shows clearly how Una was serving as the model for Hester's only half-angelic brat:

> . . . there is something that almost frightens me about the child—I know not whether elfin or angelic, but, at all events, supernatural. She steps so boldly into the midst of everything, shrinks from nothing, has such a comprehension of everything, seems at times to have but little delicacy, and anon shows that she possesses the finest essence of it; now so hard, now so tender; now so perfectly unreasonable, soon again so wise. In short, I now and then catch an aspect of her, in which I cannot believe her to be my own human child, but a spirit strangely mingled with good and evil, haunting the house where I dwell.

At this point, after brooding over the subject for eleven years or more, Hawthorne had fixed the time and place of his novel and had chosen the strands that would be woven into the plot. He had found his four essential characters: the woman condemned to public penance, the man who suffered even more from concealing his guilt, their unearthly child, and the wronged husband diabolized by his revenge. There were important technical problems still to be solved, and they happen to be the ones that particularly interest us today, but Hawthorne does not mention them in his working notebooks. Although we know that he solved them brilliantly, we cannot be certain whether it was by conscious reasoning or simply by his instinct for what, in the special circumstances, was right.

Perhaps the first of the technical problems was one of social background. The persons of Hawthorne's story existed in relation to a particular society, whose standards—

which they fully accepted—intensified their guilt and lent drama to their atonement. How could the society be brought directly into the story—not merely talked about and explained by the author, but presented in life? Hawthorne's solution was to invent a few additional characters, not to be studied in depth, but merely to be put forward as representatives of the society in its essential aspects. Three of these characters are Governor Bellingham (representing the secular authorities), the Reverend John Wilson (representing sanctity), and Mistress Hibbins the witch-lady (representing evil and rebellion inside the community). Except for the four principals—and except for Master Brackett the jailer, mentioned in passing—these are the only named persons in the story; but there are also two unnamed characters of some importance. One is a Bristol shipmaster, representing the moral freedom or indifference of the world outside, and the other is the Boston crowd, which, at the beginning and the end of the story, speaks in the voices of complacent ignorance.

The author has some comments of his own to offer, and they sometimes seem obtrusive to readers trained in the impersonal technique of more recent fiction, but they are not essential to our understanding of the story. Except in the last chapter—which is an epilogue conceived in the expository manner of other early nineteenth-century writers —Hawthorne lets his characters act out their fates. No information is needed by the reader beyond that suggested by the behavior of the characters or imparted in their dialogues. The action of the novel is completely an *interaction* among four persons in a particular environment that is also presented in its own terms. Hawthorne had solved the problem of social background in a fashion that enabled him

to write, for the first time in American literature, a novel that was a completely framed and self-subsistent work of art.

There was, however, another technical problem that required a more radical solution, arising as it did from the author's special experience and cast of mind. Until that time the novel in all its forms had been essentially a chronicle of events, and Hawthorne had no great talent or practice as a chronicler. When a very young man he had written a short and artlessly romantic novel called *Fanshawe*, which demonstrated not very much except that its author admired Sir Walter Scott and, in pure story telling, could never hope to equal him. Feeling ashamed of the little book, Hawthorne had withdrawn it from circulation and had destroyed every copy on which he could lay his hands. In the twenty years since *Fanshawe* he had written nothing else of equal length, but he had published nearly a hundred tales or sketches, and these had given a special direction to his thinking. What he had learned from writing them was, among other lessons, how to work intensively in smaller forms and how to present his subjects as moral essays or allegorical pictures rather than as continually moving narratives.

His final problem, then, was to devise some method by which a larger theme could be adjusted to his training and personality as a writer. It was the solution he found, whether by reason or instinct, that became the truly important technical innovation in *The Scarlet Letter*. Instead of conceiving the novel as a single or double narrative moving ahead in a straight or zigzag line and revealing the social landscape as if to the eyes of a traveler on horseback, Hawthorne approached it dramatistically, almost as if his char-

34

acters were appearing on a stage. Instead of dividing his book into narrative episodes—now the hero falls in love, now he fights a duel, now he escapes from prison—Hawthorne divided it into scenes, each of which is a posed tableau or a dramatic confrontation. The advantage of the method for this particular author was that it enabled him to work on each scene intensively, almost as if it were a separate tale. Although there was little movement within the separate scenes, he could create a general sense of movement by passing rapidly from one scene to another, for example, from the marketplace at night to the seashore and thence to the forest. Unity of mood was not one of his problems—that had already been achieved by his years of brooding over the central symbol—but the method enabled him to give the book architectural unity as well, by balancing one scene against another and by ending the story where it really began, on the scaffold of the pillory.

This dramatistic method followed by Hawthorne was also, in effect, the "divine principle" that Henry James would rediscover in 1895, when he went back to writing fiction after the failure of his career as a playwright. "Has a *part* of all this wasted passion and squandered time (of the last 5 years)," James would ask in his notebook shortly after having been hissed from the stage at the first night of *Guy Domville*—has part of it "been simply the precious lesson, taught me in that roundabout and devious, that cruelly expensive, way, *of the singular value for a narrative plan too* of the (I don't know *what* adequately to call it) divine principle of the Scenario?" It was the principle that enabled him to achieve what he called his *big* effects—"scenic, constructive, 'architectural'"—and he would follow it in all the novels of his later years. "Yes, I *see* thus, I

think, my little *act* of my little drama here," he said in his notebook when he was working on *What Maisie Knew.* " Ah, this *divine* conception of one's little masses and periods in the scenic light, as rounded ACTS: this patient, pious, nobly ' vindicative ' application of the scenic philosophy and method—I feel as if it *still* (above *all*, YET) had a great deal to give me and might carry me as far as I dream! "

It carried him nobly through *The Wings of the Dove* and *The Golden Bowl*, as it has carried later novelists through hundreds of more or less distinguished works. But Hawthorne in his solitude had discovered the " divine principle " almost fifty years before the first night of *Guy Domville*, and the fact seems all the more amazing when we reflect that, unlike James, he had never tried to write for the stage. As a matter of fact, he had never even engaged in amateur theatricals, having shown little talent or taste for mimicry. Although he liked going to the Boston theatres, he seems to have had no consuming interest in acted plays; at most they may have confirmed him in his taste for conveying moods by visual effects. Hawthorne's knowledge of the drama came mostly from his reading, which—according to the records of the Salem Athenaeum—included all of Racine, besides other classical French dramatists; he had been familiar with Shakespeare's works since boyhood. It might well be argued that his cast of mind was not Shakespearian, as Melville thought, but Racinian. The fact is that *The Scarlet Letter* can be read, and gains a new dimension from being read, as a Racinian drama of dark necessity.

It is a novel in twenty-four chapters, but, considered as a tragic drama, it is divided into the usual five acts and subdivided into eight scenes. (My principle would be that

an act may include two scenes if the second follows without any great lapse of time.) There are of course some chapters that fall outside the dramatic framework, since each of them deals with a single character (Chapter V with Hester, VI with Pearl, IX with Chillingworth, XI with Dimmesdale, XIII with Hester again, XX with Dimmesdale, and XXIV, the epilogue, chiefly with Hester) and since the method they follow is narrative or expository. These seven chapters serve as interludes in the dramatic action—or in one case as a postlude—and they provide some additional information about the characters that would have been difficult to incorporate into the dialogue. The essential chapters, however, are the other seventeen, in which Hawthorne is applying the scenic philosophy and method. Here is how they arrange themselves into rounded acts and scenes:

Act I, Scene 1 (Chapters I to III) is laid in the market-place of Boston, fifteen or twenty years after the founding of the city. On the right, rear, is the enormous nail-studded door of the prison, with a wild rosebush growing beside it. On the left is the meeting house, with a balcony projecting over the stage. Under the balcony is the scaffold of the pillory, which will be the effective center of the drama. Hester Prynne emerges from the blackness of the prison, with the child on her arm not hiding the letter A in scarlet cloth pinned to her breast; in the whole scene it is the one touch of brilliant color. She moves through the gray crowd and climbs the scaffold. From the balcony overhead the Reverend Mr. Dimmesdale adjures her to reveal the father of her child. "Believe me, Hester," he says, "though he were to step down from a high place and stand beside thee, on thy pedestal of shame, yet better were it so than to hide a guilty heart through life." Hester shakes her head.

Looking down at the crowd she recognizes her wronged husband, who had been missing for two years, but he puts his finger on his lips to show that she must not reveal his identity. All the named characters of the drama—including Governor Bellingham, John Wilson, and Mistress Hibbins—appear in this first scene; and there is also the Boston crowd, which speaks in strophe and antistrophe, like a Greek chorus.

Scene 2 of the first act (Chapter IV) is a room in the prison that same June evening. Here, after the public tableau of the first scene, comes a private confrontation. Hester and the child have fallen ill, a leech is summoned to care for them, and the leech is Chillingworth, the betrayed husband. He tells her that the scarlet letter is a more effective punishment than any he might have imagined. "Live, therefore," he says, "and bear about thy doom with thee." After revealing his determination to find the lover and be revenged on him, Chillingworth extracts one promise from Hester: that just as she has kept the lover's identity a secret, so she must keep the husband's.

Act II, Scene 1 (Chapter VII and VIII) is laid in the governor's hall, three years after the events of the first act. Little Pearl is thought to be such a strange and willful child that there has been talk among the Puritan magistrates of taking her away from her sinful mother. When Hester, now a seamstress, comes to deliver a pair of embroidered gloves to Governor Bellingham, there is an informal trial of her case. Chillingworth plays an ambiguous part in it, but Dimmesdale—when Hester demands that he speak—makes such an eloquent plea that she is allowed to keep the child. All the named characters are again present—down to Mistress Hibbins, who, at the end of the scene, invites Hester

to attend a witches' sabbath in the forest. Hester refuses with a triumphant smile:

"I must tarry at home," she says, "to keep watch over my little Pearl. Had they taken her from me, I would willingly have gone with thee into the forest, and signed my name in the Black Man's book, and that with mine own blood!"

This tableau and its brief epilogue are followed once more by a private confrontation. *Scene 2* of the second act (Chapter X) is set in Chillingworth's laboratory, among the retorts and crucibles. The old leech suspects Dimmesdale and has taken up residence in the same house, to continue all through the scene his relentless probing of Dimmesdale's heart. The minister will not confess, but, at the curtain, Chillingworth accidentally finds proof that he is indeed the guilty man.

Act III (Chapter XII) has only one scene, the scaffold of the pillory. Four years have passed since the second act. Subtly tortured by Chillingworth and finally driven half-insane, Dimmesdale has dressed in his ministerial robes and left his room at midnight, hoping to find relief in a private mimicry of public confession. Standing on the scaffold he shrieks aloud, but nobody recognizes his voice. Governor Bellingham and Mistress Hibbins both open their windows to peer into the night. On his way home from Governor Winthrop's deathbed, good John Wilson walks through the marketplace in a halo of lanternlight; he does not look up at the pillory. Then, coming from the same deathbed, Hester appears with little Pearl, and Dimmesdale invites them to join him on the scaffold. Holding one another's hands they form what Hawthorne calls "an electric chain,"

39

and Dimmesdale feels a new life, not his own, pouring like a torrent into his heart.

"Minister!" Pearl whispers. "Wilt thou stand here with mother and me, tomorrow noontide?"

When Dimmesdale refuses, she tries to pull her hand away. At this moment a meteor gleams through a cloud, forming a scarlet A in the heavens while it also reveals the little group on the scaffold. It is another of Hawthorne's many lighting effects, based partly on his Emersonian belief that the outer world is a visible manifestation of the inner world, but also based partly on his instinct for theatre; one might almost speak of his staginess. While the meteor is still glowing, Chillingworth appears to lead the minister back to his torture chamber. This tableau, occurring at the exact center of the drama, is the turning point of *The Scarlet Letter*; from now the tempo will be quicker. The first half of the story has covered a space of seven years; the second half will cover no more than fifteen days.

Act IV is in two intimate scenes, the second of which is the longest in the drama. Scene 1 (Chapters XIV and XV) is laid on the seashore, where Chillingworth is gathering herbs to concoct his medicines. While Pearl goes wading in a tidal pool, Hester accosts the old leech and begs him to release her from her promise not to tell Dimmesdale that he is the wronged husband. Chillingworth answers in a speech that reveals not only his own heart but the other side of Hawthorne's philosophy. The Emersonian side contributed to his stage effects, but it was his surviving Calvinism (in some ways close to Racine's Jansenism) that enabled him to conceive a tragic drama.

"Peace, Hester, peace!" the old man says. "It is not

granted me to pardon. . . . My old faith, long forgotten, comes back to me, and explains all that we do, and all we suffer. By thy first step awry thou didst plant the germ of evil; but since that moment, it has all been a dark necessity. Ye that have wronged me are not sinful, save in a kind of typical illusion; neither am I fiend-like, who have snatched a fiend's office from his hands. It is our fate. Let the black flower blossom as it may! Now go thy ways, and deal as thou wilt with yonder man."

He goes back to gathering herbs. Hester calls to Pearl, who, as they leave the stage, keeps asking her, " Mother!— Why does the minister keep his hand over his heart? "

Scene 2 of the fourth act (including four chapters, XVI to XIX) is set in the forest, which forms another contrast with the marketplace and helps to reveal the moral background of Hawthorne's drama. The forest, he tells us in what might almost be a stage direction, is an image of the moral wilderness in which Hester has long been wandering. But it was more than that for Hawthorne himself, and a close reading shows that the forest is also an image of the world men enter when they follow their passions and revolt against the community. In this sense little Pearl, the natural child, is a daughter of the forest, and we observe in this scene that she is perfectly at home there. Witches like Mistress Hibbins go into the forest to dance with Indian powwows and Lapland wizards, and Hester has been tempted to follow them. When she meets Dimmesdale in the forest, although she intends only to warn him against Chillingworth, it is natural in this setting that she should also urge him to defy the laws of the tribe and flee with her to a foreign country. The minister agrees; they will take passage on a Bristol cruiser then moored in the harbor. For a

41

moment Hester unpins the scarlet A from her dress and lets down her long black glossy hair; but Pearl, who has been called back from playing at the brookside, sulks until she pins the letter on her breast again.

On his way back to Boston (in Chapter XX) Dimmesdale meets Mistress Hibbins. "So, reverend Sir, you have made a visit into the forest," says the witch-lady, nodding her high head-dress at him. "The next time, I pray you to allow me only a fair warning, and I shall be proud to bear you company."

Act V, in a single scene (Chapters XXI to XXIII), takes place three days after the meeting in the forest and is the culmination toward which the drama has been moving. Once again it is laid in the marketplace, with all the named characters present, as well as the Bristol shipmaster and the Boston crowd that speaks with the voices of the tribe. Dimmesdale preaches the Election Sermon, the climax of his ministerial career, while Hester listens outside the meeting house. The shipmaster tells her that Chillingworth has taken passage on the same vessel; there will be no escape. Then Dimmesdale appears in a great procession of Puritan worthies and, instead of marching with them to the official banquet, he totters up the steps of the scaffold after calling on Hester to support him. At last they are standing together, in public, on the pedestal of shame.

42

"Is not this better," Dimmesdale murmurs, "than what we dreamed of in the forest?" Facing the crowd he tears open his ministerial band and shows that there is a scarlet A imprinted on his own flesh. He has made his public confession and now, at the point of death, he feels reconciled with the community. As he sinks to the scaffold, Chilling-

worth kneels over him repeating, " Thou hast escaped me." Pearl kisses her father on the lips, and the tears that she lets fall are the pledge that she will cease to be an outcast, an embodiment of the scarlet letter, a daughter of the forest, and instead will grow up among human joys and sorrows.

I spoke of Hawthorne's kinship with Racine, but at this point, if not before, one begins to feel that his drama might have another ancestry as well, even though the author was not conscious of it. He has presented us with distinguished, even noble, characters who are inevitably brought to grief for having violated the laws of heaven and the tribe. He has presented " an action that is serious and also, as having magnitude, complete in itself . . . with incidents arousing pity and fear, wherewith to accomplish its catharsis of such emotions." This familiar quotation from Aristotle seems appropriate in a discussion of *The Scarlet Letter*. In telling his story by a new method, Hawthorne had done more than to extend the unity and economy of the brief tale into the realm of the novel; and more than to discover a new architectural form that would be rediscovered by Henry James and copied by scores of respectably talented novelists after him. It is not too much to say that he had recaptured, for his New England, the essence of Greek tragedy.

43

MELVILLE, 1851

by GRANVILLE HICKS

Everyone knows the first sentence of *Moby Dick*. It is one of the grand openings in fiction, dramatic, evocative, portentous. The three words, like the first four notes of Beethoven's Fifth Symphony, cannot be reduced to banality by repetition; they still reverberate.

What may be forgotten is that the sentence does not set the tone for the paragraph in which it appears:

> Call me Ishmael. Some years ago—never mind how long precisely—having little or no money in my purse, and nothing particular to interest me on shore, I thought I would sail about a little and see the watery part of the world. It is a way I have of driving off the spleen, and regulating the circula-

tion. Whenever I find myself growing grim about
the mouth; whenever it is a damp, drizzly Novem-
ber in my soul; whenever I find myself involuntarily
pausing before coffin warehouses, and bringing up
the rear of every funeral I meet; and especially
whenever my hypos get such an upper hand of me,
that it requires a strong moral principle to prevent
me from deliberately stepping into the street, and
methodically knocking people's hats off—then, I account it high time to get to sea as soon as I can.
This is my substitute for pistol and ball. With a
philosophical flourish Cato throws himself upon his
sword; I quietly take to the ship. There is nothing
surprising in this. If they but knew it, almost all
men in their degree, some time or other, cherish
very nearly the same feelings towards the ocean
with me.

After the three challenging words, the tone changes
and we are in the midst of a passage of sardonic humor,
spiced with hyperbole. Its irony recalls the first sentence of
White Jacket: " It was not a *very* white jacket, but white
enough, in all conscience, as the sequel will show." The
narrator in *Moby Dick*, however, is preparing to attack
ambiguities more elusive than any to be found in *White
Jacket*, and he commits himself at the outset to strategies
of the most oblique sort. Is the narrator really an Ishmael,
an outcast, a wild ass of a man, with his hand against every
man and every man's hand against him? It scarcely seems
so as the story proceeds. What one feels is that the narrator
has cast himself in a Byronic role—we shall soon find him
speaking about a Childe Harold perched upon the mast-head
—and then has immediately made it clear that he has his
tongue in his cheek. He has never been in any great danger
of committing either suicide or mayhem; his desire to go

45

to sea is such as is experienced by "almost all men in their degree, some time or other."

If one were reading the paragraph aloud, one should, I think, read the first sentence rather quietly, almost casually, without any of the dramatic emphasis it seems to invite. There is much in the first chapter that is deadly serious, as the name of it, "Loomings," indicates. The reader does well to ponder what Ishmael has to say about fate and free will and "the wild conceits that swayed me to my purpose." But it is not for nothing that Melville has Ishmael use such phrases as "the invisible police officer of the Fates" and "the grand programme of Providence."

The note struck in this chapter dominates the first twenty-five chapters of the book. Newton Arvin has said of *Moby Dick* that "its warp is a tough, prosaic realism and its weft a metaphysical symbolism." This is a just account of the novel as a whole, but in the first fifth of it the weft might fairly be described as an extravaganza that comes close to farce. About the realism there can be no doubt; embedded in the narrative is a completely credible account of New Bedford and Nantucket and the setting forth of a whaling ship. But one episode after another is, and is meant to be, funny. The relationship between Ishmael and Queequeg, for example, has implications of the most complicated kind, but the account of their introduction was written with an eye for comic effects. The story of the wheelbarrow, Mrs. Hussey's chowder, and especially the encounter with Captain Bildad and Captain Peleg, these are all treated humorously. The Melville of these twenty-five chapters makes us think of Cervantes, Rabelais, and Laurence Sterne.

This is not to say that there is nothing else in the first

46

twenty-five chapters. Father Mapple's sermon alone would be enough to warn us that Melville has no intention of writing the whole book in this particular key. Queequeg, although he is used in comic passages, is anything but a comic character. Ishmael's latitudinarianism, as expounded in his defense of his worship of Yojo and in his conversations with the Quaker captains, must be taken seriously. In Peleg's observations, even more persuasively than in Elijah's warnings, there is a clear intimation that the atmosphere of the story will change once Ahab has made his appearance. Ominous notes abound in the account of the sailing of the *Pequod*, especially in the tiny chapter about Bulkington. But note that Melville follows the Bulkington chapter with a largely facetious defense of the dignity of whaling. This, it is true, modulates into a passage that is serious in intent if not in expression:

> And, as for me, if by any possibility, there be any as yet undiscovered prime thing in me; if I shall ever deserve any real repute in that small but high hushed world which I might not be unreasonably ambitious of; if hereafter I shall do anything that, upon the whole, a man might rather have done than to have left undone; if, at my death, my executors, or more properly my creditors, find any precious MSS. in my desk, then here I prospectively ascribe all the honor and glory to whaling; for a whale-ship was my Yale College and my Harvard.

47

Yet there is the ironic "Postscript" in which Ishmael offers one last argument on behalf of whaling: whale oil is used to anoint the monarchs of England.

The sardonic note is not immediately to disappear; it is heard in the first sentences describing Starbuck; but how

quickly it is subdued. In barely two pages Melville has not merely paid tribute to Starbuck and his kind but has eloquently and belligerently set forth the theory on which his tribute is based:

> If, then, to meanest mariners, and renegades and castaways, I shall hereafter ascribe high qualities, though dark; weave round them tragic graces; if even the most mournful, perchance the most abased, among them all, shall at times lift himself to the exalted mounts; if I shall touch that workman's arm with some ethereal light; if I shall spread a rainbow over his disastrous set of sun; then against all mortal critics bear me out in it, thou just Spirit of Equality, which hast spread one royal mantle of humanity over all my kind! Bear me out in it, thou great democratic God! who didst not refuse to the swart convict, Bunyan, the pale, poetic pearl; Thou who didst clothe with doubly hammered leaves of finest gold, the stumped and paupered arm of old Cervantes; Thou who didst pick up Andrew Jackson from the pebbles; who didst hurl him upon a war-horse; who didst thunder him higher than a throne! Thou who, in all Thy mighty, earthly marchings, ever cullest Thy selectest champions from the kingly commons, bear me out in it, O God!

The idea of the democratic God, which will not bear too close scrutiny on theological grounds, has the utmost literary importance for Melville. In *Mimesis* Erich Auerbach tells us that in ancient times "there could be no serious literary treatment of everyday occupations and social classes," and traces the breaking down of the theory of the separation of styles and the development through the centuries of a variety of techniques for the serious literary

48

treatment of the lower levels of society. Melville, in the passage quoted, justifies the serious treatment of "meanest mariners." He goes even further; he proclaims his right to treat such characters in an heroic, even a tragic, vein and in what Auerbach calls an exalted style.

Speaking of *Madame Bovary*, which was published in the same decade as *Moby Dick*, Auerbach writes: "The serious treatment of everyday reality, the rise of more extensive and socially inferior human groups to the position of subject matter for problematic-existential representation, on the one hand; on the other, the embedding of random persons and events in the general course of contemporary history, the fluid historical background—these, we believe, are the foundations of modern realism; and it is natural that the broad and elastic form of the novel should increasingly impose itself for a rendering comprising so many elements." In his choice of subject matter Melville accepts the prevailing trend of the nineteenth-century novel; in his methods, on the other hand, he repudiates the trend. As has been said, he is a realist when he chooses to be, but he refuses to limit himself to realism, and he particularly refuses to limit himself to any of the kinds of prose that had seemed to be adapted to the needs of contemporary fiction. He was determined to employ, as Shakespeare had done, any style that served his purpose, including the most exalted, but, unlike Shakespeare, he did not propose to treat only characters of high social station in the sublime style. And he calls upon the democratic God to bear witness that one may find on any social level men worthy of such treatment.

Again and again in the pages that immediately follow Melville calls attention to the inherent nobility of his char-

acters. The very next chapter, which describes the other mates and the three harpooners, is called "Knights and Squires." The first appearance of Ahab emphasizes the majesty of his bearing, and soon we see him sitting on a throne: "In old Norse times, the thrones of the sea-loving Danish kings were fabricated, saith tradition, of the tusks of the narwhale. How could one look at Ahab then, seated on that tripod of bones, without bethinking him of the royalty it symbolized?" Stubb's real encounter with Ahab and the one of which he dreams suggest to us a power within the captain that borders on the supernatural. Before long Melville is calling the mates Emirs and referring to King Ahab, and then he writes: "Like the Coronation banquet at Frankfort, where the German Emperor profoundly dines with the seven Imperial Electors, so these cabin meals were somehow solemn meals, eaten in awful silence."

At the end of Chapter 33 Melville observes that intellectual superiority often goes unrecognized, whereas a title or other trapping awes the masses. He goes on: "But when, as in the case of Nicholas the Czar, the ringed crown of geographical empire encircles an imperial brain; then, the plebeian herds crouch abased before the tremendous centralization." Immediately he makes clear what he is doing: "Nor, will the tragic dramatist who would depict moral indomitableness in its fullest sweep and direct swing, ever forget a hint, incidentally so important in his art, as the one now alluded to." He has not, however, lost sight of the reality he deals with: "But Ahab, my Captain, still moves before me in all his Nantucket grimness and shagginess; and in this episode touching Emperors and Kings, I must not conceal that I have only to do with a poor old whale-

hunter like him; and, therefore, all outward majestical trappings and housings are denied me." The majesty that he would portray, the majesty that warrants the exaltation of style to which he aspires, is inward and must be sought for: " Oh, Ahab! what shall be grand in thee, it must needs be plucked from the skies, and dived for in the deep, and featured in the unbodied air! "

I have been quoting from passages that lie on either side of Chapter 32, "Cetology." In the midst of developing the idea of Ahab's grandeur and the nobility of his associates, Melville pauses to offer, in the more or less jocose style of some of the early chapters, a solid block of zoological information. This is the first of the wholly expository chapters, and it gives the reader something of a start, but we soon see that Melville, in spite of a certain flippancy, is wholly serious and knows what he is doing. The expository chapters contribute to the strength of the warp of " tough, prosaic realism"; they give us knowledge we need to have if we are not to misread *Moby Dick*, in the modern manner, as merely a parable or, in the older fashion, as an adventure story with many pages that had better be skipped. Melville was not afraid to make demands upon his readers. His principal demands, of course, are upon the imagination, but he is also ready to insist that readers acquaint themselves with facts that seem to him essential to the full appreciation of his story.

51

The first lecture is a relatively brief one, a mere introductory survey of the subject, for Melville is rapidly moving on to his first great dramatic episode. Before he enters upon this episode, however, he permits his narrator again to occupy the center of the stage. We see him very much alone, for he is in the *Pequod*'s masthead. Melville begins

with a typically facetious discourse, examining the Tower of Babel, the Egyptian pyramids, the pillar of Saint Simon Stylites, and the columns of Napoleon, Washington, and Nelson as mastheads. He could have found precedents for such conceits as this in Thomas Browne and Robert Burton, but the closest parallel is the work of a contemporary, Carlyle's *Sartor Resartus*. Carlyle, of course, in spite of a certain amount of humorous inventiveness, is strictly serious. Melville is not. Yet this passage and all the passages like it are ways of reminding us that there is more than one way of looking at any object. Melville is not saying that the *Pequod* is either a microcosm or a symbol of the world, but he is warning us that we are not likely to see at first glance all that it is.

By way of a realistic passage on the nature of mastheads and crow's-nests, Melville makes a transition to the subject of Ishmael. Ishmael warns the shipowners of Nantucket: "Beware of enlisting in your vigilant fisheries any lad with lean brow and hollow eye; given to unseasonable meditativeness; and who offers to ship with the Phaedon instead of Bowditch in his head." Deliberately he strikes the Byronic note: "Childe Harold not unfrequently perches himself upon the masthead of some luckless disappointed whale-ship."

The tone is still facetious, as the offhand parody of Byron indicates, but Melville quickly becomes serious enough. A harpooner has just said to "one of these lads": "Whales are scarce as hen's teeth whenever thou art up here." Melville continues:

> "Perhaps they were; or perhaps there might have been shoals of them in the far horizon; but lulled into such an opium-like listlessness of vacant, un-

conscious reverie is this absent-minded youth by
the blending cadence of waves with thoughts, that
at last he loses his identity; takes the mystic ocean
at his feet for the visible image of that deep, blue,
bottomless soul, pervading mankind and nature;
and every strange, half-seen, gliding beautiful thing
that eludes him; every dimly-discovered, uprising
fin of some undiscernible form, seems to him the
embodiment of those elusive thoughts that only
people the soul by continually flitting through it."

But if Ishmael was once some such Platonist or pan-
theist as he describes, he is no longer, nor is Melville. Sharp
comes the warning:

"But while this sleep, this dream is on ye, move
your foot or hand an inch; slip your hold at all; and
your identity comes back in horror. And perhaps,
at mid-day, in the fairest weather, with one half-
throttled shriek you drop through that transparent
air into the summer sea, no more to rise for ever.
Heed it well, ye Pantheists!"

Having thus repudiated transcendentalism of all kinds,
having said that this world of ours is not to be trusted,
Melville is ready for an episode in which the novel rises to
a new level of intensity. The episode is given, appropriately, in dramatic form. Some critics have argued that the
novel as a whole should be regarded as a five-act tragedy,
but the argument cannot be sustained. What is certain is
that Melville wanted to bring to the novel both the dramatic intensity and the poetic power of Elizabethan drama.
There have already been many echoes of Shakespeare's plays,
and the principal scenes, including this one, remind us of
the great dramatist rather than of any novelist who had
ever lived.

53

The scene is beautifully managed, by none other than Ahab himself, who arranges the characters on the quarter-deck with an infallible eye. After the great oath come the three soliloquies—Ahab's, Starbuck's, Stubb's—followed by the scene in the forecastle. The jubilation of the sailors dies away before the quarrel between Tashtego and the Spanish sailor, which is in turn interrupted by the squall. Pip, left alone, closes the act with a speech that reminds us of the fool's speeches in the storm scene in *King Lear* and looks ahead to madder speeches.

In the scene on the quarter-deck the novel's theme, hinted at often before, is boldly stated: we know that Ahab either will kill the great white whale or will die himself. We have participated as fully in the events on the quarter-deck as a reader can in events in a novel. We can almost say with the narrator: " I, Ishmael, was one of that crew. . . . Ahab's quenchless feud seemed mine." But now, escaping from the spell, we want to know where we stand, and up to a point Melville is prepared to tell us. He begins quietly with facts about Moby Dick but quickly reaches realms of rumor and legend. About Ahab he is disconcertingly matter of fact: " The White Whale swam before him as the monomaniac incarnation of all those malicious agencies which some deep men feel eating them, till they are left living on with half a heart and half a lung. . . . All that most maddens and torments; all that stirs up the lees of things; all truth with malice in it; all that cracks the sinews and cakes the brain; all the subtle demonisms of life and thought, to crazy Ahab, were visibly personified, and made practically assailable in Moby Dick."

This is specific enough, but it seems to say that the captain is indeed " crazy Ahab," and Melville actually goes

on to tell us that, on his voyage home after losing his leg, Ahab became "a raving maniac" and had to be kept in a strait-jacket. Moreover, he recovered only in outward appearance: "his special lunacy stormed his general sanity, and carried it, and turned all its concentrated cannon upon its own mad mark." But at this we balk: if Ahab is as crazy as Melville has said he is, his tragedy lies in the past, not in the future. Melville concedes the point: "This is much; yet Ahab's larger, darker, deeper part remains unhinted." There are mysteries within mysteries, he says again when he speaks of the crew:

> "How it was that they so aboundingly responded to the old man's ire—by what evil magic their souls were possessed, that at times his hate seemed almost theirs; the White Whale as much their insufferable foe as his; how all this came to be—what the White Whale was to them, or how to their unconscious understanding, also, in some dim, unsuspected way, he might have seemed the gliding great demon on the seas of life,—all this to explain, would be to dive deeper than Ishmael can go. The subterranean miner that works in us all, how can one tell whither leads his shaft by the ever shifting, muffled sound of his pick."

We are forced to recognize, then, that if Ahab may justly be called crazy, that is a long way from being the whole truth. His monomania is felt by other men, even by the narrator. Chapter 42, "The Whiteness of the Whale," begins: "What the White Whale was to Ahab, has been hinted; what, at times, he was to me, as yet remains unsaid." What Ishmael has said is: "For one, I gave myself up to the abandonment of the time and the place; but while yet all a-rush to encounter the whale, could see naught in

55

that brute but the deadliest ill." The "but" that introduces the second clause is the word over which we must linger. On one level of his mind, Ishmael is saying, he shared in the general passion to destroy Moby Dick, but on another he dissociated himself from Ahab and the crew. In what, then, does the difference lie? Did not the others regard the whale as "the deadliest ill"? Of course they did, but as an ill that could and should be destroyed, whereas for Ishmael such evils are to be avoided.

This is the theme Melville now develops. "It was the whiteness of the whale," he writes, "that above all things appalled me." He launches at once into a long sentence, probably the longest in the book, in which he concedes that whiteness has been associated with beauty, power, innocence, and holiness, only to conclude that "there yet lurks an elusive something in the innermost idea of this hue, which strikes more of panic to the soul than that redness which affrights in blood." The defense of this thesis is not altogether convincing, as Melville seems to feel, since he has to appeal to the validity of instinctive fears, but this does not matter, for what Melville is really concerned to establish is the ambivalence of whiteness. It can, that is, be associated with either good or evil. Good and evil are both embedded in the structure of the universe: "Though in many of its aspects this visible world seems formed in love, the invisible spheres were formed in fright." Whiteness is in itself neither good nor evil but intensifies whichever it is associated with. The whiteness of Moby Dick makes him a more terrible symbol—Melville uses the word—of everything in the universe that is to be feared. The chapter ends, "Wonder ye then at the fiery hunt?" But Ishmael himself wonders on one level of his mind, as he has told us. In his calmer

moments he knows that not only the assault on Moby Dick but also the cosmic assault that it symbolizes is doomed to failure of a disastrous sort.

Having given us Ahab and shown us the depth of his obsession, and having suggested some of the meanings Moby Dick may have, Melville changes his pace. This is not a story that can rush to its climax, not if the climax is to have the force that Melville is determined to achieve.

In a series of transitional chapters Melville lays the foundation for the long middle section of the book. Chapter 43 prepares us for the emergence of Fedallah and his companions in the novel's next dramatic episode. Chapter 44 establishes once and for all Melville's right to break through the limitations of first person narrative whenever that seems necessary—to enter directly into the mind of Ahab or any other character. It and the next two chapters furnish us with many practical details pertinent to the pursuit of Moby Dick and show how Ahab can conduct the search for the whale and why he cannot immediately undertake it. The consequences of this delay are apparent even to Ahab: "he must still in a good degree continue true to the natural, nominal purpose of the *Pequod*'s voyage."

The form of the middle section is thus determined: it is to be an account of a reasonably typical whaling voyage. Melville speaks of Ahab's "having impulsively, it is probable, and perhaps somewhat prematurely revealed the prime but private purpose of the Pequod's voyage." For the sake of the novel, the revelation must come where it does, and in all that follows we are never allowed to forget it, but, having made clear that the *Pequod*'s is no ordinary voyage, Melville can proceed to treat it as if in large measure it were. He will show us how whales are killed and how their

carcasses are reduced to profitable oil, will give us much information, will introduce some more or less relevant tales. He will use this section, in short, to strengthen the realistic warp while always remembering the metaphysical weft.

That Melville does this deliberately he lets us know in Chapter 45, "The Affidavit," a chapter made up of true stories illustrating the destructive power of the sperm whale. "So ignorant are most landsmen of some of the plainest and most palpable wonders of the world, that without some hints touching the plain facts, historical and otherwise, of the fishery, they might scout at Moby Dick as a monstrous fable, or still worse and more detestable, a hideous and intolerable allegory." Whatever Moby Dick may symbolize, he is a real whale, doing nothing a real whale might not conceivably do, and the *Pequod* is a real ship with real officers and crew, who risk real lives in the course of their employment. Nor are their days and nights made up solely of perils; they are made up in large part of boredom, deprivation, and the tedium of hard and stinking work.

Melville's sense of the dramatic is illustrated by the way the first cry of "There she blows!" interrupts the idyllic scene in which Ishmael, while helping Queequeg weave a mat, meditates on chance, free will, and necessity. The appearance of the Orientals links the first lowering with Ahab's ultimate purpose, but Melville does not forget that this is our introduction to the great chase, and he summons up his resources to give us a few vivid moments. Nor does he forget that this is Ishmael's initiation, and he follows his description with a wry passage in the vein of some of the earlier chapters. "There are certain queer times and occasions," he begins, "in this strange mixed affair we call life when a man takes this whole universe for a vast

practical joke, though the wit thereof he but dimly discerns, and more than suspects that the joke is at nobody's expense but his own." Joke or no joke, we are to take Ishmael seriously when he says at the end that he has come to terms, as well as a man can, with death.

There are omens enough in the chapters that follow—the spout, the ship called the *Albatross*, the squid. The *Town-ho*'s story, presented as a massive digression with its own inner digressions, narrates events felt to be ominous by the members of the crew acquainted with the facts. The mad Shaker on the *Jeroboam* is another prophet of doom. But in this section the business of whaling and the whale himself are Melville's principal concerns. A kind of climax is reached in Chapter 87, "The Grand Armada," with its picture of the *Pequod*'s three boats in the midst of a vast school of whales, a school so large that even as some of its members are being pierced by harpoons, others are feeding, mating, bearing offspring, nursing their young. This is a world of whales, and the *Pequod*'s men are unmannerly intruders.

The tenderness that Ishmael feels at the sight of the whales engaged in their natural activities is expressed even more strongly in Chapter 94, which describes the squeezing of sperm. "I forgot all about our horrible oath; in that inexpressible sperm I washed my hands and my heart of it." This is almost the last time, until the very end of the book, that we are to see Ishmael on stage; hereafter his identity is more and more completely submerged in the role of narrator, and even the first personal pronoun appears infrequently. The character of this scene is therefore doubly important. "I squeezed that sperm till a strange sort of insanity came over me; and I found myself unwittingly

59

squeezing my co-laborers' hands in it, mistaking their hands for the gentle globules. Such an abounding, affectionate, friendly, loving feeling did this avocation beget; that at last I was continually squeezing their hands, and looking up into their eyes sentimentally; as much as to say—Oh! my dear fellow beings, why should we longer cherish any social acerbities, or know the slightest ill-humor or envy! Come; let us squeeze hands all round; nay, let us squeeze ourselves into each other; let us squeeze ourselves universally into the very milk and sperm of kindness." Strange actions, strange thoughts for a man who has called himself Ishmael!

If Ishmael has forgotten the horrible oath, Ahab has not, and with Chapter 99, "The Doubloon," we are reminded again of the old man's obsession. But Melville has not yet finished with facts; he gives us three more chapters, on the whale's skeleton, fossils of whales, and the future of the whale. The third of the chapters ends with these words: "He swam the seas before the continents broke water; he once swam over the site of the Tuileries, and Windsor Castle, and the Kremlin. In Noah's flood he despised Noah's ark; and if ever the world is to be again flooded, like the Netherlands, to kill off its rats, then the eternal whale will still survive, and rearing upon the topmost crest of the equatorial flood, spout his frothed defiance to the skies." Now Melville has said his say about whales and can turn to the struggle between Ahab and Moby Dick.

The grandeur of the sentences just quoted underlines the stylistic variety of the instructive chapters. If Melville felt it necessary to educate the reader, as obviously he did, then at least he was prepared to amuse and shock him, to beguile and uplift him, in the process. He can be sardonic, bawdy, self-consciously grandiloquent. He can laugh at

himself for trying to be "omnisciently exhaustive," can cry out, "Give me a condor's quill! Give me Vesuvius' crater for an inkstand!" "Fain am I," he writes, "to stagger to this emprise under the weightiest words of the dictionary. And here be it said, that whenever it has been convenient to consult one in the course of these dissertations, I have invariably used a huge quarto edition of Johnson, expressly purchased for that purpose; because that famous lexicographer's uncommon personal bulk more fitted him to compile a lexicon to be used by a whale author like me." But although Melville may play games with his readers while he instructs them, he is altogether serious in his determination to teach them what they need to know, and perhaps he is more than half serious in his most extravagant flights. In the midst of his mock heroics he says: "To produce a mighty book, you must choose a mighty theme. No great and enduring volume can ever be written on the flea, though many there be who have tried it." The greatness of Melville's book does not derive from the greatness of the whale, but the effort to deal justly with what he saw as "a mighty theme" helped to bring him to the highest peak of achievement.

The return to the novel's central conflict is signaled, as I have pointed out, by a chapter devoted to the doubloon that was nailed to the mast at the time of the oath. Suddenly Ahab looks closely at the coin to make out what it signifies. "And some certain significance lurks in all things," Melville comments, "else all things are little worth, and the round world itself is but an empty cipher; except to sell by the cartload, as they do hills about Boston, to fill up some morass in the Milky Way." To Ahab the inscriptions speak of pride and struggle. But others, inspired by his powerful example to examine the coin, read it differently. Starbuck

61

finds a message of religious consolation; Stubb is encouraged to be jolly; Flask sees only "a round thing made of gold." What cabalistic interpretations are made by Queequeg and Fedallah can only be surmised. Mad Pip pronounces the final judgment: "I look, you look, he looks; we look, ye look, they look." We should perhaps remember this as we move into chapters crowded with symbols; if there is an ultimate, absolute interpretation for any of them, Melville does not take it on himself to tell us what it is; he looks and we look.

The meeting with the *Samuel Enderby* brings us closer to Moby Dick. Moreover, the garrulous, good-natured captain, who has lost an arm to the whale, speaks up for common sense when Ahab asks him whether he has made a second attempt: "Didn't want to try to; ain't one limb enough?" Lapsing once more into his didactic, semifacetious vein, Melville speaks of the comforts enjoyed on British whaling ships, in order to call attention to the grim absurdity of Ahab's behavior. And yet the captain of the *Samuel Enderby*, like the captain of the fortune-favored *Bachelor*, soon to be encountered by the *Pequod*, seems mean and contemptible in comparison with Ahab.

By way of an extravagant description of a whale's skeleton used as a pagan temple, Melville moves into the last of the instructive chapters, which I have already discussed. He resumes the development of the major theme by revealing that Ahab had done some injury to his ivory leg while precipitately leaving the *Samuel Enderby*. The fabrication of the new leg gives an excuse for presenting at length two new characters, the carpenter and the blacksmith. As often, Melville is explicit about what he is doing: "the *Pequod*'s carpenter was no duplicate; hence, he now

comes in person upon the stage." The carpenter is a special-
ist, a man with a one-track mind: "Teeth he accounted bits
of ivory; heads he deemed but top-blocks; men themselves
he lightly held for capstans. . . . He was a pure manipu-
lator; his brain, if he had ever had one, must have early
oozed along into the muscles of his fingers." But let us make
no mistake: "This omni-tooled, open-and-shut carpenter,
was, after all, no mere machine of an automaton." He is
capable of making his own kind of judgment. Ahab reflects: "Here I am, proud as Greek god, and yet standing
debtor to this blockhead for a bone to stand on." The carpenter is awed: "Oh! I don't wonder he looked so scornful
on me." But he draws a sensible, if ignominious, conclusion:
"Then, a short, little old body like me, should never undertake to wade out into deep waters with tall, heron-built
captains."

The blacksmith, though introduced in connection with
the making of Ahab's leg, is described a little further on,
when he forges the harpoon with which Ahab is resolved
to kill Moby Dick. He is a man who, after many years of
prosperity and happiness, had taken to drink and thus, as
Melville puts it, "had postponedly encountered that thing
in sorrow's technicals called ruin." His response to his
predicament is resignation, and for this Ahab upbraids him:
"Thy shrunk voice sounds too calmly, sanely woful to me.
In no Paradise myself, I am impatient of all misery in others
that is not mad. Thou should'st go mad, blacksmith."

Meanwhile we have had the incident of Queequeg's
coffin, which is later transformed into a life-buoy. ("Thou
art as unprincipled as the gods," Ahab says to the carpenter,
"and as much a jack-of-all-trades," but subsequently he
considers the transformed coffin as a conceivable symbol

of immortality.) We have also had a conflict between Ahab and Starbuck, one in which the mate has won a minor victory. The *Pequod* has entered the Pacific, Ahab's harpoon has been forged and given its sacrilegious baptism, and we have heard the Parsee's predictions—no more to be believed than the prophecies of Macbeth's " juggling fiends." It seems certain that nothing can save the *Pequod* from its doom. The great storm, which, as Starbuck observes, might serve to carry the vessel home, only intensifies Ahab's determination, inspiring his great speech of defiance, perhaps the highest flight of language in the whole book.

Nothing can save the *Pequod* but Ahab's death. Starbuck knows this, and he has the musket in his hand, but he cannot kill " the wondrous old man." As Ahab has said, " Thou art but too good a fellow, Starbuck." Starbuck is what he is—a vastly better man than Ahab, and a smaller one. Ahab towers above him as Macbeth above the virtuous Banquo, Othello above the even-tempered Cassio, or Hamlet above the clear-thinking Horatio. Perhaps Starbuck could kill no one in cold blood, no matter how many lives were at stake; certainly he cannot kill Ahab.

The compass fails because of the electric storm, but Ahab proves himself " lord of the level lodestone," and calls on the seamen to look at what he has done. " In his fiery eyes of scorn and triumph, you then saw Ahab in all his fatal pride." In some ways, however, he seems less of a monomaniac as the end approaches. He befriends demented Pip, and his feeling for the little Negro is genuine, even though it causes him to boast of his superiority to those " creative libertines " the gods. The gods are much on his mind. The carpenter, after Ahab has compared him to the gods, says, " But I do not mean anything, Sir. I do as I do."

"The gods again," Ahab cries, and returns to his cabin to talk with Pip—"I do suck most wondrous philosophies from thee! "—as Lear, in *his* self-imposed loneliness, talked with the Fool.

But nothing turns Ahab from his purpose. Even the plight of the captain of the *Rachel* fails to move him. Yet even now there seems a human—if not, so to speak, a dramatic—possibility that Ahab may change. In Chapter 132, "The Symphony," one of the great chapters, there is a last pause before the storm breaks. Ahab is touched by the beauty of the day: "That glad, happy air, that winsome sky, did at last stroke and caress him; the step-mother world, so long cruel—forbidding—now threw affectionate arms round his stubborn neck, and did seem to joyously sob over him, as if over one that, however wilfull and erring, she could yet find it in her heart to save and bless." He thinks of his boyhood, of the harshness and barrenness of his long life at sea, of the cruelty with which he has robbed his girl-wife and their child of his care and affection. Starbuck grasps at the opportunity to urge the captain to turn back to Nantucket. Ahab wonders why he cannot do it but he cannot. The best he can do is to command Starbuck to stay on the *Pequod* when the attack is launched—no favor, as things turn out, but well intended.

And then, only a few pages before the end of the book, Moby Dick is sighted, and from there on there can be no hesitation. The whale, for whose entrance there has been such exhaustive and artful preparation, appears, to our amazement, not as an object of terror but as a thing of beauty:

> "A gentle joyousness—a mighty mildness of repose in swiftness, invested the gliding whale. Not the white bull Jupiter swimming away with his ravished

65

> Europa clinging to his graceful horns; his lovely,
> leering eyes sideways intent upon the maid; with
> smooth bewitching fleetness, rippling straight for
> the nuptial bower in Crete; not Jove, not that great
> majesty Supreme! did surpass the glorified White
> Whale as he so divinely swam."

That, as quickly becomes clear, is only one aspect of Moby
Dick, but, though Ahab remains oblivious of it, it is as real
as any other.

To the end the fight is all of Ahab's choosing. Even on
the third day he has a choice. "See!" Starbuck cries to him.
"Moby Dick seeks thee not. It is thou, thou, that madly
seekest him." But Ahab has already told Starbuck that for
him there can be no choice, that "this whole act's immu-
tably decreed," and he conducts himself as if he believed
this. Even the revelation that he has been cheated by the
Parsee's prophecies affects him less than Macbeth is affected
by a similar revelation. But if he sees defeat and death as
inevitable, he is by no means reconciled to them. "Oh,
lonely death on lonely life!" he cries.

> "Oh, now I feel my topmost greatness lies in my
> topmost grief. Ho, ho! from all your furthest
> bounds, pour ye now in, ye bold billows of my
> whole foregone life, and top this one piled comber
> of my death! Towards thee I roll, thou all-de-
> stroying but unconquering whale; to the last I
> grapple with thee; from hell's heart I stab at thee;
> for hate's sake I spit my last breath at thee. Sink
> all coffins and hearses to one common pool! and
> since neither can be mine, let me then tow to pieces,
> while still chasing thee, though tied to thee, thou
> damned whale! *Thus*, I give up the spear!"

66

The harpoon that Ahab hurls against the whale is the
agent of his own death, thus fulfilling the Parsee's prophecy

that he will die by hemp. Ahab is not the victim of Moby Dick's aggression but of his own monomania. All the others, all but one, Moby Dick destroys—the good Starbuck, the jolly Stubbs, gigantic Daggoo and little Pip. So far as we know, they die bravely, but they die by accident. Ahab's death is of a different order because the terms on which he is willing to live are so narrowly defined: he will live only if he can destroy Moby Dick. He will avenge himself on Moby Dick not merely for the injury the whale has done him but because he has come to regard him as the "incarnation of all those malicious agencies which some deep men feel eating them." "Vengeance on a dumb brute!" Starbuck had said on the quarter-deck, "that simply smote thee from blindest instinct! Madness!" The final act has proved that Starbuck's attitude is the only sensible one. Yet Ahab has tried to "strike through the mask," and therein lies his greatness.

That Ahab is a great tragic figure need not be argued. Not only do his natural endowments make him a king among men, as truly a king as any found in Greek tragedy; his life is absolutely consecrated to an end that only a "deep" man could conceive of. To seek to strike a final blow against the evil in the universe, this is a madness to which only great minds are liable.

There is a word to be said about the epilogue. Are we to assume that, as Ahab deserves his death, Ishmael has earned his survival? Up to a point this is a fair interpretation: Ishmael, unlike Starbuck, can recognize the evil in the universe, and yet he does not give way to Ahab's obsession; moreover, he has learned to appreciate "the very milk and sperm of kindness," whereas Ahab has sealed himself off from other men in proud and contemptuous loneliness.

Yet I think that Melville had no intention of weighing Ishmael against Ahab, and that may be one reason why Ishmael virtually vanishes from the book in the last forty chapters. His survival is an accident—"It so chanced. . . . I was he whom the Fates ordained . . ."—but not, of course, in terms of Melville's literary design. The impact of the novel would be different if there were no one to say in effect what Ishmael says specifically at the end of the *Town-ho*'s story. "So help me Heaven, and on my honor the story I have told ye, gentlemen, is in substance and in its great items, true. I know it to be true; it happened on this ball; I trod the ship; I knew the crew. . . ."

One might also say in deliberate paradox that Ishmael survives in order to remind us that he has existed. So far have we come, so completely has Ahab taken over the novel, that Ishmael has slipped away from us without our noticing it. This is part of the grand strategy of the novel. It rises to tremendous heights, and we are so awed by them that we forget the massive foundations by which they are supported. Ishmael has done his work well, domesticating us on the *Pequod*, lecturing us indefatigably on his great subject, letting us see for ourselves Ahab and his mighty antagonist not only in all their grandeur but also in all their complexity. He does his work and then makes himself invisible until suddenly he rises from the sea to speak the words of the servant in Job: "And I only am escaped alone to tell thee." We see him then revolving like another Ixion in the "slowly wheeling circle," the "closing vortex" caused by the *Pequod*'s sinking, until he reaches the "vital centre" that provides the means of salvation. And now we realize that Ishmael has a story too, but it is chiefly left to our imaginations.

WONDER FOR *HUCKLEBERRY FINN*

TWAIN, 1885

by GEORGE P. ELLIOTT

We become so used to having the famous books around that most of the time we look at them as though they were statues of generals in public parks. Americans know that *Huckleberry Finn* is there, that it is fun to read, and that there is supposed to be something great about it; and most have read it at some time or other. But how easily we pay no attention to it as though it were as dull as a stone general. Or, more subtly, how easily we fragment it into stone facts to know about ("In what magazine was *The Adventures of Huckleberry Finn* serialized and who was editor, how many issues did it run, which other novels were serialized at about the same time in the same magazine?" $64,000 or a Ph.D., take your choice). I know that

the expression of wonder demands a certain ceremony and that we are an unceremonious people. Nevertheless, I feel for *Huckleberry Finn* a special wonder which I think can be talked about: not just wonder at the mystery that it was created at all, which one feels for any masterpiece, but also at the special mystery that Mark Twain created it.

Only to Mark Twain of Americans of his age had gifts been granted in such kind and of such magnitude as to produce this book. There were a good many other entertainer-writers, such as Artemus Ward, none of whom were much more than entertainers; there were a few writers of excellence, preëminently Henry James, but they were not popular; only Mark Twain, like a lesser Dickens, combined literary excellence with popular entertainment.

His accomplishments as an entertainer are indisputable, a matter for chronicling. His books sold hugely both here and abroad, and his readings and lectures were heavily attended and loudly applauded; his jokes were quoted, his opinions were sought and respected, he made fortunes from his writing and lecturing. Furthermore, *Tom Sawyer* and *Huckleberry Finn* continue to be popular successes. His gifts as an entertainer stand objectively proved by such evidence.

But there is another sort of proof of this gift, a subjective one, for which every reader is grateful. You know by the time you have got through the first chapter that you are in the hands of a master entertainer; respectable boredom squeezes Huck toward adventure; and the style is high.

> She went on and told me all about the good place. She said all a body would have to do there was to go around all day long with a harp and sing, forever and ever. So I didn't think much of it. But I

never said so. I asked her if she reckoned Tom
Sawyer would go there and she said not by a considerable sight. I was glad about that, because I
wanted him and me to be together.

His jokes are funny, his wit is keen ("He could hear his
microbes gnaw, the place was so still"), his tall tales and
little excursions into fantastic exaggeration are time and
again amusing. But not just amusing, for he perfected his
humor to be the instrument of his comment on manners,
persons, institutions.

In Syria, once, at the head-waters of the Jordan, a camel took charge of my overcoat while the
tents were being pitched, and examined it with a
critical eye, all over, with as much interest as if he
had an idea of getting one made like it; and then,
after he was done figuring on it as an article of ap-
parel, he began to contemplate it as an article of
diet. He put his foot on it, and lifted one of the
sleeves out with his teeth, and chewed and chewed
at it, gradually taking it in, and all the while opening and closing his eyes in a kind of religious ecstasy, as if he had never tasted anything as good as
an overcoat before, in his life. Then he smacked
his lips once or twice, and reached after the other
sleeve. Next he tried the velvet collar, and smiled
a smile of such contentment that it was plain to see
that he regarded that as the daintiest thing about
an overcoat. The tails went next, along with some
percussion caps and cough candy, and some fig-
paste from Constantinople. And then my newspaper correspondence dropped out, and he took a
chance in that—manuscript letters written for the
home papers. But he was treading on dangerous
ground, now. He began to come across solid wisdom in those documents that was rather weighty
on his stomach; and occasionally he would take a

71

joke that would shake him up till it loosened his teeth; it was getting to be perilous times with him, but he held his grip with good courage and hopefully, till at last he began to stumble on statements that not even a camel could swallow with impunity. He began to gag and gasp, and his eyes to stand out, and his forelegs to spread, and in about a quarter of a minute he fell over as stiff as a carpenter's work-bench, and died of indescribable agony. I went and pulled the manuscript out of his mouth, and found that the sensitive creature had choked to death on one of the mildest and gentlest statements of fact that I ever laid before a trusting public.

All this apropos jackasses eating sagebrush in *Roughing It*.

Dickens, Dumas, Cervantes—it takes a special kind of snob to reject or disparage the pure entertainment their tales afford. The protagonists' risks are enormous, the villains are known to be bad, the reader's satisfaction at the way things turn out is unqualified, the author wrote with gusto because he enjoyed it. The entertainer, especially the comedian of any sort, works for immediate effect; if he is a novelist, the episode is his natural unit; he is apt to be weak in total construction and to string his episodes together somewhat mechanically or crudely. His novels have none of that smooth articulation and total unity of *Madame Bovary* or *Wings of the Dove*—those undelightful, frigidly admirable accomplishments of throttled men. His novels may be little more than entertaining, like *The Count of Monte Cristo* or *A Connecticut Yankee in King Arthur's Court*, and even in those which are also excellent he may at times yield to the temptation to do no more than amuse trivially as Mark Twain does in the last chapters of *Huckleberry Finn*. But I do not think we feel cheated and un-

forgiving because of such inferior chapters; just because the book is loosely held together, the defect of one part does not average out the virtue of another, as in a Jamesian novel; because Mark Twain knew exactly how much of the feuding Grangerfords to give us, we can simply forget that he gave us far too much Tom Sawyer at the end and can carry away with us undamaged the hilarious portrait of the Grangerford daughter. The entertainer, working for an effect at the moment, will seldom deny in the interest of a hoped-for artistic unity his sure-fire ideas as they occur to him; and when, as in *Huckleberry Finn*, these ideas are full of life and energy, we are willing for their sake to forgive much looseness in the construction and many defects in the parts.

For a novel is not just a work of art: it is, somehow, a work of life as well. I believe it is for this reason that recent literary criticism has done poorly by novels; ours has been a formalistic era in criticism, and novels have, notoriously, loose forms; furthermore, the greatest novels, *War and Peace* and *The Brothers Karamazov*, are formally imperfect. How maddening to a formalist critic to say: "*Huckleberry Finn* is in nearly all respects inferior to *The Bostonians* as an artifice, yet in style, event, and character it is vitally superior; therefore it is the greater book." For how can one define, account for, analyze vitality? *Here is an alive world; it delights me to learn about it.* These, I think, are the fundamental assertions to be made about a great novel; criticism comes rationalizing after.

Mark Twain was especially sensitive to words, their sounds, rhythms, implications, arrangement. His writings are not infrequently interrupted by excoriations of bad literary styles; his demolition job on James Fenimore Cooper

73

is famous. And he beat out for himself a style which is vigorous and exact—when, that is, he is not violating his own nature and putting on literary airs. His talent for reproducing vulgar language is as good as that of anyone who ever wrote English, and in *Huckleberry Finn* he constructed about that talent a great style: it is exactly the language which could best embody the story, it is a part of the world the story brings to life, and it is a pleasure in itself. I do not know what more the style of a novel can do. Grace and felicity of style, acute sensitivity to words, do not seem to be essential to greatness in a novelist; at least Tolstoy and Dostoevsky employed plain styles which do not divert the reader from the worlds they represent. Still, without overemphasizing it, I think that a style like that of *Huckleberry Finn* which itself helps create the world of the book and which is pleasurable is a thing worthy of gratitude.

> It was kind of lazy and jolly, laying off comfortable all day, smoking and fishing, and no books nor study. Two months or more run along and my clothes got to be all rags and dirt, and I didn't see how I'd ever got to like it so well at the widow's, where you had to wash and eat on a plate and comb up and go to bed and get up regular, and be forever bothering over a book and have old Miss Watson pecking at you all the time. I didn't like it, but now I took to it again because pap hadn't no objections. It was pretty good times up in the woods there, take it all around.

Really, the widow doesn't have a chance against a lazy good style like that.

Not the least of Mark Twain's gifts as a writer—important to any writer but especially to him—was a precise and vivid memory for people and happenings. *Life on the*

74

Mississippi, Roughing It, countless stories and letters attest to this gift of memory. And it was not just a factual, imaging memory; it was also the creative memory of *what it was like to be a boy.* But not even so fine a memory as his is valuable without something worth remembering. It was his fortune to grow up in a world which filled his mind with experiences suitable to his gifts.

The world of his boyhood was still being civilized; and for all his life as a writer he kicked against those civilizing forces, whose authority all the same he never really challenged.

Physically Hannibal was small and unimportant, settled in a lush wilderness from which the Indians had not long been driven. Sam Clemens as a boy had been free to ramble half-wild, and free to mix with the slaves and learn their uncivilized superstitions and stories. The original Huck Finn, son of the town drunk and envy of the boys of respectable families, did not have to go to school, wash, or go to bed at bedtime; yet so far from graduating, as he would be likely to nowadays in one of our cities or even in Hannibal itself, from juvenile delinquency into crime, he wound up a justice of the peace in Montana.

The humid heat of the Missouri summers enforced a fine indolence. Mark Twain the writer, remembering what it had been like to be Sam Clemens the boy, provided his imagined boys with indolent summers to lazy away; the man himself was driven, like a proper American, to ceaseless work, more than he could do justice to; yet the boys lolled in perpetual summer in a luxuriance of doing nothing. (Strange, the energy with which Eliot's Prufrock demonstrated that he was enervated, and the great energy which

Mark Twain expended to extol, among other things, laziness.)

When Mark Twain was a boy, Hannibal was a town recently of the frontier. The special frontier excitement recreated itself in the middle-aged man writing in safe, settled Connecticut. The people of Missouri had had to be independent to get along at all; they had been hopeful and restless because there was money to be made; they had been free, or at least unpoliced. Mark Twain himself enjoyed these special opportunities, so much that when he lost his work as a pilot because of the Civil War he lit out for the rawer frontier of Nevada and California. But criminals also are attracted by money, independence, and the lack of police; Mark Twain knew them by long experience, and as a child he experienced much violence, that white violence which had ravaged the Atlantic Coast from the Indians, advanced its rule to the Pacific, enslaved and imported Negroes, and has not disappeared. His fantasy books are drenched in mayhem; Satan, the angel in *The Mysterious Stranger*, is portrayed as obliterating with utter indifference the tiny people he makes, and the carnage in *A Connecticut Yankee* destroys nearly all the knights of England. Likewise the most real, authentic, of his books contain as a matter of course killings or injuries or thefts in nearly every episode; and only a man accustomed to cruel violence could find Tom Sawyer's game of freeing Jim, to Jim's anguish of suspense, so simply funny as Mark Twain found it.

However, the frontier violence generated in the people of Missouri its own antithesis, repressiveness. There was the obvious repression of slavery itself, which does not in Mark Twain's writings breed retributive violence among the slaves, though the masters assume the slaves would be vio-

lent if they could; and of course slavery is a conditioner and shaper of *Huckleberry Finn* as of *Pudd'nhead Wilson*. And there was the pervasive, law-making repressiveness of Calvinistic respectability. This was not that ferocious Calvinism which had animated the Puritans, though it rather thought it was; this was a vigorous, Bible-belt version of that respectability which in those days told the nation what was right, and tells most of it still; *good* is what the respectable say it is. This respectability shod Huck's bare feet, dragged him sometimes into church where he itched, and taught him he should betray his best friend into slavery; furthermore, not all Huck's own true goodness, relative freedom from its dominion, and experience to the contrary allowed him to rebel against the laws of respectability, only to try to slide out from under.

Freedom, violence, respectability—and the river. The river was wonderful to Mark Twain no matter how well he knew it, and, as he relates in *Life on the Mississippi*, he knew it well. The river provides Huck and Jim with their escape and they love it; it nearly kills them and they fear it. It is the object of an awe that is more genuinely religious than anything else in the book. If it is a symbol, it is that kind of symbol which is not recognized as such by the characters whose lives are subject to its power, or by the writer who presents it, and which intellect can not inspect in the glare of prose exposition.

77

Yet even though Mark Twain had such gifts and such experiences, I think that one who had read his other books, even the best of them, could not have guessed that he would write his great one—as one could not guess it of a good many other writers, Melville and *Moby Dick* or Coleridge

and *The Rime of the Ancient Mariner* and *Kubla Khan*; it is the chasm between good and great in art. *Life on the Mississippi* demonstrated Mark Twain's profound knowledge of the river and its people, *The Adventures of Tom Sawyer* his pleasure in boyhood, *Pudd'nhead Wilson* his understanding of slavery, these and *Connecticut Yankee* and a number of stories his taleteller's gift, a thousand asides and especially *The Mysterious Stranger* his angry and bitter satire. But not even an anthology of all his best other work could bridge the chasm that separates them from *Huckleberry Finn*. For he was severely limited in his capacities as a writer, and it would be easy and tempting to suppose that the genius restrained by these limitations could never free itself into a book worthy of it.

He had so little critical judgment of his own writings that he believed his masterpieces to be those frigid contrivances *The Prince and the Pauper* and *Joan of Arc*, that he intended *Tom Sawyer* to be a book for adults and *Huckleberry Finn* merely its companion-piece, and that he chose of all his masterpieces the only shallow section for his platform favorite, the game of rescuing Jim from his prison. This gross defect of taste is manifest in everything of importance he wrote. As a comic entertainer he yielded to each comic impulse as it arose, not only to the damage of the total unity of the work but also, frequently, to the distress of the reader; for many of these ideas were just gags, the sort of thing he had become famous for in his newspaper articles. For example, *A Connecticut Yankee* contains a lot of advertising and journalistic gags which are pretty poor stuff: "Camelot *Weekly Hosannah and Literary Volcano*!—latest irruption—only two cents—all about the big miracle in the Valley of Holiness!" A good many of Tom

Sawyer's tricks and games, truth to tell, are better than this sort of thing only because they are a boy's. Mark Twain's satiric passages are usually spoiled by an outburst of unironic anger or else by a lapse back into funnyman anecdote and gagging. Even *The Mysterious Stranger*, which he wrote from great bitterness and from no desire to please the masses, dissolves into a rigged-up plot quite unworthy of the irony of the opening. A writer's critical judgment ought not to refrigerate him until he turns out, if anything, works of exquisite ice. Yet neither should it be so feeble as to permit him to yield to every impulse; for though the novel is not formally strict, yet it is an art; there are some things that can't be fit into it. A talent, such as Thomas Wolfe's, that cannot contain itself even within the hospitable limits of the novel is denied greatness of accomplishment; and most of the time Mark Twain's talent is uncontained in a way that a harder self-criticism could have helped to remedy.

But, as I see it, a source of greater shortcoming in Mark Twain was his acceptance of standards of value—moral, social, literary—which in his heart he disbelieved in. That he was divided within himself there is overwhelming evidence: the identical appearing prince and pauper, "Those Extraordinary Twins," in *Pudd'nhead Wilson* the infants changed in their cradle and also the Italian twins, the pseudonym Mark Twain itself. I think that this split may be taken, in some sense, as the war of powerful impulses with a code of conscience put on from without. I do not believe that this code was imposed upon him against his will and that he fought it. This may have been the case when he was a boy, but as a man and writer he actively sought respectability and voluntarily restricted himself to its laws. The

79

famous story of all his manuscripts' being submitted to his wife's censorship, from which they emerged, if at all, expunged and maimed, was originally his joke and only a joke. In truth, he sometimes, as he himself described it, planted censorable words and passages to delight his children and to give his wife the feeling she had helped him by censoring them; but sometimes she missed a word or two, which he then himself struck out. He was a vigorous man sexually, whose books contain no love affairs or sexually desirable women. He wrote an entire book on the Mississippi and its pleasure boats without so much as hinting at the flagrant prostitution on the boats. He swore with zest and imagination, but his characters are denied a goddam. Contradictions like these, some trivial, some large, are not in themselves enough to damage a writer; indeed, most writers are full of them. But Mark Twain was full of desires which he had always been taught were bad and needed controlling —anger, for example, alcohol, laziness, tobacco, sex. He decided that a good many of his impulses were innocent because natural, but he knew that others needed controlling, and he could find no governing principles which he could accept fully and happily. He rejected Calvinism; yet in 1897, in *Following the Equator*, this occurs in "Pudd'nhead Wilson's New Calendar":

> The spirit of wrath—not the words—is the sin; and the spirit of wrath is cursing. We begin to swear before we can talk.

He largely accepted the canons of respectability—he married and loved a highly respectable wife, lived conventionally in Hartford, accepted Howells as his mentor; yet respectability is the chief object of his chronic satire, as in his best short tale, "The Man That Corrupted Hadleyburg."

Optimism and faith in democracy and progress he made his creed; but as this creed failed him he descended into a pessimistic determinism which was a sort of Calvinist metaphysics with God left out. A Connecticut Yankee has not the slightest doubt that he is right to obliterate the nobility of Britain in order to introduce nineteenth-century American democracy and inventions; but fifteen years later The Mysterious Stranger says that even when a man

> "is trying to make up his mind as to whether he will do a thing or not, that is itself a link, an act, and has its proper place in his chain; and when he finally decides an act, that also was the thing which he was absolutely certain to do. You see now that a man will never drop a link in his chain. He cannot. If he made up his mind to try, that project would itself be an unavoidable link—a thought bound to occur to him at that precise moment, and made certain by the first act of his babyhood."
>
> It seemed so dismal!

Literarily he was both fortunate and unfortunate. Having a weak sense of self-criticism, and knowing it, he not only voluntarily submitted to the censorship of the age but also set himself romantic, high-flown models of literary style; hence, he could not only write *Personal Recollections of Joan of Arc* but admire it over *Huckleberry Finn*. Yet the censorship and models were not so binding on him as they might have been; fortunately he came to literature late, without a university training, and also fortunately he came to it through journalism; he learned to please the people before he tried to please the cultivated. In a letter to Andrew Lang he wrote:

> I have never tried in even one single little instance to help cultivate the cultivated classes. I was not

81

equipped for it, either by native gifts or training. And I never had any ambition in that direction, but always hunted for bigger game—the masses. I have seldom deliberately tried to instruct them but have done my best to entertain them. To simply amuse them would have satisfied my dearest ambition at any time.

And from "Pudd'nhead Wilson's New Calendar":

There is no such thing as "the Queen's English." The property has gone into the hands of a joint stock company and we own the bulk of the shares.

Here the great Mark Twain was speaking, albeit with exaggeration, but there is also the voluminous Mark Twain who wrote *The Prince and the Pauper*. Even when he sets out to spoof such a style as he there employed, as in *A Connecticut Yankee*, he frequently gets caught up in it or else burlesques it into tedium. If the Brahmins had trained him, they might very well have vitiated him down to their own level—that of Holmes, Lowell, Longfellow—because he was certainly corruptible. But they got to him too late to do real harm, and furthermore it was Howells who, as editor of the *Atlantic Monthly*, directly influenced him, Howells the most generous and perspicacious of them all.

The gravest charge to be brought against Mark Twain's work outside *Huckleberry Finn* is its lack of sustained moral seriousness. For the moralizing and anger in which he indulged do not, when given their head, produce works of true seriousness. A great deal of the time, to be sure, he was intending only to entertain; even at its best, as in *Tom Sawyer*, pure entertainment makes little claim on our moral sense; our excitement at the danger Tom and Becky run in the cave with Injun Joe (hazards of nature and a black

black villain) dies when they are saved and leaves scarcely a trace behind. But frequently he deals with profounder subjects, and it is in them that the lack of sustained moral seriousness is most damaging. His satire is usually flawed by vitriol or frivolities; his philosophizing is confused and jejune; the stories he tells do not embody within themselves a moral issue clearly involving the characters and morally resolved. *Pudd'nhead Wilson* is a partial exception to this last charge; there he treats miscegenation and slavery; but the treatment is so gaunt that the bare bones of the plot show through pretty badly; and Roxy, the pivotal character, the slave who traded the babies in the cradle, though she is strong and well portrayed, is still morally of no greater interest than melodrama ever allows.

Yet there on the far side of the chasm, in the company of the great, *Huckleberry Finn* wonderfully stands.

Granted his gifts, his material, his shortcomings, he needed a most delicate and special combination to be able to write at the top of his bent; and I believe that one of the two essential elements in this combination was his choosing to write as Huck. No other point of view would do, and he tried many. Being a violent and headstrong man, Sam Clemens needed severe restraints to accomplish a work of art; the restraint of putting on the mask " Mark Twain " was not enough, for the man modified the writer into himself; the restraint of writing as a yankee in King Arthur's England might have done it, but the fantasy was too wild; the restraint of telling tales was never enough, nor of writing satire. In all these guises his intemperance was insufficiently constrained; he would philosophize, wisecrack, melodramatize. Only in the person of Huck Finn could he be

83

true to himself, to the character, and to the story, and also be profoundly serious.

There is the style. Held to Huck's language, Mark Twain could not lapse into a high-flown passage, except to satirize it when other characters used such bombast. And then the delight of assuming Huck's language must also have guarded Mark Twain from wandering, for his fidelity in suggesting dialects is not the dry exactitude of a word-scholar but the joyous making of a poet. Yet Huck's language is wholly adequate for every demand put upon it, for description and narration obviously and also for such introspection as Huck is obliged to do, about as much as Mark Twain was capable of handling well.

There is Huck's social status—the bottom. (Negroes had no status at all.) Huck, because of the money he and Tom found in *Tom Sawyer*, has had thrust upon him a certain status; but when his father reappears, in the fourth chapter of *Huckleberry Finn*, he sells his money to Judge Thatcher for a dollar, happy to get rid of it and all that goes with it. His poverty is voluntary. Mark Twain had portrayed himself as a boy in Tom Sawyer, the child of respectability; yet, by good fortune, in this book he chose to write in the person of Huck the outcast. Huck did not need to rebel against or dream of subverting that respectability which Tom (i. e., Sam, i. e., Mark) could not get out from under even if he wanted to; Huck had been civilized for only a short while by people to whom he had no strong obligation, who were doing their duty to a boy that had come into some money and who cannot be said to have loved him. Therefore Huck could be (i. e., Mark could be) easy and offhand in his observations of the ways of righteous people; he would not need to moralize, to shout with anger,

or to condemn any but the most outrageous rascal. Hence Huck's presentation of manners and character is direct and uninterfered with, Sam Clemens' idyl of boyhood remembered is wholly unselfconscious, and Mark Twain's satire is stronger than it otherwise could have been.

When Huck arrives at the Phelpses, Tom Sawyer's relatives, and is taken for Tom, he excuses himself for arriving late by telling Aunt Sally there had been a steamboat accident.

> "Good gracious! anybody hurt?"
> "No'm. Killed a nigger."
> "Well, its lucky; because sometimes people do get hurt. Two years ago last Christmas your Uncle Silas was coming up from Newrleans on the old *Lally Rook*, and she blowed out a cylinder-head and crippled a man. And I think he died afterwards. He was a Baptist. Your Uncle Silas knowed a family in Baton Rouge that knowed his people very well. Yes, I remember now, he *did* die. Mortification set in, and they had to amputate him. But it didn't save him. Yes, it was mortification—that was it. He turned blue all over and died in the hope of a glorious resurrection. They say he was a sight to look at."

Surely this patch of dialogue between a boy we know to be generous and good and a woman we learn to be decent and kindly is not only casually probable but also as powerfully satiric as any other passage of its length this side of Swift. To Huck himself, as to a child reading it, this is merely Huck's reporting of an exciting (though imaginary) accident and of Aunt Sally's comments on another accident which this suggests to her, and it is not satire. To Sam Clemens remembering, as to an adult reading for simple

85

entertainment, this is a part of a nostalgic world where astonishment is everywhere to be found, and it is not satire. But to Mark Twain, as to a partly detached mature reader, the disparity between this matter-of-fact dialogue with all its assumptions and any humane code of moral values is frightful; his choosing so coolly to emphasize this brutal disparity, to hold it up for censure, is derived from his hot anger, and the effect of such a passage, beneath the excitement and astonishment and delight, is that of great satire.

There are other, lesser accidents of Huck's condition that were of good use to Mark Twain, especially his age; however old he may be, he is certainly before the age of open sexual activity. However, there is, above all, Huck's character, the salient elements of which both restrained and liberated Mark Twain.

Huck ordinarily uses the code of values he has been taught, for example, that slaves were not fully human; yet he responds to people just as people. Seeing Jim mourn one morning, he writes:

> He was thinking about his wife and his children, away up yonder, and he was low and homesick; because he hadn't ever been away from home before in his life; and I do believe he cared just as much for his people as white folks does for their'n. It don't seem natural but I reckon it's so.

How casually in this passage Huck recognizes and responds to Jim's humanity and at the same time sees the disparity between this and the code of conscience he has been taught. This very disparity is the source of most of the profound comment implied in the book.

Huck is alive to other people, sharp-eyed for details of furnishing and dress, and intelligent in winnowing the

hypocrisies from the truths—as Mark Twain was. But Huck is also, partly by his station in life and partly by nature, not in the least interested in manipulating people in any way, as Tom Sawyer is. A good many times during the course of the book Huck says he wishes Tom were with him to rig up a better trick than Huck himself has managed, and for the last nine chapters Tom is present. More than present—Mark Twain, who had restricted himself to Huck's character, could restrain himself no longer, and Tom takes over in directing the course of events. Huck is passive; he does not even try to save himself, in his numerous adventures, until things have come to quite desperate straits; yet he is not sluggishly indifferent; on the contrary, he is keenly responsive to all the world about him, social and natural. Because of this quality in Huck, Mark Twain's own manipulative impulses could be reduced to a minimum, to the engineering of melodramatic episodes, which, however, are *seen* unmelodramatically. Huck accepts the world as he finds it, until a part of it is about to destroy him, at which point he runs off and hides till things calm down; such acceptance by a live intelligence is a high kind of love, the sort that leaves the object of its love alone. To be sure, there are a great many characters in the course of the book whom no one could be expected to love in any active sense; but whatever Mark Twain, or Sam Clemens as a comic entertainer, might have thought of them, however he in real life might have dealt with them as actual people, however he intended us readers to feel about them, the important thing is that Huck, who is telling the story, observes them acutely, does not want to change them, would like to accept them for what they think they are, and does accept them for what he sees them as being. Never does he

tell the reader: Here, this is what you should be thinking about so-and-so.

> I went right along, not fixing up any particular plan but just trusting to Providence to put the right words in my mouth when the time come; for I'd noticed that Providence always did put the right words in my mouth if I left it alone.

Well, Huck left it alone, as Mark Twain seldom managed to.

And Huck is moral, highly moral. By this I do not mean that he is " good " but that he is concerned with discriminating between good and evil and with behaving well. The world of *Tom Sawyer* opposes good to naughty, and the only evil is natural evil, danger, damage; even Injun Joe in the cave, because he is seen melodramatically, is like a bear, scary. The cheat of the last portion of *Huckleberry Finn* is just that Tom Sawyer brings with him his simpler way of acting, so that he converts Jim's escape from a matter which can occasion genuine moral anguish into a game. But a cruel, unmorally cruel, game; for the reader does not forget so easily as Mark Twain does the extremity of Jim's danger; the reader remembers Huck's genuine contrition, a contrition of which Tom was not capable, after cruelly teasing Jim in the fog early in their adventures on the river.

88

> It was fifteen minutes before I could work myself up to go and humble myself to a nigger—but I done it and I warn't ever sorry for it afterward, neither. I didn't do him no more mean tricks, and I wouldn't done that one if I'd ' a ' knowed it would make him feel that way.

Huck's moral perplexities come from his difficulty—it is everybody's difficulty—in distinguishing between the

right and wrong of convention and the good and bad of morality. He is split as Mark Twain was between convention and morality; but Huck's impulses leaned him steadily away from convention or respectable conscience.

> It don't make no difference whether you do right or wrong, a person's conscience ain't got no sense and just goes for him *anyway*. If I had a yaller dog that didn't know no more than a person's conscience does I would pison him. It takes up more room than all the rest of a person's insides and yet ain't no good, nohow.

The righteous are those who identify their right with good and their wrong with bad, as Huck has endless opportunity to observe; furthermore they do not see themselves in other sinners, as Huck sees himself.

> I begun to think how dreadful it was, even for murderers, to be in such a fix. I says to myself, there ain't no telling but I might come to be a murderer myself yet, and then how would I like it?

In the early part of the story moral issues are not so important to Huck as just surviving. His escaping from his father and from proper society and Jim's escaping from Miss Watson and being sold down the river are scarcely moral acts; but the difficulties and dangers of actually escaping force Huck to steal and lie even more than usual. (Jim is exempted from these because he must hide from everyone.)

89

> Mornings before daylight I slipped into corn-fields and borrowed a watermelon or a mushmelon or a punkin, or some new corn or things of that kind. Pap always said it warn't no harm to borrow things if you was meaning to pay them back some time,

> but the widow said it warn't anything but a soft
> name for stealing and no decent body would do it.
> Jim said he reckoned the widow was partly right
> and pap was partly right, so the best way would be
> for us to pick out two or three things from the list
> and say we wouldn't borrow them any more—then
> he reckoned it wouldn't be no harm to borrow the
> others.

Clearly Huck's pap is wrong and the widow is right; but
equally clearly the stealing will not, in this opulent land,
hurt the farmers much and will permit Huck and Jim to
survive. So, as a sort of propitiation to the right they are
violating, they

> concluded to drop crabapples and p'simmons. We
> warn't feeling just right before that but it was all
> comfortable now. I was glad the way it come out,
> too, because crabapples ain't ever good and the
> p'simmons wouldn't be ripe for two or three
> months yet.

Right has its due, crabapples and green persimmons.

Huck enjoys lying, and never regrets it when it does
its work, and it usually does. "She done it [apologized] so
beautiful it was good to hear, and I wished I could tell her
a thousand lies, so she could do it again." He must lie to
survive, he sometimes lies for the fun of it, but he never
lies to injure; that is, his lying is, as he sees it, wrong but
never bad. And he always knows when he is lying, and he
can judge the effects of the lying well enough. When the
king and duke pretend to be the English brothers of Peter
Wilks, for the purpose of defrauding his daughters, Huck
says "it was enough to make a body ashamed of the human
race." Huck's own lying is sometimes gratuitous and even
cruel. It is not that he does no evil, but that he knows

when he has done it and repents. And he does not judge others. He gives Jim's unfailing patience and loving kindness its full due, and he gives wicked deeds their proper epithets; but he is sickened to see even the king and duke run out of town, tarred and feathered, on a rail. "Human beings *can* be awful cruel to one another."

Finally, Huck is capable of, and endures, moral agony. Like no other character in Mark Twain's books, he reaches the point of having to make in full consciousness a choice which will affect the whole life of the person he most loves and therefore his own life; he has the power to send Jim back a slave to Miss Watson merely by writing a letter, and he is prompted by all the force of conscience, of right-wrong conscience, to do this. Also, he says,

> think of me! It would get all around that Huck Finn helped a nigger to get his freedom, and if I was to ever see anybody from that town again I'd be ready to get down and lick his boots for shame.

Furthermore, all that he comprehends by providence and God direct him to this. So he writes the letter, and feels "good and all washed clean of sin for the first time I had ever felt so in my life, and I knowed I could pray now." But memories of Jim's love arise and confound him till he is all in a tremble looking at the paper on which he has written the words of betrayal/righteousness.

91

> "All right, then, I'll go to hell"—and tore it up.
> It was awful thoughts and awful words but they was said. And I let them stay said; and never thought no more about reforming. I shoved the whole thing out of my head and said I would take up wickedness again, which was in my line, being brung up to it, and the other warn't. And for a starter, I would go to work and steal Jim out of

slavery again; and if I could think up anything worse, I would do that, too; because as long as I was in and in for good, I might as well go the whole hog.

Here is a person we have come to know, in the true thick of decision, pushed by religion, society, and his own weakness toward a righteous action which, though he cannot say so, he feels to be bad; his humanity saves him and he does the wrong/good thing. But not only is the reader moved by Huck's perplexity, struggle, and final decision; he also, prepared for it by act and comment throughout the novel, is moved by the dreadful irony of this good person's anguish at having to defy conscience in order to resist doing the worst deed of which he is capable. Right tempts him to evil.

And by the fortune of his writing in the person of Huck, who accepts, Mark Twain could not weaken his case by railing against convention, hypocrisy, slavery, as he normally would have done; nor could he slough off the painfulness of this irony with a joke as he sometimes did. Huck's acceptance contains Mark's hatred. The tension holds.

Yet writing in Huck's person was not in itself enough to give Mark Twain the free constraint he needed. For Huck is the narrator of *Tom Sawyer, Detective*, set on Tom's Uncle Silas's farm in Arkansas, and of *Tom Sawyer Abroad*, in which they wander with Jim across the Sahara and Egypt in a balloon. Neither is worth much as a story, and for the most part Huck's style deteriorates accordingly. These are the inventions of Mark Twain the popular entertainer, just as the mock-rescue of Jim in *Huckleberry Finn* was the invention of Tom (Sam, Mark).

The other essential element which permitted Mark Twain to fulfill himself as a writer was a wandering through the world he knew: the river. Staying put in St. Petersburg, as in *Tom Sawyer*, overstrained his ability to join episodes together plausibly within one unity. But floating too freely, as in *Tom Sawyer Abroad*, tempted him to superficiality, a sort of touristing across the Atlantic, the Sahara, the high points of Egypt, and Mt. Sinai. What he needed was the opportunity to hang episodes together in the form of a romance, to move from one set of people to another so that he would not try developing the characters of a single group as a novelist ordinarily does, and to present variations on a few basic themes. He needed small river-towns in the South to set his romance in, for only in this world, the one Mark knew and loved best, could Huck become involved in an occasion that mattered fully and morally.

Meanwhile, the reader is delighted by episodes of un-abashed adventure; by hilarious portraits of respectable folly and low buffoonery; by lazy days; by dozens of splendidly sketched characterizations; by the best and liveliest sug-gestion of dialects written in America; by the warm friend-ship of Huck and Jim; by a mass of folklore and super-stition, included because it is a part of the characters' lives and not for its own sake; by slapstick and high satire; by brutal cruelty and delicate forgiveness. And there is no problem about transitions: at the very outset Huck and Jim must get away, and every stop by the way is only an interruption of their flight. The river is the natural agent of their escape, and Mark Twain knew the river, as boy and pilot, with a lover's intimacy. He knew the river, the life along the riverbanks, the customs of that South; he knew slaves, footloose boys, murderers, bossy housewives,

93

cheats, absent-minded preachers, feuding gentle families; he knew the language of that world.

From the disappearance of Tom in the third chapter to his reëmergence in the thirty-fourth, the book is adequately motivated, as no other book of Mark Twain's is and therefore its action is true, not tricky. Amazing how alive with action even the indolence is.

> We would watch the lonesomeness of the river, and kind of lazy along and by and by lazy off to sleep. Wake up by and by, and look to see what done it and maybe see a steamboat coughing along up-stream, so far off towards the other side you couldn't tell nothing about her only whether she was a stern-wheel or a side-wheel; then for about an hour there wouldn't be nothing to hear nor nothing to see—just solid lonesomeness. Next you'd see a raft sliding by, away off yonder, and maybe a galoot on it chopping, because they're most always doing it on a raft; you'd see the ax flash and come down—you don't hear nothing; you see that ax go up again, and by the time it's above the man's head then you hear the *k'chunk!*—it had took all that time to come over the water. So we would put in the day, lazying around, listening to the stillness.

And the hushing fog that Huck and Jim are parted in—that lovely evocation of the experience of thick fog—is given us by action, not by set-piece description. The descriptions of the river, say at sunset, in *Life on the Mississippi* are admirable; but this evocation of the fog on the river is unexcelled in the genre anywhere. Huck whoops for Jim; paddles; listens; watches snags; whoops; pushes off from the islands' banks; gives up and sleeps. And these actions are not only the best way to communicate the

experience, but also they are strongly motivated; for finding Jim again matters, on every score.

Under it all is the river itself, the cohering, unifying force of the book. For even greater than Huck's moral struggle and victory is the force of the river, that fascination which *Life on the Mississippi* talks about to us but which *Huckleberry Finn* creates in us. The river, in the book, makes their escape possible; they refresh themselves by swimming in it; they drink it; they live at its slow pace; it brings them adventures; it tears away the towns built on its shores; it is beyond imagining powerful. Huck will defy the Presbyterian God, but the river he fears and loves past any defiance; God is above and separate from him, but the river is about him and in him; God is righteousness but the river is mover and comforter and savior.

Although I am grateful that Mark Twain chose to write in the person of Huckleberry Finn about the world he knew best, I have no idea how he came to make the choice—chance, fortune, providence. It happened. It was his gift of gifts.

THE RED BADGE OF COURAGE

CRANE, 1895

by BERNARD WEISBERGER

The year 1893 was hardly the moment for an American literary event. The United States was painfully preoccupied with a simmering political rebellion in its Mid-west and with a nationwide economic collapse. The social problems swept under the carpet in the Gilded Age were about to explode into new violence. A culture still staggering under the impact of the age of steam was confidently, but somewhat groggily, preparing to grapple with the consequences of electricity and internal combustion. It seemed unlikely that a small artistic revolution could attract much attention.

Creativity, however, has a way of choosing its own auspices. In that year's summer, a twenty-one year old native of Newark, New Jersey, the son of a minister with

a solid American ancestry two and one half centuries long, covered one hundred and seventy-six sheets of blue, ruled paper with a novelette. He called it *The Red Badge of Courage: An Episode of the American Civil War*. Its theme of courage was timeless. Its setting was a nineteenth-century war, already haloed with erroneous romance. Its technique and conception were uncompromisingly modern, unshakably identifying it with the literature of the century ahead. To these apparently unrelated parts, Stephen Crane added the intangible element of his talent and the sum of them was a kind of greatness. The book was, and is, a brief classic.

It had overwhelming consequences for Crane; in fact, it stamped out the pattern for the remainder of his life. Published first in a newspaper and then in hard covers, it was a sensational success. Because of it, he was able in 1896 to bring out *Maggie, A Girl of the Streets* under his own name. Because *Maggie* dealt with slum life in a way that was then considered too sordid for propriety, it had first seen print anonymously. With two widely read novels to his credit, Crane could now select his own writing assignments from a variety of offers. His choice led him into an existence which was a study in irony. He hungered for a broader experience of life than the New Jersey parsonages of his childhood had given him. He elected, therefore, to become a roving newspaper correspondent. In 1896 he went out to the Far West. There he looked among the ghosts of mining camp, Indian war and cattle trail, hoping to find some violence left in them. But the West was already freezing into maturity. The next year Crane headed for Cuba, where a native insurrection against the Spanish was blazing. His ship was wrecked off the coast, and he spent

97

nearly two days at sea in an open boat. Later he translated that horror into a famous short story. His compulsive curiosity for "experience" was still unsatisfied. He went to Greece before the year was out, and covered a Greco-Turkish war. In 1898 he was in Cuba again to report on the American campaign against Spain. The irony was most apparent here. Stephen Crane, the writer of *The Red Badge of Courage*, should have turned a searchlight on that fustian adventure and exposed it for the shabby thing it was. Instead, Stephen Crane, the man, could not get too close to the "glory" of the front. He was cited in dispatches for bravery under fire. The next year he went to England to rest up and meditate new undertakings. But his health was wrecked by his Cuban exposures. In June of 1900, still only twenty-eight years old, he died of consumption on the continent.

Out of this untimely cutting-off rose a paradox. Crane was a pioneer in "realism," and *The Red Badge of Courage* should have done to heroic epics of the Civil War what *Don Quixote* is supposed to have done to romances of chivalry. Moreover Crane was a hard-working literary man, who published enough in eight years to fill twelve volumes of collected works. And Crane was successful and recognized and well paid for his endeavors from the time he brought out his second novel. His newspaper career and early death veiled these facts, however. In his manner of living and dying he emerged as a stereotype of popular fiction—an amalgam of Richard Harding Davis and Lord Byron, who dared all, drank deeply of life and died while yet a boy, unfulfilled. As an artist, Stephen Crane would sharply have rejected anything so palpably phony as his own legend.

What is more, no man ever dealt so cruel a blow to his own favorite literary theory. It was Crane's feeling that the author must be as close as possible to the experience which he crystallized in words; that one could do nothing good aesthetically unless it had once meant something important to him. Yet his two most lasting novels, *Maggie* and *The Red Badge of Courage* were spun out of imagination, during unagitated afternoons in small-town family residences. Nothing could better illustrate the fallacy of believing that the "slice of life" offered by a realistic author need be in any way a slice of his own exterior history.

The fact is that *The Red Badge of Courage* is both realistic and modern precisely because of its masterly handling of interior action. This is the first of its claims to be ranked with the best fiction of the present. It is a story with movement and with crises, but the movements are of images within the mind, and the crises are crises of soul. For the story, taken merely as a story, is a lean one. Briefly, it is the history of a member of a fictitious regiment, fighting a nameless Civil War battle. The hero is a youthful soldier, whom we first meet, beset by fears, as the regiment is moving into action. He wonders if he can stand the naked shock of battle, and he makes fumbling and frustrated efforts to shore up his nerve by seeking out others as frightened as himself. But he cannot break through the defensive wall with which each man is invisibly surrounding himself, and his turmoil increases as they get nearer to the fighting. The troops line up and repulse one attack, but when the second wave of the enemy hurtles through the smoke, the boy bolts and runs away—or rather, gallops away in the blind, terrible, unreasoned thrashing of animal terror. Soon

he is mingling with a motley crowd of couriers, teamsters, other skulkers and walking wounded, the normal refuse of the front line. He meets a wounded man who torments him by solicitously asking where he has been hurt. He finds a friend from his own company who, in the final agonies of a mortal injury, dies before his eyes. Then he meets another cluster of retreating soldiers. When he tries to stop one of the frenzied men to get some information, he is clubbed with a rifle butt. Stumbling and jerking about in a daze, he is discovered by a cheerful trooper who leads him back to his outfit. There, to his vast relief, it is assumed merely that he got lost during the action and suffered a head wound.

Next day there is more fighting, but this time the youth plays his part well. In one charge he advances the flag with a recklessness that wins the regimental commander's notice. After a day of confused motion, the regiment is ordered away from its new position, with the usual pointlessness of war from the private's unillusioned point of view. As they leave the place of "blood and wrath," the soul of Henry Fleming changes. He has been to touch the great death and found that, after all, it is but the great death. He is a man. And so, he "came from hot ploughshares to prospects of clover tranquilly, and it was as if hot ploughshares were not. Scars faded as flowers."

This is hardly a story with a sweeping focus. In form, it is compressed. Its foreground is never wider than the view taken in by the single pair of eyes belonging to the hero. Its action is not of a kind for satisfactory dispatches and six-column headlines. Yet *behind* these eyes there is continuous and detailed motion, adding up to development. The book is really a rich and complete story of a successful search for identity. It is, in fact, significant that the full

name of Henry Fleming is not revealed until well along in the tale. What is most important, there are no pauses in this action, no suspended moments between charges and bombardments, or halts by the roadside. Every impression, every word, every shape, color, sound and smell is in some direct way related to the emotional experience of the boy. So tight is the construction, and so continuous the flow of impression and mental reaction, that the book could easily be re-written as a monologue by Fleming in stream-of-consciousness style.

There is no character in these pages except for the frightened soldier. Almost immediately, we are introduced to the "youthful private." Within another few paragraphs we learn of the fictitious image of himself that he created before his enlistment and during his early days of service. He saw war as a series of "large pictures extravagant in color, lurid with breathless deeds," and in the first weeks of strutting in uniform, he had "believed that he must be a hero." In the following months of drill and encampment, that original image has been lost, and he has sunk into the anonymity of the army; he is "part of a vast blue demonstration." Now, confronted by action, he is aware of himself again. In a sense the other soldiers, loud and swaggering or stubbornly refusing to speculate on the impalpable tomorrow, are personifications of the various protective attitudes which he himself has adopted. But the question abides. He can no longer find rest in military depersonalization. "Now, with the newborn question in his mind, he was compelled to sink back into his old place as part of a blue demonstration." Compelled to do what was previously voluntary, he is unsatisfied. And so he continually tries "to measure himself by his comrades."

101

Yet his aloneness continues to be overwhelming. As they move up towards the line he is suddenly obsessed with the idea that they are headed for a trap, and that he alone knows it. "He thought that he must break from the ranks and harangue his comrades. . . . There was but one pair of eyes in the corps. He would step forth and make a speech." But of course he does not. In the first fighting he finds temporary reassurance in being a part of the regiment, "welded into a common personality which was dominated by a single desire." But then the rage of battle sweeps around him, cutting him off from the others. He is dazed and suffocated—sensations like those of being buried alive, cut off from the living earth. The words of another soldier ring in his mind: "I didn't come here to fight the hull damned rebel army." The vision of himself alone against the gray lines is all too intense. When he finally breaks and runs, he loses his sense of direction. There is no longer any comfort in the thought of others at his side, or support troops behind. Rather, "destruction threatened him *from all points*." He is in the direct center of the stage.

In his odyssey through the rear area, this is made even more clear. The tattered soldier whom Henry meets, wounded in the head and the arm, can easily be taken for the romantic hero parading through those large and colorful pictures of war in Henry's mind as a raw recruit. There is a hint of this in the fact that the tattered soldier is first encountered gawking, his mouth "agape in yokel fashion," at a bearded sergeant who is telling a story. This is a flashback to the wide-eyed greenhorn that Henry has been. But now this pristine and virginal personage is tattered, fouled with blood and powder stains, and, wounded in the *head* and *arm*, unable to think or act sensibly. From this ghost of

himself the boy hears an insistent question that racks him with shame. "Where yeh hit, ol' boy?" The answer which he cannot give, of course, is "in his manhood."

Henry escapes from this inquisitor, and meets the wounded "tall soldier," mumbling and lurching toward his death spasm, minutes away. Jim Conklin is not described as an older man, but it is clear earlier in the book that Fleming looks up to him and leans on him for reassurance. He seems to represent the consolations and supports of those who are respected in youth—parents, elders, teachers, and ministers. Now he dies, with horrible contortions, leaving Henry with a childish desire "to screech out his grief." One more refuge is gone. The tattered soldier then reappears. This time, he has become partly identified with Conklin, since he hints that he is an older man, with children. He is visibly getting weaker from his own hurts. He begins to babble and to confuse Henry with one of his own friends, highlighting Henry's further alienation from his past and from others who have shaped him. Remorselessly, the tattered man presses his question, until Henry snaps, "Oh, don't bother me!" and leaves him. But this is a fresh crime to add to cowardice. He is deserting a wounded comrade, and further deserting both his idealized self and the standards set for him before he put on the blue.

A climax is approaching. Henry is buffeted by emotions. He wishes that the army would lose the battle and share his disgrace. Then he recoils from the idea, because his need to believe in certain success for "that mighty blue machine" is overwhelming. A man cannot hide his own failure by pulling the universe down around his ears; the will to order is too strong. Next, he wishes to die. Suddenly, he is agonized by a fantasy in which the whole

regiment is discussing his cowardice. In a sense, he is going through the crisis of guilt felt by the " convicted " sinner of a revival. He is thinking of " rules for the guidance of the damned," in Crane's own phrase. And the fact is that he is about to be, in the words of a Christian, " born again."

There is going to be a rebirth, indeed, but not a supernatural one. What happens, rather, is that he meets another panicky refugee, with livid face and rolling eyes. When he tries to intercept this flying fragment of an organization, the man smashes his rifle across Henry's head. This is a turning point. For the frightened soldier is precisely what Henry was himself in the moment when he began to speed toward the rear " in great leaps." Up to now the boy has angrily turned aside the tattered man's question, refusing to recognize the reality of his act. Now he is face to face with his own image at last, and what happens? Clubbed over the skull, he has at last received a wound—a " red badge of courage." From that very moment, the direction of the story changes. The trek *back* to the front begins. The wound is a first stage in redemption, and for all practical purposes, it is self-inflicted.

The next redemptive step comes soon. Henry wanders aimlessly, deliriously thinking of home. He remembers days as a schoolboy, swimming in a favorite pool. He can feel " the swash of the fragrant water upon his body." This is his baptism, and the redeemer is at hand. A cheery voice at the boy's shoulder hails him, his arm is firmly taken, and he is walked along in the darkness towards his regiment. The man with him is a tower of strength, threading the mazes of the tangled forest, avoiding guards and patrols, beating " ways and means out of sullen things," steadily guiding them both on the road back to the campfire—to light, and

most of all, to companionship. All the while he is delivering a long, rambling monologue, the whole point of which is that it says nothing coherent. The core of it is in a sentence that spells out the pointlessness of battle.

> . . . By dad, I give myself up fer dead any number 'a times. There was shootin' here an' shootin' there, an' hollerin' here an' hollerin' there, in th' damn darkness, until I couldn't tell t' save m' soul which side I was on.

What a shock the Reverend J. T. Crane would have experienced, had he lived to read and understand these lines by his son. "*I couldn't tell t' save m' soul which side I was on.*" The gospel that saves Henry Fleming is no assurance of purpose and ultimate salvation in an ordered universe, where good and evil are definable. No; it is the statement of the fact that there *is* no fathomable purpose, that the souls, wandering and crying in the damned darkness, never know their own side. Here is a negation of the Christian conversion, in which one sees the light and is enrolled among the saints. Yet from this negation, the boy will take strength. A man is courageous, at last, because he must be. He has no prop but himself. But let him prove himself once, and then he can never be betrayed.

And who offers this counsel of iron? No prophet, no saint, no elder—in effect nobody. For there is one enormously important detail. Once Henry has found his old outfit, the voice disappears in the darkness. And suddenly the youth realizes that not once has he seen his benefactor's face. His journey has been one of *self*-discovery. His injury has come from his own hand. Either the cure for it has come from the same place, or else from nothingness. There

105

is no saviour to whom he can offer a prayer of thanks, just as there was no devil to blame for his wound.

One final step remains. He hesitates about going back to the campfire, trembling at the thought of the "barbed missiles of ridicule" which will be aimed his way. But he finds that he does not need to invent a story. His friends assume that he was misplaced in action, and they make a satisfying to-do about nursing his bruise, which they assume is from a bullet-graze. So he makes a final connection. He had been alone, true. But there is compensation for the isolation. Weakness, if it goes unnoticed, makes no more of a ripple in society or the universe than unseen courage. "He had performed his mistakes in the dark, so he was still a man." At first he had created a false hero-image of himself, tailored to meet false standards. The image and the standards are now as dead as Jim Conklin. The facts of the situation are plain. There is man, and there is impersonal fate. If fate is kind, the favor is accepted gratefully. If not, a man does the best he can. In neither case is there much purpose in looking further.

> In the present, he declared to himself that it was only the doomed and the damned who roared with sincerity at circumstance. Few but they ever did it. A man with a full stomach and the respect of his fellows had no business to scold about anything that he might think to be wrong in the ways of the universe, or even with the ways of society. Let the unfortunates rail; the others may play marbles.

He does not have to worry any longer about future battles. "It was not essential that he should plan his ways in regard to them. He had been taught that many obligations of a life were easily avoided." So much for the re-

sponsibilities of the "saved." Freed from fear, he knows
that the necessary evil will come when it will come. Meanwhile he can sink again into the anonymity of the company,
moved aimlessly here and there, and perform heroically.

His conversion has led him to a kind of traditional
religion in reverse. He can take his loss of identity in battle,
because he is reconciled to his own character. If he has no
control over his fate, neither has anyone else. He can be a
conventional warrior, because he knows that the conventions of fictitious war do not really exist, and cannot make
impossible demands. So the goal of an essentially psychological story is reached. The rest of the book is merely to
prove the change in Henry.

Crane's story is one of the first robins of a literary
spring, in which hundreds of bewildered young men will
hunt for bearings in a world they never made and are not
hopeful about mending. But there is a second seal of the
contemporary age stamped into the narrative, by the very
manner of its telling. Crane constructed the tale with
devices which were to become the badges of several schools
of modern fiction. For one thing, the careful descriptions
of scenery and climate are intended to create a tone match-
ing that of the hero's mind at any given moment. In this
kind of environmental symbolism, the ideas will be implicit
in the action and the setting. They will not be lifted out
by the intervening hand of the writer, and examined. The
communication from the invented character to the reader
will be direct, but carried on through suggestions.

The very start of the book—the cold, passing "re-
luctantly from the earth"—immediately establishes a chill,
foreboding atmosphere; a sense of 3 A. M., when the muscles

197

are torpid, the body's juices congealed, and every prospect vile. And when, in the final sentence, a golden ray of sun bursts through "hosts of leaden rain clouds," it is almost too pat, too much of a celluloid bromide. In between, this parallel construction of mood and setting reappears again and again. When the regiment is hurrying into action, it is during the "rushing yellow of the developing day." But even as the sun "strikes mellowingly" on the earth, two columns of soldiers moving across a hill look like "two serpents crawling from the cavern of the night." Readers will not be allowed to forget that encroaching darkness. As the troops make a crossing of the river by night, a fire gives to its waters a winelike tint. But the tint of wine is also that of blood, suggesting the kind of river that is going to run through the action of the next day. It is well to notice again the occurrence of two images from the evangelical literature of conversion—the river which must be crossed for salvation, and the blood in which the sinner must be washed. When the regiment has managed to meet the first charges bravely, the boy notices that "the sky is blue and pure, and the sun gleaming." But when he is running away, as the crisis of darkness draws on, the same sun is emitting "slanted bronze rays," and when Jim Conklin dies, it is red and "pasted in the sky like a wafer."

Another development in "new" writing at this time was the effort to break down barriers between art forms and fuse different sensory images of experience. It was especially notable in symbolist poetry, where words were used for their musical effects rather than their meaning, in some cases, and certain sounds were identified with particular colors and the emotions which they evoked. *The Red Badge of Courage* is in step with this trend because in good part it is a painting.

Crane uses colors almost compulsively. In the very first paragraph the sun rises and turns the landscape from brown to green. An amber-tinted river purls at the army's feet, and at night hostile campfires gleam like red eyes. We learn later that when Henry had his first dreams of martial glory, his mother discouraged him, throwing "a yellow light" on his ambitions. The army is a "blue demonstration." But the most effective use of color is in the scene when Henry stumbles on a decaying corpse in the woods. The overarching boughs make a little chapel of the place, entered through "green doors," with a "gentle brown carpet" of pine needles. In this cloister-like atmosphere of warm browns and greens, the boy is paralyzed with terror when he discovers a long-dead soldier. The uniform has faded to a melancholy, sick green—not the fresh hue of the grass. The eyes are the color of a dead fish. The mouth has turned yellow; black ants parade hungrily over the gray skin of the face. This abrupt precipitation into violent greens, yellows, blacks and grays burns the symbol of rejection of conventional religious supports—the "church" containing only a moldering carcass—deeply into the consciousness. Towards the end of the book, when Henry is exhilarated and bold in the final fighting, pieces of the battleground are fought over as if they were "gold thrones or pearl bedsteads"—colors again taken from the popular impression of the heavenly city—and the battle flags fly "like crimson foam," setting the triumphant tone of final salvation.

A third brand identifies *The Red Badge of Courage* with writing styles that were breaking down the conventions of the novel as the nineteenth century ended. Crane is included by critics among the "naturalists" of that period

—writers who made man something of a cipher in a world ruled by a "nature" which had no respect for his purposes, and which as often as not crushed him in its blind movements. *The Red Badge of Courage* seems entitled to the label. Certainly, Henry is carried, in his personal retreat, towards the conclusion that the cosmos is not interested in him. The theme is presented most directly when he stumbles into a wood, "as if resolved to bury himself" in nature, the great consoler of so many romantics. But this is not the benign nature of Transcendentalism. As Henry forces his way along, vines cling to his legs and branches shout his secret shame. He cannot "conciliate the forest." He pushes further, looking for "dark and intricate places" and it needs no profound acquaintance with psychoanalysis to guess what they are. Suddenly there is a flash of false hope. He shies a pine cone at a squirrel, which sensibly runs away and does not remain to "die with an upward glance at the sympathetic heavens." This is cheering. Here is nature supporting his own craven action with a demonstration of instinct at work. "She re-enforced his arguments with proofs that lived where the sun shone."

But immediately he blunders into a swamp, where a small animal is observed, pouncing into some *black* water, and emerging with a fish. It is a quite conventional reminder of the cruelty of the struggle for life. The thickets get deeper, but then there is a second illusion of hope. He reaches the little chapel in the forest, with the "high, arching boughs" through which a "religious half-light" is falling. Here is another conventional scene. The groves, after all, were God's first temples. The stage is set for the formal rite of purification and prayer. And what leaps out as the branches are pulled aside? The ant-eaten corpse!

The shock underlines the sardonic joke, like the grin of a skull suddenly discovered. Henry runs for his life. Nature may not take the trouble to be an enemy, but she is no friend.

Crane also hammers repeatedly on the theme of the frustration of the individual will in the collective personality of the regiment. The military units are *things*—sometimes living organisms, sometimes machines. A column of stragglers and wounded is " a flow of blood from the torn body of the brigade." After one action, the regiment lies "heaving from its hot exertions." A battle in the distance is a contest between beings who strike savagely and powerfully at each other." But on the other hand, mechanistic images are frequent. The boy imagines that the charging Confederates are "machines of steel." He never quite loses his faith in the final victory of his "mighty blue machine." His company, tired out by repeated charges, is "a machine run down." Most of these similes are pedestrian, but occasionally Crane is capable of greater polish in his imagery, as when he describes bullets which "buff" into men with "serene regularity, as if controlled by a schedule."

The soldiers sense their helplessness and frustration. "The slaves toiling in the temple of this god began to feel rebellion at his harsh tasks," Crane says in one of his more awkward and inexperienced passages. Later, he returns to his proper technique of letting feelings escape in the words and deeds of his characters. (His writing is worst when he is untrue to the style he is creating.) Rebellion simmers effectively in Henry's outburst:

> 'Good Gawd,' the youth grumbled, 'we're always being chased around like rats! It makes me sick. Nobody seems to know where we go or why

111

we go. We just get fired around from pillar to post and get licked here and get licked there, and nobody knows what it's done for. It makes a man feel like a damn' kitten in a bag.'

This is Thomas Hardy or Omar Khayyam, flavored with the American countryside. The lieutenant gives the proper naturalistic answer. "'You boys shut right up! There no need 'a your wastin' your breath in long-winded arguments about this an' that an' th' other.'" In the end, frustration is dominant. After a successful charge, the regiment is reproached by the commanding general, who knows it only as a number, for not having gone far enough. It is as senseless as the rebuke of God for alleged sins, committed in ignorance. And what is more, when all is over, the regiment goes back across the river, presumably to its starting point. Yet there is victory of a kind, but the victory of these veterans is in their acceptance of this real war in place of the fraudulent heroic illusion towards which they bravely marched two days before. They are disenchanted but not beaten. And the moral is plain that man does not choose his destination. He cannot even hold on to the scarred bit of ground which he has won at the price of his youth.

A final hallmark of the book is its "realism." Here, Crane was something less of an innovator. Symbolism and naturalism were somewhat new in 1893. But the pedigree of the novel's fidelity to detail goes back to the "local color" tradition which Crane inherited from the writers who were forging their fame during his childhood—Mark Twain, George Cable, Sarah Orne Jewett, and their like. These authors differed considerably from each other, but they were all trying to re-create accurately the dialects and mannerisms of certain sections and classes of the country.

Crane and others were to marry this technique to a more liverish view of life than the seventies and eighties had thought fashionable. They helped to link realism with what was, in the stock phrase, "hard-boiled," and they laid down a road which some have followed all the way to Erskine Caldwell and James T. Farrell.

However, the "ash-can" school of writing was not necessarily implicit in the "realistic" writing of Crane's day. The modern thinker recognizes many "realities." Crane and his contemporaries were after a kind of "realism" which was particular and had boundaries. Sometimes it was called "copyistic," sometimes "veritistic," and sometimes more simply, "photographic." Its aim was to copy objective surroundings as faithfully as possible, and as impersonally as a wet plate. The impact was made on the audience by making the external resemblance between fact and fiction so exact, that the original sensations of an actual event were rekindled. It did not intend to shock deliberately, but it did not flinch from whatever was necessary to complete the sensation of a genuine experience, verifiable by life. One recent edition of *The Red Badge*, in fact, is illustrated by some of Matthew Brady's photographs, and no love-match of text and illustration could be happier.

Crane's method of achieving this special kind of realism was to record his soldier talk in what he considered a reproduction of Eastern rural speech. It is hard to tell whether or not the longer spoken passages accomplished his mission. After a time, such words as " sech," " hull," and " dumbed," and the persistent omission of final sounds, as in " t' " and " an' " become rather stylized themselves. Stenographic accuracy has a way of dating with appalling quickness. The dialogue is a weak link.

But the language of gesture and expletive, on the other hand, is timeless. There is a sense of imminence and closeness in some of Crane's prose because of what his characters do and say in their more terse moments. When we first meet the troops, they are in an argument with the tall soldier, who has picked up a rumor of impending movement, while in the unheroic act of washing his shirt. When Henry leaves his mother to rally to freedom's starry flag, she furnishes counterpoint to his fantasies by making her parting remarks to him as she peels potatoes. When he is lying in his tent, seeing visions of a "thousand-tongued fear" that will betray him the next day, the voices of his fellows are heard in a card game.

Even these homey touches can, by themselves, fade quickly into picturesque, Norman-Rockwell-like effects. Crane avoids this by contrasting them with the crashing events around them, thus making them powerful. The thunder of battle reinforces the intensely human quality of the trivial action. The flyspeck of detail underscores the solemnity of an entire scene. We are all conscious of this contrast in life between the sublime occasion and the ridiculous human animals taking part in it. Crane digs out the full dramatic value hidden in such linked opposites as the sneeze at the funeral, the nervous banality at the scene of an accident, or the drop of perspiration on the upper lip of the great orator.

These antitheses are superbly used. When the first Confederates come charging across the fields, a soldier is seen knotting a red handkerchief about his throat, giving "exquisite attention to its position." Even better, when the second wave comes over, a cry goes up: "Here they come ag'in!" Upon this, one soldier leaps to his feet and utters

a simple, single word. He says, "Gosh!" It is a conversational two-cent piece, but standing out alone, it has the impact of a shout. When Jim Conklin feels his life draining away through a side which looks as if it had been chewed by wolves, he can only murmur: "An', b'jiminey, I got shot—I got shot. Yes, b'jiminey, I got shot." To deglamorize war further, Crane has the generals, in their occasional appearances, talk in the same rural patois as the men, which is historically correct as well as artistically satisfying. And as a last example of this, one of the more potent speeches in the book is made by Henry's lieutenant when a new order for a charge is carried to the exhausted and thoroughly bloodied regiment. "Charge?" he says. "Well, b'Gawd!"

Oddly, it is this kind of detail which spells out the really remarkable feat of the boy Crane's imagination. He himself might well have undergone the central struggle of his hero to find manhood. Certainly the book's moral is a rejection of his own upbringing. The fight for emancipation needed no special setting. But it is remarkable that the imagined backdrop is so convincing.

It is tempting to wonder what his sources were. There was some realistic war writing for him to draw on, but not much, and it is hard to know what he had gotten hold of. John W. De Forest had printed some vivid letters describing infantry combat, which were buried in bound volumes of *Harper's*. He had also, soon after the war, published *Miss Ravenel's Conversion From Secession to Loyalty*, a superb and unsparing (and mostly unsold) novel of the high and low levels of military life. Walt Whitman had put out *Specimen Days*, which treated, without gloves, the hor-

rors of military hospitals. There were some good reporters in the war, and one of them, George A. Townsend, had, in 1866, written *Campaigns of a Non-Combatant*, which set forth the fevers, the plundering, the filth and the pain of parts of the war in unsparing terms. Brady's photographs were widely known. And there were the veterans—men only in their forties, then—who might have given an unlacquered account of camp and battle to a wide-eyed little boy in Port Jervis, or Newark, or Asbury Park, assuming that they chose to.

But the point is that even if we could isolate Crane's raw material, we must still credit him with amazing discernment, for he would have to weigh his truth against a mass of more conventional military reminiscence which dominated the market. There was far more of this than of useful material, for it was the age of formal military portraiture, in high collars and well-combed beards. The style of most non-fictional war writing was being set by the "Battles and Leaders" series of generals' memoirs appearing in the *Century Magazine*, where the war was fought over bloodlessly and with dignity ninety per cent of the time. (The other ten per cent was fine.) The fiction was mostly of the kind typified by the boys' histories emitted from the pen of Charles Carleton Coffin, a saintly Bostonian newspaperman, whose style was considered admirably suited to the task of embalming the nation's past, thus:

> The men throw aside everything which will hinder them, fix their bayonets, and prepare for the work. Their blood is up. They know that it is to be a desperate struggle. But it is not death they are thinking of, but victory.

Crane would normally acquire tons of this kind of

116

forget-me-not kind of romance to every ounce of genuine depiction he found. He had to do an enormous job of sifting. Then he had to break up what he had sifted, and re-fuse it in the heat of his imagination to make it a fit vehicle for his central struggle. This is the really astounding part of his youthful achievement. It still stands amazingly free of minor flaws. If *The Red Badge of Courage* is read and laid alongside a really good non-fictional memoir of the war, such as De Forest's, it matches up amazingly well.

There is no doubt that the credit for this achievement goes to Crane's genius. It is no ordinary thing to create a small masterpiece of imagination first, and wait for experience to validate it later—a little like digesting first and eating afterwards. Even more impressive is the universality of a book by a writer of such limited attendance at the school of life. *The Red Badge of Courage* rises above the times both of Henry Fleming and Stephen Crane. It paints the experience of all young men who go into battle, familiar with fright but strangers to themselves, and who come out of it touched with sin but somehow stronger. Its baptism in war might have taken place anywhere between the Trojan plain and Pork Chop Hill. Sometimes it almost seems as if it could do altogether without the background of war. The real story is in the emotional storm which divides maturity from innocence.

Yet even if we grant the truth of this, no creative work can be sliced entirely out of its context. Crane is a writer of his times, and he did not invent symbolism, or naturalism, or copyism, however much of them he unearthed on his own. But more than this, *The Red Badge of Courage* tells

117

a story which marks a new approach to the literary treatment of the Civil War. It is a special landmark in the history of our taste, the placement of which raises some absorbing questions. And in addition, the story of Henry Fleming is not in free flight, entirely independent of its setting in the Union army of the sixties. The book is great in part just *because* it takes place when and where it does.

The first of these points is of special interest to history. *The Red Badge of Courage* is the first novel to scrub the war of moonbeams and still find wide acceptance in the market place. It is the first widely accepted work in which a writer who sees life in its rank and primal conditions sees the war in the same light as a part of the whole of that life.

As we have seen, there were a few books which did expose the ugly realities of a fighting man's life, written by men who had taken part in the Civil War. These books died on the sales counters. Twenty years after the peace of 1865, there were realists like Garland, Howells, Ed Howe, Joseph Kirkland and others who did not hesitate to point out the defects of postwar society and to paint the unpleasant features of victorious materialism and sordid politics leering over the American scene. (The Gilded Age, after all, got its name from a novel by Mark Twain and Charles Dudley Warner.) Yet the two streams of realism do not run together. There is no single school of writers to take the two contrasting opposites—the idealism of the war for freedom and the Union and the corruption of national reconstruction—and push them up to confront each other.

There were men who could face the basic unpleasantness of combat without blinking. Yet such men cling to the idealism with which they enlisted. Oliver Wendell Holmes, Jr., of the 20th Massachusetts Infantry, survived the worst

fighting of the war and three severe wounds. In his old age, however, he could still recall the experience as one which touched his heart with fire. At the opposite end of the social scale is Private Ben Falls, of the 19th Massachusetts. He re-enlisted in 1864, commenting simply: "Well, if new men won't finish the job, old men must, and as long as Uncle Sam wants a man, here is Ben Falls." It did not occur to him that a job which cost so much in human agony might simply not be worth finishing. Nor does any veteran, looking around him in later years at what happened, announce publicly that the job might as well not have been done in the first place.

On the other hand, the writers who lash out at the grinding of the poor and the preening of respectable plutocracy in the eighties and nineties do not argue that the betrayal of American democracy and idealism began with the war itself. They accept the official valuation. There is almost a mutual agreement that the war will stay encased in a moment of time, forever different from what follows it. There was the war, with its lights and shadows; there is the acknowledged evil in what follows; but in the popular mind neither will be allowed to tarnish the other.

There is the sharpest kind of contrast between this literary situation and that of the twenties. The writers like Cummings, Hemingway, Dos Passos and their kin (to mention only the Americans involved), who found American society vulgar, craven, fraudulent or hollow in their day, also wrote books which debunked the war as a trick played upon them by their elders. The sell-out of what they were taught to believe in as children began when they put on their uniforms, not after they had laid them in mothballs, to judge by much of their writing. But the Civil War itself

119

does not fall victim to this kind of hostile recollection by its veterans, or even by their children. No one says that the war itself is the tree which has borne the bitter fruit.

The Red Badge of Courage changed all this only slightly. It is not a " debunking " book in any sense. It does not deride courage as the false coinage of a propaganda machine. Rather, it simply says that courage, like the fear which it overcomes, has animal reasons for being. Yet Crane's book is free of the conventional posturing of the war fiction then current. The reader of 1895 could not really accept the death of Jim Conklin and simultaneously believe in the fairy-tale heroes in blue who expired with eyes heavenward and a dying message to Mother on their lips. Crane had made a small breach in the wall of myth surrounding the war.

The question is, Why could readers of 1895 accept even that breach? Was it merely because nothing central in the myth was sacrificed? Or did the war already seem safely remote from anything in which they were concerned—a fight between Greeks and Trojans, in which bones could splinter and bowels spill without impropriety? Had the legend done enough work in the politics of justifying the *status quo* to be safely trimmed at the edges? Or was the world of Hanna and McKinley simply too busy to care one way or another? For that matter, why does our own age still enshrine the era of Lee and Grant with legend, when it has learned long since that the years of 1861 to 1865 were as bloody, brutal and stupid as any other war years?

These questions are merely variations on a basic inquiry—what is the effect of culture on literature? The fact remains that a fundamental national experience such as war itself is translated into different kinds of art under dif-

ferent conditions. What circumstances must be ripe to produce "real" wars, and "useless" wars and "noble" wars
in fiction? In the case of *The Red Badge of Courage*, it
took twenty-eight years for a popular market to be ready
for a work which said that the Civil War could be, for
the common soldier, a cruel and purposeless war at times.
The timing of the book gives it the status of a special
problem in the sociology of art.

There is one other way in which the story receives a
special impact from its Civil War setting. If it is the story
of innocence transformed into maturity, then it means more
because the boy soldiers of the sixties were especially innocent in a way that our world cannot entirely re-create.
The teen-ager of a century ago, especially in the farm
world, lived in unimaginable isolation. He was a realist
about many things—pain, hard work, death. But his *vicarious* experiences were limited. He read little. He had to
find types of humanity by digging them out from behind
the masks worn by his few immediate kinfolk and neighbors.
He did not see movies, hear programs or read articles describing the lives and labors of statesmen, safe-crackers,
cowboys, spies, evangelists, mountain climbers and confidence men.

This put him under a handicap. The self which he
would discover in the tragedy of war was somewhat cramped
imaginatively. The rural boy of that time could not play
the game of identifying himself with characters of fiction,
and trying on their supposed attitudes for size, which is
one way for an adolescent to learn something of life. If
he read much about war, it was in popular romance which
said simply that a young man in battle should be chival-

rous and fearless. It was precisely this image which he would try to force over his own craven and stubbornly resisting body, and his failure to get a good fit would terrify him.

By the time of the first and second World Wars, however, the situation had changed. In 1917 the early movies and the popular magazines had helped to create roles for boys to practice imaginatively—the wise guy, the tough mug, the strong and silent type and the others in the gallery of cheap fiction. And by 1941, the new soldiers were drenched with vicarious experience. Many of them lived in a world shaped entirely by comics, radio and movies. The more literate ones had read the realistic portraits of the war of Woodrow Wilson's day. The depression had brought its own disillusionments to their childhood. Popular psychoanalysis told them of unsuspected deeps in their souls. Comics, radio and the movies had inured them to violence from babyhood. The government thoughtfully provided them with canned and cellophane-wrapped entertainment, mostly freshly exported comics, radio programs and movies, to distract them up to the moment of combat from thinking any thoughts of their own.

Their problem, in fact, was the reverse of Henry Fleming's. Henry and his comrades did not know of the many forms which the self might take. The soldiers of MacArthur and Eisenhower had tried on so many imaginative suits that they were unable, in some cases, to decide among them. Their personalities were more deeply buried under layers of pretense, borrowed from the world of popular entertainment which rarely left them alone. The world was too much with them, just as it was too little with the soldiers of *The Red Badge of Courage*.

In the end, the essential experience may have been the same. War peeled the layers of pseudo-sophistication from the armed children of the nineteen-forties with as much finality as it stripped the posed romantic valor from youngsters in blue and gray. But it is still significant that innocence and maturity were not so badly confused by Private Fleming's generation. Fleming was more alone because, in battle, he had fewer stylized responses, fewer *learned* attitudes to adopt. And yet, on the other hand, perhaps he was more tough-minded in the long run. Was the boy bred close to the earth more aware of the permanence under the flux? More habituated to tragedy? Was he readier to examine his experiences more deeply and realistically under pressure, simply because they were fewer? Was his "self" more accessible and more resilient than the complex and many-faceted ego of the soldier who followed him into war eighty years later?

These questions are raised when the hero of Crane's novel is transferred from a universal setting and seen as the simple fighting man of a pastoral republic in 1861. Soldier and republic alike are entering battle full of strong and simple notions. Neither of them has yet any awareness of the catastrophe which will overwhelm those notions. It may be a classic of war anywhere and anytime, to be sure, but *The Red Badge of Courage* has the additional distinction of being specifically an epic of America's national tragedy, the Civil War.

123

by RICHARD CHASE

Like *The Wings of the Dove* and *The Golden Bowl*, its companion pieces among Henry James' late works, *The Ambassadors* is, one might say, a notoriously great novel. It was completed in 1901, when Henry James was sixty-one, and published in book form in 1903. It is the first and most popular of the three late novels. Any sympathetic reader with a versatile sense of literary values must surely admit that these works are great in conception and that they are often true, beautiful, and show astonishing virtuosity in their execution. Yet even admitting so much, not all readers are ready to accommodate themselves to the famous " difficulty " of James' late style, to the tenuously elaborate language in which the late novels are written. There is so

124

overwhelming and obtrusive a sense of a total intricate *expression* that one is not always able to remember or to discover what is being expressed. Then, too, the poetry of the Jamesian novel—the enriched and shimmering texture of language, the involved metaphors, the tantalizing suggestion of symbol and allegory—is present to charm and haunt and often to baffle the reader. There is no notoriety, no problematic quality, about the greatness of an earlier novel like *The Portrait of a Lady*. Everyone can agree that although it too is a relatively complicated work, its greatness comes through unequivocally. But of the three novels of the late period *The Ambassadors* is the least exotic, the most straightforwardly novelistic, as *The Portrait* is novelistic.

James wrote to Howells during the composition of *The Ambassadors* that the book was "human, dramatic, international, exquisitely 'pure,' exquisitely everything." And he joyously declared that "my genius, I may even say, absolutely thrives." This note of confidence, of renewed connection with his best talent and strongest energies, was by no means illusory. He was leaving behind him the period of social melodrama and of dark questionings of perverse morality and psychology which produced such works—all fine successes in their way—as *The Princess Casamassima*, *What Maisie Knew*, and *The Turn of the Screw*. He had returned to that characteristic subject which could usually be counted on to elicit his best powers, the international scene. Once again his theme would be Americans and Europeans. As always the Americans would be shown to be innocent and righteous and the Europeans would be more flexible, more disillusioned, more corrupt, but more deeply wise in the ways of the world and, in that sense, more humane. As always James' fable would trace the fall from

125

innocence of the Americans—and Lambert Strether, the hero, and young Chad Newsome are eminently ready to fall, although their American friends and relatives remain sturdily immune. Once again the moral transcendence of the American initiated into the mysteries of Europe would be seen as a rebirth—not in a mythic or religious sense, but as an amplification of the qualities of aesthetic understanding, moral flexibility, indulgence of human foible, released and consolidated maturity, comic and tragic assessment of the fate of man as a social being. Once again James' innate Americanism would be expressed by his insistence that if American innocence was incomplete without European wisdom, European sophistication needed the moral dimension the Americans could give it. The theme would be more intimately and poignantly rendered than had been possible in an earlier work like *The Portrait of a Lady*, because in *The Ambassadors* the central figure was to be a man much like James himself. Strether would have James' wistfulness, his sense of losing out on the chances of life, his timidity and moral scruples, his limitless self-cultivation and awareness, his gentlemanly sensibility. As the preface to *The Ambassadors* insists, Strether is a " man of imagination," though of course he lacks the powerful will of James' literary genius.

As we learn from James' preface and from his notebook entries, the idea of *The Ambassadors* came to him when a friend told him about an exhortation "to live" that had been impulsively delivered by William Dean Howells at a garden party given by the painter Whistler in Paris. The aging Howells, his wistful impulse toward the free and full emotional life tragicomically at odds with his Puritan scruples, and anxious that the young man to whom he

spoke should not, as he had, "miss out" on life, provided James with Strether and the scene in Gloriani's garden where Strether delivers *his* impassioned exhortation to Little Bilham. This occurs in the second chapter of Book Five, and from this scene, which is "planted," as James says, "or 'sunk,' stiffly and saliently, in the centre of the stream," the whole novel flows. Thus to break out unhappily at the age of fifty-five in favor of "living" is an admission on the part of the hero that he is in a "false position." The action of the novel will consist not so much in the episodes of the hero's sojourn in Paris as of his growing awareness, in relation to these episodes, of this "false position." For the first time Strether begins to "see" his fate, which, like that of John Marcher in *The Beast in the Jungle*, is *not* to have lived, not to have shared in full degree the common chances of humanity. "So that the business of my tale," James writes, "and the march of my action, not to say the precious moral of everything, is just my demonstration of this process of vision."

But the "false position" must be objectified in plot and character, if the "demonstration" is to provide the qualities James most wanted the novel to have: "intensity" and "drama." Thus the "poor gentleman" will inevitably come from New England. He will be dispatched from Woollett, Massachusetts, to Paris "to save" young Chadwick Newsome, who is ominously reluctant to return to the family business firm and Mamie Pocock, the flower of Woollett, whom Woollett wishes him to marry. The automatic assumption is that he has fallen into the clutches of a loose woman. Strether is sent on his embassy by his friend and patroness Mrs. Newsome, Chad's mother, and an important part of his false position is that he is to marry Mrs. New-

some, and thus gain the financial ease he lacks, if he succeeds in " saving " Chad. What he soon discovers, of course, is the inapplicability, as well as the vulgar prurience, of Woollett's fantasied moral melodrama. Chad is not " lost." Strether sees that he has changed for the better; he has matured and deepened. It is true that he has been taken in hand by a woman or women, among whom a countess, Mme. de Vionnet, and her eighteen-year old daughter Jeanne, appear to figure prominently. Accepting provisionally the shadowy liaison, without understanding it yet, Strether begins to give it his approval. Seeing in Chad his own lost youth, seeing in Chad also a young man such as his dead son might have become, Strether naturally cultivates the pleasant sense of living vicariously through the charming young friend for whom " Paris " has done so much.

Meanwhile the people in Woollett wonder why their ambassador lingers so long abroad, and concluding that he has himself been made captive in Babylon, Mrs. Newsome commissions the Pococks to investigate. They find a changed Strether, who instead of urging Chad to return to Massachusetts, urges him to stay in Paris. All that remains now, beyond the comic failure of the second contingent of ambassadors, is the full demonstration of Strether's ever growing awareness. He must discover, at last, and also approve, the liaison between Chad and Mme. de Vionnet. At the end he lingers to make his obeisances to the woman whom his Woollett categories had assumed to be a—how shall one say? —courtesan.

128

As James writes in the preface, certain other characters are necessitated by the decision that the whole story is to be seen through the eyes of a third-person point of view. Since he does not speak as " I," and therefore cannot address the

reader, he must have "confidants." The main confidant is Maria Gostrey; the minor one is Waymarsh. But although James says these characters belong rather to the "treatment" than to the "subject," they do gradually assert a life of their own, besides being merely brought in to listen whenever Strether starts to talk. Since Strether addresses people in the book, rather than the unknown reader, the ordinary inhibitions of social intercourse obtain and this, says James, will save the novel from "the terrible *fluidity* of self-revelation." As the phrase suggests, James appears to have two objections to the stream-of-consciousness technique which he banishes from *The Ambassadors:* it too readily encourages the expression of improper thoughts and it makes for formlessness.

Although our hero, Lewis Lambert Strether, is named after one of Balzac's characters and although one of James' ideals was to be ever emulous of the father of the modern social novel, *The Ambassadors* does not encompass anything like the full available range of Parisian life. James' Paris is that of the *haute monde*, and usually what we see is not a real city but a city converted in the act of Strether's perception of it into an unfolding aesthetic and moral experience—the "rush" or "flow" of experience, as James often writes.

The Ambassadors is not intended to be a full-blown social novel; it is a novel of manners. Despite the general sense of profundity and poetic significance, its spirit, as F. W. Dupee says, is of "urbane comedy." *The Ambassadors* is a comic work in the general tradition of Molière and Jane Austen. As such it looks back to James' fine early novel *The Europeans.* Strether's ideal friend Mme. de Vionnet is a finer version of the Baroness Münster of the earlier

129

work; Strether is a more intelligent and susceptible Robert Acton; Chad a more powerful version of young Wentworth. As in all high comedy what we have is the tale of how illusions and pretensions are squared with social reality. Personal biases, crotchets, moral rigidities, implicitly brutal, prurient or selfish suspicions (such as the Woollett people entertain with respect to Mme. de Vionnet) are corrected— in those susceptible of correction—by the decreed manners and morals of an emancipated upper social order.

In his preface James has this to say about Strether and the squaring of his precepts with reality:

> *The* false position, for our belated man of the world—belated because he has endeavoured so long to escape being one, and now at last has really to face his doom—the false position for him, I say, was obviously to have presented himself at the gate of that boundless menagerie primed with a moral scheme of the most approved pattern which was yet framed to break down on any approach to vivid facts; that is to any at all liberal appreciation of them.

We are reminded how common is this possibly Puritan theme in American literature. In the works of Hawthorne, Melville, and James we have innumerable examples of people who come to grief because they try in their innocence or monomania to impose a "moral scheme" upon a world which is more various, treacherous, and complicated than they know. In Melville's compulsive heroes and in Hawthorne's obsessed inquisitors the attempted imposition is cruel and malignant. In many of James' characters, the attempted imposition is benign, although in some it is not. For example, one might imagine a spectrum of decreasing obsessiveness and perversity in three of James' women who

try to grasp reality with minds too highly "primed with a moral scheme": the governess in *The Turn of the Screw*, Olive Chancellor in *The Bostonians*, and (charming and guileless as she is) Isabel Archer in *The Portrait of a Lady*. But Strether is merely innocent; he is mistaken but not malign. Hence it is proper that his story should be told with a lightness of tone.

But as in all enduring comedy there is a tragic note. In the classic Molière style, the comedy turns to tragedy in the suffering of a gifted woman—in this case, Mme. de Vionnet—who symbolizes all that is best in the ancient tradition and culture of her way of life. Her sacrificial suffering suggests the human cost and the high value of her social order. From her implicitly emanate all moral judgment and all standards of taste. By contrast the other players of the piece are in one degree or another like the fools, gulls, and fops of the stage comedies.

As for James' famous if somewhat elusive humor, which none of the critics has been able to describe very well, it is abundantly present in *The Ambassadors*. It is not the epigrammatic wit of Molière or Congreve or even of Jane Austen. James used the terse *mot* effectively in *The Bostonians* (as when he says of Miss Birdseye, the feminist and reformer, that with her, "charity began at home and ended nowhere"). But the concise witticism is not James' characteristic style. His style of humor is an elaborate levity, a mock-serious playing with language. An incapacity to follow James' elaborate joking is more often than not the reason why some readers fail to penetrate the famous difficult style of late works like *The Ambassadors*. Much gentlemanly and some cattily female fun is poked at Strether's friend Waymarsh, the grand aboriginal American who re-

131

minds people of Daniel Webster and Sitting Bull and who is so unhappy and homesick a tourist. He is, Strether concludes, in his very nature " extremely, almost wilfully, uncomfortable." A mild enough stroke, but before Strether has got through telling us his impressions, we have this Jamesian aperçu about Waymarsh, the tired businessman, who has come to Europe on the verge of a nervous breakdown:

> What it expressed at midnight in the gas-glaring bedroom at Chester was that the subject of it had, at the end of years, barely escaped, by flight in time, a general nervous collapse. But this very proof of the full life, as the full life was understood at Milrose, would have made, to Strether's imagination, an element in which Waymarsh could have floated easily had he only consented to float. Alas, nothing so little resembled floating as the rigor with which, on the edge of his bed, he hugged his posture of prolonged impermanence. It suggested to his comrade something that always, when kept up, worried him—a person established in a railway-coach with a forward inclination. It represented the angle at which poor Waymarsh was to sit through the ordeal of Europe.

James' humor mostly comes down to a play on metaphor (like the one about Waymarsh floating), by means of which James makes the metaphor admit its own absurdity, usually by following it through at least one more step than the reader is prepared for. The purpose is not to deny the significance of what is being said, but rather by opening up the metaphor, as it were—by making us note how outrageous it is, taken literally, but also how perfectly expressive it is—to make us feel not only its standard significance

132

but also fresh and exact significances which we were not aware the metaphor could be made to express.

The Ambassadors, like all of James' best books, boasts many successful examples of inspired linguistic playfulness. Needless to say the trick does not always come off. There is, for instance, the passage near the beginning where Strether meets Maria Gostrey. Strether soon realized—as a plainer man would put it—that he had been lucky to meet such an accomplished woman. But James makes Strether reflect that

> What had come as straight to him as a ball in a well-played game—and caught, moreover, not less neatly—was just the air, in the person of his friend, of having seen and chosen, the air of achieved possession of those vague qualities that figured to him, collectively, as the advantage snatched from lucky chances.

We don't much want to catch that ball, particularly since it changes into an " air " just as we reach for it. And although there are certainly qualities and quantities that figure for us as vague, the phrase may unhappily remind us of a notorious sentence in *The Wings of the Dove*: " Milly, let loose among them in a wonderful white dress, brought them somehow into relation with something that made them more finely genial."

But James is a master of significant levity, of the elaborately serious joke, and in this we notice a kinship with Hawthorne, Mark Twain, Melville, Whitman, and Faulkner. Despite their highly individualistic styles, the love of mock-serious word-play, of complicated and sustained parody and metaphor, is shared by these writers, who on one side of their genius are all " American humorists."

133

To mention Hawthorne, Mark Twain, and Melville—romancers all—is to be reminded of how little of a romance, how fully novelistic *The Ambassadors* is. There is no impulse to escape to the frontier, down the river, or to the Pacific; there is, on the part of the author, no dark melodrama of good and evil. As Strether tells Chad's friend, Little Bilham, he thinks of Chad, now much influenced by Mme. de Vionnet, in terms of "his manners and morals, his character and life. I'm speaking of him as a person to deal with and talk with and live with—speaking of him as a social animal." This is, of course, the way the novelist, as distinguished from the romancer, conceives of character. Again, thinking of James in relation to the American romancers, whose fictional world is so largely masculine, we are struck by the omnipresence of woman in James' novel. It would seem that as an exaggerated reaction to the neglect of women in American fiction before his time, James' works are permeated by the feminine presence, *The Ambassadors* almost totally so. Waymarsh, long separated from his wife, is the only untamed man's man in *The Ambassadors*. It is as if James had set out to test and affirm the validity of old Mr. Touchett's prophecy in *The Portrait of a Lady* that "the ladies will save us." When the Pococks—Jim, Sarah, and Mamie—come from Woollett to Paris, Strether, with his new sense of Jim's middle-aged juvenility, reflects that "the society, over there, of which Sarah and Mamie—and in a more eminent way, Mrs. Newsome herself—were specimens, was essentially a society of women." Before he comes under the influence of Maria Gostrey and Mme. de Vionnet, and even afterwards, Strether is positively haunted by Mrs. Newsome. He cannot sit down to lunch by himself without an almost supernatural sense of her fine, sensitive,

134

morally taut presence sitting across the table from him, and, as everyone notices (including James, who crows over it in his preface), one of the triumphs of the novel is the vivid idea we have of Mrs. Newsome even though she never actually appears on the scene. Miss Gostrey, who is among the women who should know, says to Strether, "You owe more to women than any man I ever saw." And Strether himself notes of the Chad who has been made somewhat strange to him by his Parisian experiences that here is a "young man marked out by women." Nor can he help seeing that Mme. de Vionnet's way of "marking out" men is (although he doesn't use the word) culturally superior to the way of Massachusetts women. The effect on Strether of Mme. de Vionnet and of Maria Gostrey, the European-ized expatriate, is to "complicate his vision," to make more flexible his naive moral categories, to prepare him for a tragi-comic, rather than merely a wistfully righteous, view of life, whereas the effect of Mrs. Newsome, fine and attractive as she is, is to isolate him from both the chances and the awareness of life.

But although women affect men, men do not affect women, with the single important exception of Chad's effect on Mme. de Vionnet. Her capacity to be affected by men is of the essence of her fate as of her simple humanity—that simple humanity which Strether perceives anew when he visits her for the last time, now fully conscious of her unhappy passion for Chad. "It was almost appalling," he reflects

135

> that a creature so fine could be, by mysterious forces, a creature so exploited . . . she was as much as ever the finest and subtlest creature, the happiest apparition, it had been given him, in all his years,

> to meet; and yet he could see her there as vulgarly troubled, in very truth, as a maid-servant crying for her young man.

The general lack of masculine reciprocation, especially in Strether himself, accounts in part for the somewhat tenuous quality—the softness at the center—of life as depicted in James' novel, a tenuousness and softness we cannot help feeling despite the wealth of reported observation. In *The Ambassadors* experience itself, in its subtle flow, seems essentially feminine; there is little sense of abrupt dimension, of anything massive or architectural, no delineated empty or static space. Except where James strives directly to "frame" the picture, all angular and geometric quantities are broken down and dispersed into the flow of musing perception.

Compared with any novel by Balzac, compared, for that matter, with *The Portrait of a Lady* or *The Bostonians*, there is too little dialectic of passion and will. Generally speaking, only one side of the dialectic, the feminine side, works with full vigor, and the novel suffers thereby in dramatic interest. The comparison may seem at first a little far fetched, yet one may further measure the quality of life in *The Ambassadors* by thinking of it in relation to Shakespeare's *Antony and Cleopatra*. James momentarily induces us to do so by saying that Mme. de Vionnet, when Strether first meets her, strikes him as the ideal of the *femme du monde*. She is "like Cleopatra in the play, indeed various and multifold. She had aspects, characters, days nights . . . she had taken all his categories by surprize." "Age cannot wither, nor custom stale her infinite variety" is the measure of the similarity between Mme. de Vionnet and Shakespeare's heroine. And indeed *Antony and Cleo-*

136

patra has to do with a man from a new and somewhat superficial culture, legalistic and stoic in its ethos, who gets entangled with a foreign woman in an older, more corrupt, more aesthetically interesting civilization, so that ambassadors have to be sent out to save him and bring him home. The great clash of passions is all here before us in Shakespeare's play. We see the dialectic of wills and of cultures direct. It is not filtered through the sensibility of "a poor sensitive gentleman," as James called those several characters in his stories who resemble Strether. Not that one wishes by this invidious comparison to suggest that, given the time, place, and the available forms of language and of imaginative representation, it would have been easy for James to treat the subject otherwise than as he did.

Strether has had his chances with women. He had married early and then tenderly mourned the young wife who had died. His feeling for Mrs. Newsome is scarcely passionate; but when he leaves Woollett the marriage at least looms before him in its realism. He distantly loves Mme. de Vionnet. He has stirred the heart of Maria Gostrey so that at the end of the book she virtually throws herself at him. Yet he rejects her, because he has rigorously promised himself at the beginning of his embassy, "not, out of the whole affair, to have got anything for myself." We gather, too, from James' notebooks that the insistent public demand for happy endings clamored in the author's mind and that once again this "vulgar" demand was not to be satisfied by making Strether marry Maria. There must be few readers, however, who would not give three cheers for Strether if he had gone back on his quixotic promise and given us the happy (but scarcely delirious) ending which would certainly not strike anyone as vulgar. Instead we are

137

left with the sensation of witnessing another one of those all too gratuitous renunciations that James prizes so highly—which strongly suggests that however much James may provisionally admire a great French lady who lives in sin, however much he may cherish the full and free life, he clearly applauds the "rightness" that Strether insistently attributes to his renunciation of Miss Gostrey and to his consequent return to Massachusetts and a life he envisions as probably bleak and empty.

As in all of James' major novels, we find in *The Ambassadors* certain great recognition scenes, framed and presented with the utmost care and skill. The three most memorable scenes take place in Gloriani's garden, in the countryside by the lake where Strether sees Mme. de Vionnet and Chad in a rowboat, and in Mme. de Vionnet's drawing-room on the occasion of Strether's last visit to her. In such scenes we reap the full benefit, in dramatic excitement, of the beautifully planned preparations that have been made for them—the elaborate "picture," in James' terminology, that leads up to the "scene." Each of the three scenes constitutes a sort of station along the path of Strether's ordeal. Each has the impact of a newly heightened awareness that approaches, as James wants us to feel, the force of revelation.

The leading images of *The Ambassadors* are of penetration into the labyrinth of life and of immersion in the flow of experience. Strether and his friends play an endless tune, or rather—since James' imagination is more akin to plastic art than to music—they weave a rich tapestry out of these images. A Freudian generation will be constantly aware of a sexual component in both images, possibly too much aware, since the sexual meaning is so intricately sublimated. In order to comment on the three main scenes, let us briefly notice the way the images are used.

138

The idea of penetrating a labyrinth is noticeable from the beginning. For example, there is the visit to Chester, with its "tortuous wall . . . rises and drops, steps up and steps down, queer twists, queer contacts, peeps into homely streets and under the brows of gables." Nothing like that in Woollett. But it will soon be apparent that penetrated labyrinths are not merely images but subject and treatment as well. That is, Strether's gradual progress towards full awareness of the life of Europe is the progress, also, of the novel towards the full representation of its subject. It is natural that James should repeatedly think of Balzac in writing a novel about Paris, and his essay, "The Lesson of Balzac," written in the years just after *The Ambassadors*, helps us to understand his intentions, particularly the following long paragraph:

> The question of the color of Balzac's air and the time of *his* day would indeed here easily solicit our ingenuity—were I at liberty to say more than one thing about it. It is rich and thick, the mixture of sun and shade diffused through the *Comedie Humaine*—a mixture richer and thicker and representing an absolute greater quantity of "atmosphere," than we shall find prevailing within the compass of any other suspended frame. That is how we see him, living in his garden, and it is by reason of the restless energy with which he circulated there that I hold his fortune and his privilege, in spite of the burden of his toil and the brevity of his toil and the brevity of his immediate reward, to have been before any others enviable. It is strange enough, but what most abides with us, as we follow his steps, is a sense of the intellectual luxury he enjoyed. To focus him at all, for a single occasion, we have to simplify, and this wealth of his vicarious experience forms the side, moreover, on which

139

he is most attaching for those who take an interest
in the real play of the imagination. From the moment our imagination plays at all, of course, and
from the moment we try to catch and preserve the
pictures it throws off, from that moment we too,
in our comparatively feeble way, live vicariously—
succeed in opening a series of dusky passages in
which, with a more or less childlike ingenuity, we
can romp to and fro. Our passages are mainly
short and dark, however; we soon come to the end
of them—dead walls, without resonance, in presence
of which the candle goes out and the game stops,
and we have to retrace our steps. Balzac's luxury,
as I call it, was in the extraordinary number and
length of his radiating and ramifying corridors—
the labyrinth in which he finally lost himself.
What it comes back to, in other words, is the intensity with which we live—and his intensity is
recorded for us on every page of his work.

It is a question, you see, of *penetrating* into a
subject; his corridors always went further and further and further.

The references here to the pictorial imagination, to the rich
sense of atmosphere, to the " frame " which shapes experience, to " intellectual luxury," to " the real play of the
imagination," and to the penetration of corridors all illuminate what James hoped to achieve in *The Ambassadors*.

To come from Woollett to England is exciting for
Strether, but " Europe " is really Paris, and Paris, as he first
sees it, " hangs before him . . . the vast bright Babylon, like
some huge iridescent object, a jewel bright and hard. . . .
It twinkled and trembled and melted together, and what
seemed all surface one moment seemed all depth the next."
Paris, alternately a jewel, a trap, a vortex, a sea, a maze, is
for Strether generally " a fathomless medium," in which, as

he extravagantly muses, people seem to "bump against him as a sinking swimmer might brush a submarine object." Partly because our point of view is so much that of the rather vaguely, if exquisitely, appreciative Strether, partly because *The Ambassadors* is so much in the aesthetic spirit of its time, the novel continually reminds us of impressionist art. If Balzac is really to be felt in James' novel, it is a Balzac whose powerful, flamboyant, three-dimensional effects have been atomized, almost homogenized, into the flowing, shimmering chiaroscuro of the age of Renoir, Pissarro, Maeterlinck, Whistler, and Debussy. No wonder Strether's categories break down in the flow of the seductive medium; sometimes we think the danger is that in this so destructive element *all* categories must break down. We are therefore thankful for the great scenes, because these are framed and given dimension.

Gloriani's garden, where Strether joins the cosmopolitan gathering and meets Mme. de Vionnet, is "far back from streets and unsuspected by crowds, reached by a long passage and quiet court." The life of these privileged Parisians speaks to Strether of "survival, transmission, association, a strong, indifferent, persistent order"—of everything that American social life lacks. Strether is much moved by the great sculptor, who has had so full a life, who has had fame and adulation and self-expression, who has had women (Strether allows himself the perception under the tutelage of Chad). He is struck by "the deep human expertness in Gloriani's charming smile." He is struck by the "special flare" of all these brilliant people for a humane worldly wisdom which he thinks of as a "long, straight shaft sunk by a personal acuteness that life had seasoned to steel." Much moved, and feeling, as a Massachusetts gentle-

141

man, rather out of it all, Strether delivers his famous speech to Little Bilham, exhorting him " to live " before, as it is for Strether, it is too late.

The scene by the lake makes the dramatic, if not the ethical, climax of the novel. Everything is prepared for the overt revelation which at this late stage of the book is positively in demand. Nothing " happens," except that Strether chances to see Chad and Mme. de Vionnet in a rowboat and he realizes that, as we groundlings say, they have been living together. But the revelation is made to carry the full weight and concentration of Strether's mild adventures. The drama of the international experience is secured by making Strether hold in his mind at the same time his sense of the lovely French countryside and his memory of " a certain small Lambinet " landscape he hauntingly remembers having seen long ago at a Boston art dealer's. The remembered Lambinet " frames " the present experience. And the illicit union of lovers, as Strether now contemplates it, makes everything that has happened to him fall into place. It is his crowning experience, it is the crisis of his story, it is the final step in the humanization and release, as far as this is destined to occur, of his character. He has now only to go through the ritual obeisance of the pilgrim. He must pay his final visit to Mme. de Vionnet and receive the ritual accolade of the great lady, admitting now, as he firmly does, that whatever Massachusetts morality may say, " he could trust her to make deception right. As she presented things the ugliness—goodness knew why—went out of them."

Although the reader is likely to feel that the lake scene is the real climax of the novel, James himself insisted, in his notebook, that the last interview between the hero and

142

Mme. de Vionnet is "really the climax . . . towards which the action marches straight from the first." It is true, at least, that in this scene the most general significance of the book is expressed. In relaxing at last his Puritan righteousness, and ashamed of his suspicions, Strether can now with full sincerity defer to the high civilization represented by Mme. de Vionnet. He can now relax enough to love and pity her. Pity, indeed, is in order, for as she says with perfect simplicity, her "only certainty is that I shall be the loser in the end." Love, too, is in order. But Strether loves her not as a lover, but as someone who has been led by her, as James illuminatingly says in his notebook, "to revise and imaginatively reconstruct, morally reconsider, so to speak, civilization." Reconsidering the ancient, traditional, Catholic civilization of which Mme. de Vionnet is the flower, Strether understands, for the first time, the human cost at which it has been won.

By the end of the novel Strether has come to resemble James' friend Henry Adams more than he resembles Howells. Like the aging Adams, Strether has completed his education by worshipping at the shrine of the goddess of civilization. In *Mont-St.-Michel and Chartres*, the pilgrim from New England finds that the Virgin, as she was conceived in thirteenth-century Chartres, absorbs and reconciles all the galling contradictions of the moral life and clothes in aesthetic splendor the sparse Puritan categories. Like the Virgin herself, Mme. de Vionnet is unity, humanity, culture, the ideal culmination of history.

143

The last of the three great scenes is, then, the ethical, if not the dramatic climax, for the drama must be somewhat diminished for us by its coming so close on the heels of the lake scene. Yet taken by itself it is dramatic enough, and it

calls forth, as the talk between Strether and Mme. de Vionnet is being led up to, one of the supreme concentrated expressions of James' art.

> Between nine and ten, at last, in the high, clear picture—he was moving in these days, as in a gallery, from clever canvas to clever canvas—he drew a long breath: it was so presented to him from the first that the spell of his luxury wouldn't be broken. He wouldn't have, that is, to become responsible—this was, admirably, in the air: she had sent for him, precisely, to let him feel it, so that he might go on with the comfort—comfort already established, hadn't it been?—of regarding his ordeal, the ordeal of the weeks of Sarah's stay and of their climax, as safely traversed and left behind him. Didn't she just wish to assure him that *she* now took it all and so kept it; that he was absolutely not to worry any more, was only to rest on his laurels and continue generously to help her? The light in her beautiful, formal room was dim, though it would do, as everything would always do; the hot night had kept out lamps, but there was a pair of clusters of candles that glimmered over the chimney-piece like the tall tapers of an altar. The windows were all open, their redundant hangings swaying a little, and he heard once more, from the empty court, the small plash of the fountain. From beyond this, and as from a great distance—beyond the court, beyond the *corps de logis* forming the front—came, as if excited and exciting, the vague voice of Paris. Strether had all along been subject to sudden gusts of fancy in connection with such matters as these—odd starts of the historic sense, suppositions and divinations with no warrant but their intensity. Thus and so, on the eve of the great recorded dates, the days and nights of revolution, the sounds had come in, the omens, the beginnings

broken out. They were the smell of revolution, the smell of the public temper—or perhaps simply the smell of blood.

It was at present queer beyond words, "subtle," he would have risked saying, that such suggestions should keep crossing the scene; but it was doubtless the effect of the thunder in the air, which had hung about all day without release. His hostess was dressed as for thunderous times, and it fell in with the kind of imagination we have just attributed to him that she should be in simplest, coolest white, of a character so old-fashioned, if he were not mistaken, that Madame Roland, on the scaffold, must have worn something like it. This effect was enhanced by a small black fichu, or scarf, of crape or gauze, disposed quaintly round her bosom and now completing, as by a mystic touch, the pathetic, the noble analogy.

If, as some readers complain, Strether sees Paris as a sort of museum instead of a city, this has the advantage of making us think of the above passage in relation to James' famous dream of the Louvre, which strikes us as being the concentrated symbol of James' characteristic imagination. As James tells us in *A Small Boy and Others*, he had once dreamed of overpowering and putting to flight a hideous monster of vague purport but apparently representing madness, chaos, or death. This he does by a suddenly marshalled act of will, confronting the intruder and then pursuing him down a long corridor, which he recognizes as the Galerie d'Apollon in the Louvre and from the high windows of which thunder reverberates. Exultingly, he feels "a general sense of *glory*. The glory meant ever so many things at once, not only beauty and art and supreme design, but history and fame and power, the world in fine raised to the richest and noblest expression."

145

In this vivid dream are the main components of the modern American imagination as we see it in its " genteel " aristocratic development. In its picture of fright and scruples overcome, its alliance of the imagination with the great traditions of European art and culture, in its sense of the ominous reverberations of revolution and of history, as well as of thunder, it reminds us not only of Strether paying his visit to Mme. de Vionnet, but of the final years of Henry Adams' pilgrimage and also of the lost modern spirit seeking salvation in T. S. Eliot's " Portrait of a Lady " and " Waste Land."

James thought that *The Ambassadors* was " quite the best, ' all round,' of my productions." His preface goes on to speak of the ease, the almost automatic facility with which everything fell into place, once he got the idea of a fifty-five year old American " man of imagination " giving a speech about " living." There is no doubt that James should have been a little suspicious about his blithesome feelings, as any writer ought to be when he feels too good about something he has written. The error will usually be that the writer does not see the overindulgence of his own habits of mind and tricks of style. We wish that in the writing of the book James' automatic facility had encountered a more punishing opposition from an ever-renewed sense of reality.

146

The germinal idea certainly offered James fine possibilities, and yet we cannot help reflecting that the wistful longings and regrets of a man like Strether, though strong on pathos and exact sentiment, are going to be lacking in drama. It is going to be a matter of what might have been, not of what can be. The modern American reader will need to dissociate Strether as much as may be possible from

his uninspiring descendant, the timid gentleman of contemporary middlebrow or *New-Yorker* culture. And then, too, James might well have been wary of his view of the book as a " demonstration." *The Ambassadors* is so much a demonstration of the sensibility of its hero that it sometimes seems to be not only a novel but a sort of handbook of manners and morals by a new Castiglione, an exposition and portrait of the ideal gentleman of the late nineteenth-century Anglo-Saxon upper middle class. It is possible to take the book in this way and to enjoy it as such. But of course it is a fine novel too—offering us, as we gladly admit, its peculiarly effective sort of drama, its realized characters, its endlessly fascinating resources of language, of sensibility, of humor, and of pathos. Rather than agreeing with James in his own judgment of the book, one wants to set down one's own list of his best productions: *The Portrait of a Lady, The Bostonians, the Europeans, The Ambassadors, The Aspern Papers, The Turn of the Screw*—and more.

EDITH WHARTON'S *THE HOUSE OF MIRTH*

WHARTON, 1905

by WALTER B. RIDEOUT

One reason for our failure still to give Edith Wharton her due may be simply the accident of chronology. With the publication of *The House of Mirth* in 1905, she entered on her "major phase" as a novelist at the beginning of that fictionally inferior decade just before the First World War when Twain and James had ceased to publish long fiction, when Howells had fought his best fights and written most of his best novels, when the lively young naturalists and impressionists of the nineties had prematurely died or written themselves out, and when only a few lonely figures like Dreiser and Ellen Glasgow were left to prepare the way for the burst of talent just after the war. We have tended to reduce Edith Wharton to the period, at most to

dismiss her as one of the best in a bad time, without quite realizing how good in an absolute sense that best could be. A detailed examination of *The House of Mirth* may do something toward reinstating her.

What Edith Wharton achieved in this novel had not been too frequent in American fiction up to the time she wrote, and her achievement helped make it more possible thereafter; it was to unite a strong sense of form and a robust sense for the details of experience. Not so towering a figure as either James or Dreiser, she nevertheless succeeded in fusing at a lower level of intensity the particular quality uppermost in each man: James's conscious, sensitive control and Dreiser's immersement in concrete fact. A close analysis of *The House of Mirth* will show that her sense of form manifests itself primarily in terms of structure, while her delight in the "specific density" of details is particularly noticeable in the way she interweaves the individual and the social life. Out of both design and detail grows the meaning of the novel.

Since the characters of *The House of Mirth*, like those of *The Custom of the Country* and *The Age of Innocence*, are carefully related to a particular stage of development in the society in which Edith Wharton herself grew up, it is important to place the novel according to time. *The Age of Innocence* was, of course, to describe the New York mercantile aristocracy of the seventies, that monotonous but solid brownstone-fronted world of her girlhood, that old social order of the "Aborigines," as Ralph Marvell wryly terms them in *The Custom of the Country*. During the eighties had come the first waves of the "Invaders," or as Edith Wharton was to specify in her autobiography, *A Backward Glance*, " the earliest detachment of big money-

149

makers from the West"; and the nineties brought more and greater waves of these new men of money, along with their wives. But *The House of Mirth* is a novel of even more nearly contemporaneous life, for the book's dating details place the action fairly certainly in 1900-1901, by which time the Aborigines had gone down before the Invaders, or rather, when these two antagonistic forces had coalesced by a species of social dialectic into a third force dominated by wealth rather than tradition or family name.

This social development in New York upper class society was objectified by an architectural development of which we are often made aware in *The House of Mirth*, the rise of the huge, eclectically-designed mansions of the new rich along Fifth Avenue, east of Central Park and north of that uniformly brownstone section of the avenue where the Aborigines had dwelt. When Paul Bourget, the French novelist who became one of Edith Wharton's best friends, saw Fifth Avenue in the middle 1890's, it already could impress him as a sign of "too much" money. In *Outre-Mer* (1895), he wrote:

> The interminable succession of luxurious mansions which line Fifth Avenue proclaim its [money's] mad abundance. . . . Here and there are vast constructions which reproduce the palaces and châteaux of Europe. I recognize one French country seat of the sixteenth century; another, a red and white house, is in the style of the time of Louis XIII. The absence of unity in this architecture is a sufficient reminder that this is the country of the individual will, as the absence of gardens and trees around these sumptuous residences proves the newness of all this wealth and of the city. This avenue has visibly been willed and created by sheer force of millions. . . .

Considering Edith Wharton's sensitivity toward houses and their decoration, both in her private life and in this novel, it is not being over-analytical to suggest that her title was intended to call up in the reader's mind just such a literal image of ostentatious stonework.

The title, of course, has several implications. Robert Morss Lovett noted that it was derived from Ecclesiastes 7:4, "The heart of fools is in the house of mirth"; and on the obvious level "the house" is the inclosed, exclusive society where Lily foolishly longs to dwell. Edith Wharton's temperament, however, was one that delighted in sharp contrasts. By contrast "mirth" becomes an ironic word with which to describe the empty routine of pleasure followed by her leisure class characters, to whom, incidentally, the book containing Ecclesiastes is merely a costume accessory at a Sunday social ritual. Lily's own sojourn in the "house" is of uncertain mirthfulness, she is soon shut out, and her end is mirthless enough. Even the title, then, is carefully integrated with the intent of the novel.

In her article, "The Criticism of Fiction," published in the *Times* Literary Supplement for May 14, 1914, Edith Wharton was to insist that "the conclusion of [a] tale should be contained in germ in its first page." Following that suggestion, it is worth while to examine, not only the first page, but the whole first chapter in order to show how skillfully the author prepared her subsequent action there. Granted the circumstances of serial publication which forced her to commit her initial chapters to the public before writing the remainder and granted the concern she expressed to W. C. Brownell over the loose ends of her design, she nevertheless managed to establish many of the elements of that design in the first chapter and to carry them out vigorously through almost all of the book.

The first chapter is comprised of three major parts: the chance meeting of Lily Bart and Lawrence Selden in Grand Central Station, her visit to his apartment, and her discomfiture by Rosedale on the street as she emerges from Selden's apartment house. What strikes one at once is the carefulness with which Edith Wharton has picked her settings to make implications about her characters and their subsequent fates. The initial placing of Lily in Grand Central Station suggests two aspects of Lily's situation which will become part of the book's pattern. In the first place, Lily is seen here in momentary isolation, related to but separated from her accustomed luxurious environment, and also set apart by her "highly specialized" appearance from the "dinginess" of the average women crowding past her. Throughout the book the author will repeatedly emphasize Lily's manifold isolation, illustrating it for the last time in the very last chapter of the book. In the second place, the fact that Lily is only pausing in a characteristic passage from one country house to another underlines the rootlessness of her life, her lack of a securely fixed place either in a tradition or a social class. *The House of Mirth* is, to a surprising degree, a book designed to depict motion.

The selection of Selden's apartment as her next setting allows Edith Wharton to establish in plot terms the beginning of the relationship between Selden and Lily, but it also puts into a concrete image a constant alternative to the "house of mirth." Selden's bachelor apartment, like his clothing, is slightly shabby; yet it expresses in its fireside and book-lined walls an intimacy and an elegance of the spirit lacking in any other dwelling which Lily will enter. It is the apartment, too, of a person who is fastidious, who prefers to observe rather than participate, and these are

qualities which will influence Selden's attitude toward a woman who both attracts and puzzles him. Lily's unconventional presence in the apartment has resulted from a spontaneous, natural impulse on the part of both people. This is to be characteristic of their relationship at its best, though, reader of La Bruyère that Selden is, " he could never be long with her without trying to find a reason for what she was doing." Typically in this visit she is open and friendly toward him while at the same time picking his brains to help herself in a scheme for marriage to a wealthy man. It should also be noted that after leaving Selden's apartment Lily has a mildly unpleasant encounter with a scrubwoman that is to involve a later, much more unpleasant encounter with her, which in turn relates to Lily's one other visit to this apartment near the end of the book.

Finally, the street meeting with Rosedale is a specific instance of Lily's real social insecurity, her vulnerability to the constant reproving presence of convention, which ultimately will exclude her from the charmed circle of her aspiration. Appropriately both Selden and Rosedale appear in this first chapter, for they are eventually to become her two possible choices as husbands and ways of life. Their characters are already set in contrast. Where Selden carefully observed all the proprieties while Lily was an unchaperoned guest in his apartment, Rosedale even in a meeting in a public street manages to speak to her "in a tone which had the familiarity of a touch." Where Selden is outwardly shabby and inwardly elegant, Rosedale is "upholstered" in "smart London clothes" and betrays an inner shabbiness through his eyes, "which gave him the air of appraising people as if they were bric-a-brac." Unlike Selden, who has been primarily shown fitted into the back-

153

ground of his apartment, Rosedale is shown only in the open street, detached from any background except Selden's apartment house, which he owns but does not inhabit.

Edith Wharton's insistence on Rosedale's Jewishness unpleasantly reveals her own social snobberies, but that insistence clarifies her implied comment on contemporary upper-class society as it is made through Rosedale's subsequent fortunes. At the beginning of the book Rosedale is the " outsider " by " race " as well as background. That so scorned a person can, even if slowly, scale the social heights by using his increasing financial success to establish ever more helpful social connections, we can see how fluid, how lacking in sense of family tradition, how solely dependent for its cohesiveness on the plain cash nexus, how utterly lacking in admirable qualities Edith Wharton believed this society to be. Such a frivolous society could acquire " dramatic significance " and " tragic implication," as she later wrote in *A Backward Glance*, " only through what its frivolity destroys " and " in its power of debasing people and ideals." So Lily Bart must be destroyed, and here we come upon one of the most important structural elements of the book. As Lily, an unsecure " insider " at the beginning, slopes downward from the heights, Rosedale rises slowly toward her. Their lines of progress meet, cross and continue, each in its established direction so that the pattern of their paths traced through the book is almost exactly that of an " X " laid on its side. When the pattern is consciously excerpted from the book and commented on, it may seem too pat and insistent, even mathematically plotted, but the triumph of the device lies in the apparent casualness with which the author keeps Lily and Rosedale related to each other at successive steps throughout the book. Here in

Chapter I they are at their greatest social distance apart, until their positions are reversed at the end of the book; yet immediately Lily is linked to him almost as fatedly as she is to Selden. Because of her hasty rebuff to him on the street in front of Selden's apartment, she has placed her reputation to a certain extent within his power. Acts are always caused and have consequences in this novel, and here we see set in motion part of the social machinery which will end with the exclusion of Lily Bart from " the house of mirth." So the end of Chapter I will later be seen to have sounded again the theme of Lily's isolation already implied on the first page of the book.

Scene, character, the beginnings of plot elements and of an important structural relationship—all these Edith Wharton has compressed into her first chapter, and she has managed to do even more. For one thing, the conversation between Lily and Selden has introduced, with appropriate emphasis for each, many persons to be importantly involved in Lily's subsequent career—Selden's cousin, Gerty Farish; Lily's aunt, Mrs. Peniston; the Trenors and the Dorsets. One of Edith Wharton's real abilities is to keep large numbers of characters in a wide, carefully controlled set of relationships one with the other. Again, money, the foundation of this upperclass society, is alluded to in this chapter so many times either in itself or in the shape of what it will buy that the sound of it almost rises from the pages. Lily consults a " little jewelled watch " while waiting to finish her journey from one great country house to another. She openly admits to Selden that her choice of a husband is governed by the fact that she is " very expensive " and " must have a great deal of money." The conversation over books is primarily over their money value, while Lily points

155

out that Selden may dress a bit shabbily whereas a woman " is asked out as much for her clothes as for herself."

The constantly reiterated motif of material wealth is explicitly connected by Selden at one point to a prophetic explanation of Lily's relationship to her environment. As he watches her well-groomed hand with " the sapphire bracelet slipping over the wrist," he thinks: " She was so evidently the victim of the civilization which had produced her, that the links of her bracelet seemed like manacles chaining her to her fate." Once again we find the end of the story in its beginning, for Lily is indeed predestined by a frivolous society to be that society's victim; yet what attracts us to Lily is what attracts Selden to her, the contraries in her temperament with which she will go to meet her particular doom:

> She paused before the mantlepiece, studying herself in the mirror while she adjusted her veil. The attitude revealed the long slope of her slender sides, which gave a kind of wild-wood grace to her outline—as though she were a captured dryad subdued to the conventions of the drawing-room; and Selden reflected that it was the same streak of sylvan freedom in her nature that lent such savour to her artificiality.

Chapter I is a masterpiece of planning, but it is only the first in a group of three chapters united by the facts that their action takes place on a single day in early September and that they form an introduction to the case of Lily Bart. In Chapter II we see Lily on the train, successfully initiating marriage operations against Percy Gryce, the wealthy and timid collector of books of Americana, operations which are impeded by the appearance of Mrs. George Dorset. Edith Wharton is skilled, as we have already seen,

at interrelating setting, character, and action to make implications for the future; and Bertha Dorset's imperious, self-centered entry of the railroad car, the chill which she casts over the cozy intimacy Lily has carefully established between Percy and herself, prefigure her role as destructive agent in Lily's subsequent career.

Having shown Lily Bart in the present from several angles, Edith Wharton uses the third and last chapter of the first chapter-group to reinforce our view of her through a quick survey of the home environment which produced her. Even this mainly retrospective chapter is given dramatic quality, however, by three highly functional paragraphs at the beginning which describe the luxurious interior of the Trenors' house, Bellomont, the evening of Lily's arrival there from New York. Coming as they do just before her extended remembrance of the marginal existence enforced on her mother and herself by her father's financial ruin and death, these introductory paragraphs are charged with ironic contrast. Pausing, alone, on the broad stairway, Lily looks down on the last card-players, to whom she has just lost more money than she can afford. The main hall, with its crimson carpet and columns of pale yellow marble columns, represents congealed money, as it were; and the author notes the silver collars about the decanters which the butler has just brought in and the jewels which flash from the women's hair. Lily herself is conscious of the contrast between this scene, which gratifies "her sense of beauty and her craving for the external finish of life," and "the meagreness of her own opportunities." Then as she watches, Bertha Dorset, "glittering in serpentine spangles," draws Percy Gryce after her "to a confidential nook beneath the gallery." Admittedly the word "serpentine"

157

is too obvious a hint of Bertha's deviousness and danger-ousness; still this introduction sets off even more sharply the tale of drab defeat to follow and makes the reader com-prehend more feelingly that Lily " hated dinginess as much as her mother had hated it, and to her last breath she meant to fight against it, dragging herself up again and again above its flood till she gained the bright pinnacles of success which presented such a slippery surface to her clutch."

This retrospective third chapter makes one more im-portant point about Lily in order that her actions at the end of the book will not seem to result from the author's arbi-trary management. In contrast to her more crudely am-bitious mother, Lily has " a vein of sentiment," perhaps transmitted to her by her father's dilettantish interest in books in his early days of marriage, a quality " which gave an idealizing touch to her most prosaic purposes." So " lost causes had a romantic charm for her, and she liked to picture herself as standing aloof from the vulgar press of the Quirinal, and sacrificing her pleasure to the claims of an immemorial tradition. . . ." This is, in effect, what her fate is to be.

The first three chapters, then, have formed a tightly knit group introducing us to the basic elements of Lily Bart's case. As one way of imposing order on the possible chaos of characters and events, Edith Wharton continues the grouping device so that the remaining twelve chapters in Book I fall into four more groups of three chapters each, each group rising to a climax in its third chapter, and the five groups as a whole rising to a grand climax at the end of Book I. We have, as it were, five acts in the first half of Lily's drama. Another device for order is the careful control of the time scheme, which is also used to produce

emphasis and concentration. This time scheme often subtly reinforces the grouping device, but does not parallel it mechanically. The first three chapters, except of course for the flashback in Chapter III, cover the events of a single day; Chapters IV through VII occupy one week; Chapters VIII through XI go fairly quickly over three months; while Chapters XII through XV deal with the happenings of only three days to allow for greater expansion of detail at a crucial point. It may be noted here that the same device of concentrating in time the actions of the first three and last four chapters is employed in Book II, thus giving the entire novel a certain formal symmetry.

To turn to the second chapter group (IV through VI) of Book I, we here see Edith Wharton preparing for and then describing the first crisis in the relations between Selden and Lily, a crisis which is carefully located in Chapter VI. The two previous chapters are essentially devoted to illustrating Lily's lack of inner stability as she is now annoyed by, now attracted to, the well-dressed, vacuous society at Bellomont. In addition the author suggests through these emotional shifts the earlier motif of Lily's peculiar kind of isolation; she is in this society, yet not in; related to it, but separate. When Selden arrives at Bellomont, he sharply "readjusts her vision." At dinner she looks through his eyes at Gus Trenor, the master of the house, who "with his heavy carnivorous head sunk between his shoulders . . . preyed on a jellied plover," and at his wife Judy "suggestive, with her glaring good-looks, of a jeweller's window lit by electricity." From this new angle of vision Lily sees "under the glitter of their opportunities . . . the poverty of their achievement." But while clarifying the effect of Selden on Lily, underlining his role in the

159

drama, Edith Wharton does not forget to keep certain other characters related to Lily and her situation. So Sim Rosedale is jokingly named as the probable best man at Lily's wedding—not too many chapters away he will be named as groom—and Bertha Dorset, who has already begun to turn Percy Gryce away from Lily, is explicitly shown twice as standing between Lily and Selden.

Chapter VI, in which Selden makes his first offer of marriage to Lily, is a set piece that gives an appropriate climax to the second chapter-group. "The afternoon," it opens with latent irony, "was perfect." The careful detailing of the countryside's natural beauty underlines skillfully the contrast between the potential seriousness and naturalness of Selden's and Lily's relationship on the one hand and on the other the empty, artificial society at Bellomont, of ironic name. The conversation, too, contrasts two ideas of success, whether one should inhabit Lily's "house of mirth" or Selden's "republic of the spirit." Selden becomes, in fact, the author's *raisonneur*, admitting the value of "the decorative side of life," yet excoriating the waste of human nature by which it is produced. Challenged by Lily to cease being merely the objective observer, to give her something beyond the diminution of her goals, Selden is surprised into making, rather indirectly, the offer of marriage, and Lily as indirectly accepts. At that moment Edith Wharton deliberately introduces references to the natural setting and the "soft isolation of the falling day" to emphasize that the two have momentarily found together a proper separation from society, have briefly entered "the republic of the spirit." Then the silence is broken by the sound of an automobile, one of the expensive toys of the rich, and Lily drops them back to their former relationship

160

by urging their immediate return to Bellomont. The "perfect afternoon" has passed into twilight, and Selden closes
the scene with a remark full of his own and his creator's
irony: "'Let us go down.'"

The second chapter-group has set the pattern for the
remaining three of Book I: two chapters prepare for a third
in which Lily rises momentarily to a crisis that calls out
some inner fineness, fails to sustain herself at the level of
spirit, and drops to a lower level of security in the society
she has been shaped from birth to inhabit. In each case
Selden is in some way linked to a fixed realm above, or to
one side of, "the house of mirth," and in each case as
Lily's social fortunes continue to slope downward, they
more nearly approach a point of convergence with those of
the tortuously ascending Rosedale. In Chapter VII a relationship to a third man develops when, made rash by her
"renewed sense of power in handling men"—she has, in
fact, just lost Selden because of her interest in Gryce and
Gryce because of her interest in Selden—Lily lets, or gets,
Gus Trenor to speculate for her on the stock market, Gus
having just done so well on a tip from Rosedale that he is
now willing to sponsor him socially—within limits. Unob-
trusively but relentlessly, Edith Wharton extends what
might be called the "lines of force" produced by these
three men in relation to Lily. In Chapter VIII Lily attends
the wedding of a Van Osburgh girl cousin, sees Selden in a
nearby pew, and experiences mingled attraction and resistance to the man whose "presence always had the effect of
cheapening her aspirations, of throwing her whole world
out of focus." At the wedding reception, having learned
that Percy Gryce is engaged to another Van Osburgh girl
and hence permanently out of her marriage schemes, she

161

is told by Trenor that Judy will have Rosedale to dine at the Trenor town house, though not at Bellomont. Shortly thereafter she finds herself standing with the three men who in different ways have some kind of power over her: Trenor for his financial investment, Selden for his " readjustment of her vision," Rosedale for his compromising knowledge of her unchaperoned visit to Selden's apartment. By a tableau device the relationships are objectified: Trenor speaks to her with an unpleasant "note of conjugal familiarity"; Selden leans against the window, "a detached observer of the scene"; Rosedale, after a boorish reference to their earlier meeting, triumphs by having her as companion in a walk to the conservatories at the farther end of the Van Osburgh house.

Almost as though these causes were producing their effect, we learn in Chapter IX, the climax chapter of the third group, that this autumn Lily is receiving fewer invitations than usual to her friend's country houses, and the slow descent of Lily toward " dinginess " is emphasized by the necessity of her staying in her aunt's house in New York during the physically distasteful annual orgy of house cleaning. As always, setting contributes actively to scene, for it is in these surroundings that Lily meets for the second and last time with Mrs. Haffen, the unattractive charwoman who had blocked her descent on the stairs outside Selden's apartment. Mrs. Haffen is under the impression, disgusting enough to Lily in itself, that Lily is the writer of certain letters sent by Bertha Dorset to Selden in an attempt to renew an old affair. The charwoman has saved these letters from Selden's wastebasket and now attempts to blackmail Lily with them for money. (We may note, incidentally, that the motif of money is introduced in

yet another pejorative context.) Lily believes that she must protect Selden in this matter and, rising to the crisis, bargains successfully in cold disgust for the packet of letters appropriately wrapped in a dirty newspaper. Just after this interview, Mrs. Peniston returns to her house and in her absent-minded chatter informs Lily that Bertha Dorset had arranged the Percy Gryce—Evie Van Osburgh engagement. So Lily learns that her attempt to dwell secure in "the house of mirth" through marriage to Gryce has been thwarted by the woman whose incriminating letters she holds. Her decision not to burn them, as she had been about to do, shows again her inability to remain at the height of her grand moment of defending Selden's name. Putting away the letters as a reserve weapon against Bertha, she reflects with conscious irony that she has been able to buy them with money from Gus Trenor. The physical, and moral, repugnance of the scene is complete.

Once again Lily has risen momentarily to a crisis of the spirit, has failed to sustain herself there, and has dropped to a lower social plane, this time to the point where, at the beginning of the fourth chapter-group, she is willing to spend Thanksgiving week at a camp in the Adirondacks with the Wellington Brys. At this point we realize that the supposedly stable background against which has been projected Lily's never-resting, downward-sloping career is itself a constantly shifting one. The Brys represent a new wave of Invaders who, like Rosedale, are moving upward out of obscure social origins with the assistance of the Stock Exchange, that source of quick, spectacular wealth. The secure, uniform world represented by the brownstone fronts, we are ever more reminded, has completely given way to that of the huge, ornate mansions, "visibly willed

163

and created," in Bourget's phrase, "by sheer force of millions." Even Mrs. Peniston, that stolid guardian of outworn forms, knows that society is in flux and watches the successive groups of "new people" struggle through the social surf either to sink or reach the security of dry land. But Edith Wharton's particular skill is not simply in describing a society in flux as it is caught fixed at any one moment, but also in suggesting the intricate shifts and changes of motion of which flux is made up. Lily moves down as the Brys and Rosedale move up, but even those ascending do so at different rates of speed. The relative speed with which the paths of Lily and Rosedale are converging is demonstrated in this fourth chapter-group when Lily must endure an actual visit from him in the privacy of her aunt's home and must go publicly to the opera with him and Trenor because of the threat of power each holds over her. Now when she visits Bellomont, caustic remarks linking her and Rosedale are made, not behind her back, but directly to her.

It is with this sense of social flux and incipient disaster that Edith Wharton begins her twelfth chapter, the climax of the next to last chapter-group in Book I. In this chapter comes Lily's last triumph within "the house of mirth" and the second crisis in the relationship between her and Selden. The triumph comes with her part in the *tableaux vivants* staged at the Brys' recently built town house, a vast, opulent structure which is as much a piece of stagecraft as the *tableaux*. When the curtain rises on a Lily supple in the pale draperies of a Reynolds' portrait, her loveliness brings gasps of admiration from the audience, a goatish remark from old Ned Van Alstyne, and from Selden a recognition of "the real Lily Bart, divested of the trivialities of her little world, and catching for a moment a note of that

eternal harmony of which her beauty was a part." For a second time he is willing to go beyond his role as detached observer, for he feels "the whole tragedy of her life," her peculiar isolation.

> It was as though her beauty, thus detached from all that cheapened and vulgarized it, had held out suppliant hands to him from the world in which he and she had once met for a moment, and where he felt an overmastering longing to be with her again.

As on the hill above Bellomont, Selden and Lily seem ready to enter together "the republic of the spirit"; yet when they meet after the *tableaux*, Edith Wharton brilliantly emphasizes, not the ideal quality of the scene, but its unreality. Dream-like they move into a great, dimly-lit conservatory. They are alone as before in a place of beauty; yet, ironically, this is an enclosed, man-made garden, the weather outside is in reality winter-cold, "the distant drift of music that might have been blown across a sleeping lake" is the music from Mrs. Bry's expensive orchestra from a farther room. Selden speaks his love directly, their lips meet for the first and only time in a kiss, but Lily breaks the spell by accepting and rejecting his love simultaneously. Then she slips away and disappears "in the brightness of the room beyond." And as the chapter began with a review of Lily's social precariousness, so the author firmly completes the contrast by returning us to reality again. Gus Trenor, struggling into his coat at the door, speaks broadly of Lily's bodily beauty and of the waste of time it takes to break new people in socially.

165

Now Edith Wharton moves into the last three chapters, which, rising in intensity within themselves, form a powerful climax to Book I. Several structural devices are used to

help increase the effect. The shortening of time is one; Chapter XIII begins on the morning after the *tableaux*, while Chapter XV ends only three days later. Again, development by scene greatly predominates over development by narrative, and several scenes overlap each other in time. Finally, scenes are often juxtaposed with deliberate irony. Chapter XIII is almost entirely given over to Trenor's trapping of Lily in his Fifth Avenue house and Lily's full realization that she must pay her debt in cash lest Trenor force it from her in kind. With the sound of the Furies' iron wings in her brain, she flees toward the apartment of Gerty Farish, Selden's cousin, who has just learned that Selden's new tenderness is directed toward Lily rather than herself. Gerty must give her distraught rival protection for the night. But as Selden is trying to find Lily earlier that evening, he by chance observes her leaving Trenor's house. If the author has timed this chance event somewhat too relentlessly, still we should admire the scene for the way Edith Wharton suddenly compresses the whole social background behind the personal drama into an idle harangue on the architecture of Fifth Avenue houses made by Ned Van Alstyne to Selden as they approach the Trenor mansion.

First, Van Alstyne points out the utter eclecticism of the Greiner house, " ' a typical rung in the social ladder,' " which Rosedale has bought, the man who now, according to Van Alstyne, might conceivably marry Lily Bart. Next they pass the Brys' mansion, which, in its pretense of copying the Trianon, represents a higher stage in the social ascent. Finally they observe the Trenors' house—" ' the Corinthian exuberant, but based on the best precedent ' "; and as Van Alstyne chatters on about the grandiose alterations to be made on this " Corinthian " structure, the door opens

to let out Lily and to show Trenor "black and bulky . . . persistently projected against the light." The fitting of Lily's individual fate into the social milieu has been so concretely imaged that we are not surprised when Selden, clearly jumping to conclusions about Lily's presence in Trenor's house at night, turns abruptly away. One last point: the scene ironically echoes Lily's visit to Selden's apartment in Chapter I and the chance meeting between her and Rosedale outside on the street. It is Selden's mistake, of course, to assume of the event what Rosedale and society assume. Lily Bart is a puzzling personality to him, but he, like Lily, has been influenced by his environment. Selden, too, is a victim.

Chapter XV brings the book to its halfway climax. Returned from Gerty's apartment the following day, Lily for the first time reckons up the exact sum of money she has carelessly accepted from Trenor and shamefully recognizes that she must repay the nine thousand dollars in order to restore her self-respect. She partly confesses her distress to the unsympathetic Mrs. Peniston and realizes that Selden is her only hope. While she waits vainly for Selden, unaware that he has turned from her because of his chance sight the night before, she instead receives a visit from Rosedale. The latter, unconscious of the irony, speaks of his wealth and crudely proposes marriage. The thought of Selden makes Rosedale's offer seem to her grotesque, but because of his power over her reputation she dismisses him with a polite intimation of future possibilities. Then she learns from a newspaper that Selden has sailed for Havana, and she is about to write to Rosedale " to tell him to come to her." It is at this point, only a little beyond the exact middle of the novel by page count, that the paths of Rose-

dale and Lily intersect to make the first half of the "X" figure. Lily is apparently saved from her dilemma by the arrival of the telegram from Bertha Dorset inviting her on a Mediterranean cruise; but just as in *The Age of Innocence*, the end of Book I sets the novel's major character firmly on the path to ultimate fate. We shall shortly see that what appears to be a reëntrance into the house of mirth is actually a formal banishment from it.

Edith Wharton learned much from Henry James, but she rarely shows in her novels the rigorous concern with "point of view" which characterizes particularly James's later fiction. Her approach to this technical matter seems much more pragmatic, as though at any point she would use any character as the center of consciousness so long as doing so could advance her story; yet she is often able to achieve certain limited effects by the manipulation of point of view. One impressive instance is the beginning of Book II through the eyes of Selden after holding the final chapter of Book I exclusively within the consciousness of Lily. Three months have elapsed between the books, and the scene has moved temporarily to the Riviera, where Selden is viewing a stage-setting-like Monte Carlo with "the renewed zest of spectatorship that is the solace of those who take an objective interest in life." So begins the second half of Lily's tragedy.

It is in the second half of *The House of Mirth* that Edith Wharton's material at times escapes the superb control which, as we have seen, she exercised over it in the first half; even so, the first group of three chapters in Book II represents a sustainedly brilliant piece of work. When Lily lands with the Dorsets and their friends from the yacht *Sabrina*—if one recalls Milton's *Comus*, he will recognize

another instance of the author's delight in ironic names— Selden sees with his own changed eyes that " a subtle change had passed over the quality of her beauty "; its formerly transparent surface has crystallized " into one hard brilliant substance." Although the blunt divorcée Carry Fisher has suggested that " at heart, [Lily] despises the thing she's trying for," Selden now believes that she has disciplined down any of such " rebellious impulses " as he had previously hoped to encourage in her. And as he comes to this conclusion, he suddenly perceives that Lily's situation is desperate, that she seems " poised on the brink of a chasm " with one foot advanced over it. That Lily is at least at the edge of corruption is emphasized by the conclusion to this first chapter wherein the American un-innocents abroad watch fireworks over the dark bay at Nice, Bertha Dorset and her lover slip away in a carriage, and the bored wastrel Lord Hubert Dacy, after losing a heap of gold at baccarat, laments briefly that Lily is abroad without the protection of Mrs. Peniston's sturdy obtuseness. In its mixture of glamor and corruption, its picture of Americans confronting Europe, this scene curiously fills in a gap in a development from *The Ambassadors* to *Tender Is the Night*, though Edith Wharton's own firm and clear moral condemnation of the situation differs both from James's intense sensibility and Fitzgerald's immersion in the glamor.

169

Despite the natural beauty of sea and shore at Nice, which Lily observes from the yacht on the following morning, Chapter II details a set of contrasting moral uglinesses: Lily has left her unpleasant remembrance of financial obligation to Trenor back among old scenes in New York; Carry Fisher now persuades her to take over the direction of the Brys' assault on international Society;

George Dorset sickly confesses to Lily his outrage at Bertha's misconduct; and Bertha, ruthlessly employing attack on Lily as the best defense of her own precarious situation, accuses her of misconduct with her husband. With the chasm opening beneath her foot, Lily moves like a queen, in Chapter III, to the elaborate dinner given in a public restaurant by the egregious Mrs. Bry; and Selden again notes her peculiar isolation, detached as she is "by a hundred undefinable shades" from the costly stupidity of the very society she still aspires to, so that "he saw her definitely divided from him by the crudeness of a choice which seemed to deny the very differences he felt in her." Now he is able to view her with real detachment rather than with the passionate disenchantment he had experienced back in New York. It is this detachment from Lily and his nagging, convention-bred suspicion of Lily's equivocal position in the Dorset trouble which prevent him from giving her more than a gentleman's assistance when Bertha Dorset publicly forbids her to return to the yacht. Character is always shaped by environment and once shaped cannot choose to act at will.

From this point on Lily's descent takes on the speed of momentum, and the author begins to present views of her at selected stages in this descent rather than trying to suggest, as in Book I, the continuity of a downward slope. The grouping of chapters becomes irregular or ceases to exist at all, considerable intervals of time appear between chapters, and in fact where the action of Book I occupied only three months, that of Book II covers twelve in somewhat fewer pages.

The next stage in Lily's descent is linked explicitly with money; just before dying, her aunt has disinherited

her as a result of the rumors about her conduct in Europe. Although Lily's conduct has been in certain respects innocent, she was in an equivocal position as viewed by outside eyes even before Bertha Dorset's dissembling attack on her, and she has furthermore consciously abetted Bertha's love affair by distracting the husband's attention. This, as always, she realistically admits to herself after the event, and she accepts her disinheritance with grace. After the reading of Mrs. Peniston's will, Gerty Farish asks her where her European mishap began, and Lily tells her with acute self-perception: "'Why, the beginning was in my cradle, I suppose—in the way I was brought up, and the things I was taught to care for.'" Like her creator, Lily sees causation in terms, not simply of character, but of character as formed by environment. If she is betrayed by what is false within, the falseness was originally placed there by a world she never made.

Isolation now becomes a constant motif in Lily's story, recurring in various forms. In the scene of the reading of the will, Lily deliberately seats herself apart from her relatives and at the conclusion is deliberately avoided by everyone in the room except Gerty. Next she is practically cut by the Trenors in a restaurant. Advancing the "X" shaped lines of movement set up in Book I, the author includes in the Trenor party Rosedale, who "flushed as he was with the importance of keeping such company, at once took the temperature of Mrs. Trenor's cordiality, and reflected it in his off-hand greeting of Miss Bart." To complete the tableau at the restaurant, Trenor is seen breaking off his greeting to Lily abruptly; Selden is simply not there.

Isolation from relatives and friends brings isolation from her whole social group, and Lily is forced down to the

level of the Gormers, who in Europe had been much less far along the social ascent than the Brys and who present to her a world that is only a " flamboyant copy of her own." Here, of course, Edith Wharton runs into an artistic dilemma. She wishes to show that Lily's moral sensibilities are slowly losing their edge as she passes downward from stage to stage; yet to give us the full weight of this loss, she should develop the point in a succession of scenes. On the other hand, to do so would be to run the risk, as she must have conceived it, of over-emphasizing the Gormer milieu in terms of the rest of the book. She obviously preferred not to take that risk. The Gormer world is given us in acute, condensed summary, but the relative sketchiness of this section makes the author appear to be hastening through her potential material in order to reach the end. We are told, rather than shown, that " a hard glaze of indifference was fast forming over her delicacies and susceptibilities, and each concession to expediency hardened the surface a little more."

All motion in this novel is relative, however, and as the Gormers rise, Lily's path slopes downward even below them. Her one recourse is to try to induce Rosedale to propose to her. The scene of Rosedale's " proposal " is carefully built up by Edith Wharton in an intricately ironic set of contrasts to Selden's proposal to Lily at Bellomont. The season is late fall rather than late summer when she goes to walk with him, although there is a haze in the air which reminds her of the earlier walk with Selden; and the natural scene, which hardly impinges on her or the reader's consciousness, is " a rocky glen above the lake " instead of the fertile opulence of the hills around the Trenors' country house. The participants in the scene are much

172

different. Lily is changed in social condition, and she carefully maneuvers the conversation rather than, as with Selden, falling into it unpremeditatedly. Rosedale is a complete opposite to Selden. He is dapperly self-confident and
draws attention to his wealth by groping for a gold-tipped
cigarette in a gold case "with plump jewelled fingers."
Instead of entrance into "the republic of the spirit," he
offers Lily's mind escape from "fluctuating ethical esti-
mates . . . into a region of concrete weights and measures";
provided Lily rehabilitates herself socially by blackmailing
Bertha Dorset into cooperation through the letters he knows
she holds, Rosedale will marry her and thus assure her
security. In disgust Lily refuses what is not a marriage proposal so much as a financial proposition. Her attachment
to decency loses her Rosedale as her attachment to wealth
lost her Selden, and Rosedale produces the final contrast by
a violent reference to the other man: "'Well, I'll be damned
if I see what thanks you've got from him!'"

By the mere act of listening to Rosedale's offer, Lily
shows that "she had learned to live with ideas which would
once have been intolerable to her"; and quite suitably she
next drops to the bizarre world of Mrs. Norma Hatch and
the fashionable New York hotel. In this aimless atmosphere
of "torrid splendour," the young Undine Spragg of *The
Custom of the Country* would have thrived; but Lily cannot, though she proudly rejects Selden's too-disinterested
attempt to help her, and she takes the next step down. In a
single chapter Lily appears as an unskillful working woman
in a shop where hats are made for her former friends.
Driven by fatigue and the dread of "dinginess," she is
tempted more and more frequently to use Bertha Dorset's
letters in a last desperate attempt to save herself. Then just

173

as the structure of the novel appears ready to break into fragments, Edith Wharton moves securely into the final climactic section of the book, concentrates the action of four chapters into three days time, and draws the themes of the book together.

The final section begins, in Chapter XI, almost exactly a year after Lily's catastrophe on the Riviera. Lily stands at a corner of Fifth Avenue, the complete outsider now, watching the passing carriages of the wealthy and recognizing a few familiar faces that in themselves almost recapitulate her fall—Mrs. Percy Gryce, Judy Trenor, and, characteristically in an electric victoria, Mrs. Norma Hatch. An ironic contrast is thus set up for the remainder of Lily Bart's drama, which is played out for the most part among dingier surroundings. For the last time Rosedale appears in her life, and the crossed pattern of their careers is now completed with his announced intention of going to Europe as a step in his continued ascent of the social heights and Lily's refusal to take from him the money with which she could repay Trenor. In this final moment of meeting, Edith Wharton makes recompense to Rosedale, for she has Lily realize that her dislike of the man is breaking down before her recognition here, as on other recent occasions, of qualities of kindliness and fidelity beneath his materialism. It is as though the author herself were becoming more tolerant through describing the sufferings of her heroine.

Having refused help from Rosedale, Lily sets off in the cold grey evening of the following day, resolved to confront Bertha Dorset with the letters. Instead she makes her second unconventional visit to Selden's apartment, a visit which balances and contrasts with the first. The scene is "unchanged," but a year and a half ago "the wide Septem-

174

ber light had filled the room, making it seem a part of the outer world: now the shaded lamps and the warm hearth, detaching it from the gathering darkness of the street, gave it a sweeter touch of intimacy." As before Selden acts toward her with restraint, but this time the restraint comes from old disillusion rather than from the habit of detachment. Lily is the more changed of the two, for her body is wasted and her loneliness at being excluded from her social world is intensified by the sense of being shut out of his as well. Now she speaks to him directly and sincerely without her old light irony, thanking him for letting her see and know the folly of wishing to dwell in the house of mirth. Where in the first visit he had been lightly drawn to her impervious charm, now she feels for him "the love his love had kindled." Her proof that "she had saved herself whole from the seeming ruin of her life" comes when she secretly drops the packet of letters in the fire, a gesture which escapes melodrama only by the fact that it is in accord with her "vein of sentimentality." The letters have appropriately been destroyed in the room where they were found, and she has paid Selden her spiritual debt.

On the same evening Lily is also able to pay her financial debt to Trenor because of the chance arrival of the check for the total sum of her inheritance. But if Edith Wharton will make that much concession to an arbitrary manipulation of events, she refuses to go the easy step further, to produce the conventionally happy ending. Instead she relentlessly works out the fate of Lily and Selden in terms of their characters as environment has shaped them. Quite typically, Lily takes the calculated risk of an extra dose of sleeping drops to overcome the expected insomnia and sinks into darkness at the moment when Selden, quite

175

as typically, is slowly resolving to offer her his love once more. That he comes too late results inevitably, as he forces himself to see the following morning, from the iron fact "that all the conditions of life had conspired to keep them apart." Even when she had caught his attention months ago, waiting in Grand Central Station, lovely, enigmatic, and alive, they had both been marked as victims. Their end was in their beginning.

JENNIE GERHARDT: THE AMERICAN FAMILY AND THE AMERICAN DREAM

DREISER, 1911

by CHARLES SHAPIRO

> "Life is to be learned as much from books and art as from life itself—almost more so, in my judgment. Art is the stored honey of the human soul, gathered on the wings of misery and travail. Shall the dull and self-seeking and the self-advertising close this store on the groping human mind?"
>
> —Theodore Dreiser
> "Life, Art and America."

There is a stuffy myth, perpetuated and intensified by scholarly magazines as well as critical journals, that makes Theodore Dreiser simply a great shaggy monkey pounding the keys of a typewriter, stumbling upon his words—wild words, unbeautiful, unkempt words which, by a transcendental trick left over from the Romantic Period, would pile upon each other and somehow total a powerful novel. A

disorganized, crudely written novel, but one with strength and insight. To our regret, however, we are not living in an age of many miracles, and bad sentences, stretched end to end, will never equal a good book. Dreiser realized this, and while he was an uneven writer, he was conscious of his craftsmanship, and as a result his stories and novels were carefully planned and carefully written. Above all, they were part of his lifelong inquiry—his continual grabbing at what he considered to be the vital problems inherent in American life.

Dreiser's novels have an important design, significant because he was a keen, if often naïve, observer of the social and political realities of his day. He saw America as being at middle age, and he was concerned with a culture which, by creating and encouraging artificial goals, was perverting its worthwhile institutions and, more important, was robbing the individual of his chance to live up to a full, meaningful potential. Each of Dreiser's novels illustrates a different aspect of what he felt was a crucial misdirection of American energy. Often his insights were vague and muddied: in *The Genius*, for example, he attempts to explain the forces harmful to the creative artist, and since he places the blame on a curious mixture of capitalism and eroticism his novel rests on a faulty base. Which is to say that Dreiser is usually a bad writer at the point where he leaps over his immediate feelings and his own past. In his first two books, *Sister Carrie* and *Jennie Gerhardt*, Dreiser studies the failure of the American as an individual and of Americans as a family group, and his theme provides a valid and compassionate foundation for the novels. He was writing out of the misery and passion of his own experiences.

Dreiser's works, while exploring many sides to a prob-

178

lem, would adhere to a single point of view, and the focus, often shifting, from book to book, in various economic and philosophical directions, would originate in what he believed at the moment to be the deepest roots of American unhappiness. As his work matured he became akin to the character in one of Virginia Woolf's novels of whom it was said that as he grew older there was a compensation ". . . simply this; that the passions remain as strong as ever, but one has gained—at last! the power which adds the supreme flavor to existence—the power of turning it round, slowly, in the light." It is untrue to state, as has one prominent critic, that Dreiser's art betrays " a sheer incapacity for development." His art was never static: only his critics.

Dreiser's technique, while remaining in the naturalistic tradition, varies with the American experience explored. The experience which is turned round in *The Bulwark* (Dreiser's last novel), the disastrous careers of the children of a bedrock Quaker, is set on a relatively bare stage, while in earlier novels Dreiser's background is a cluttered one, filled with people, facts, musings, and street signs. This profusion of details accentuates the point of view, producing a kaleidoscopic effect. With *The Bulwark* Dreiser settled on a different framework. An almost naked story is told, and the simplicity only adds to the final terror. But this is not true in the first novels, books of tragic courage and predoomed struggle. In these works the well-filled background provides the tone and excuse for the plot.

In *Sister Carrie*, Dreiser's first novel, the details, believed by reviewers to indicate a lack of " style," were ridiculed and parodied, and ever since he has been a sitting duck for critics whose only criterion is a self-oriented meticulousness. Sinclair Lewis, in his Nobel Prize speech,

179

hinted at the shortsightedness of those who would evaluate a new work of art in terms of the standards set up on the basis of other excellent but different efforts. He speculated at the sensation that might have been created if Dreiser had received the award, and Lewis added his own high tribute to a man he saw in the tradition of Whitman and Twain. Only today are we finally understanding that America's rich fictional heritage has a broad enough base to include the shrewd observations of both a Henry James and a Theodore Dreiser. Art, as Edmund Wilson points out, "is that which gives meaning to experience." And our experiences and their translation into fiction are many and diverse.

In *Sister Carrie*, the characters, the symbols, the action, and even the details are attuned to a basic theme, an elaboration of Emerson's complaint that "things" dominate the American scene. "Things are in the saddle and ride mankind." Only the "things" had become more elaborate, more slippery to grasp. In later books the burden on the individual would lead to violence and murder. In *Sister Carrie* the rewards are self-destruction, a nagging unhappiness, and a poverty made worse by the visions of former days which promised future glories.

Francis Fergusson defines "action" as that "which points to the object which the dramatist is trying to show us, and that we must, in some sense, grasp if we are to understand his complex art; plotting, characterization, versification, thought, and their coherence." In the same sense the themes of Dreiser's novels underlie the books, and unless this is understood, the details and dialogue will give us little more than melodrama. Dreiser's details are carefully injected, seldom robbing his novels of the force of the plots or characterizations which are interesting in them-

selves. And his details, strategically placed and skillfully ordered, are used to point up his key themes. In *Sister Carrie* the theme is the effect, on the individual consciousness, of the misdirection of the American success dream, and the novel is a logical precursor to *Jennie Gerhardt.*

Details in *Sister Carrie* play up not only the characters but the over-all perception of the novel. Each sordid item is in order, adding illumination to the chapters and adding evidence to the underlying theme—the shame of a society whose structure rested, according to Dreiser, on the shaky premise that guided a man by rewards not in keeping with his potentialities and his promise. And these details are kept from becoming a soapbox squawk against capitalism because Dreiser understands the essential dignity of Hurstwood. Hurstwood, unlike the autonomous figures of "labor" pictured in WPA murals, is detailed into being more than a symbol, and for this reason he is a truer representation of a person and a better symbol.

Dreiser has captured, in the story of Hurstwood and his decline, an almost ideal man and situation to epitomize the essence of early 20th century industrial America. Possessing the fatal American yearning for a top role in society, but hindered by his strict middle-class concepts, Hurstwood is forced into various jobs which, by their eclectic nature, put him in focus from several points of observation. The first picture catches him as the restauranteur, and as his social status plunges and he switches jobs, we see him increasingly handicapped by his preconceptions of his social position. Hurstwood's downward movement is reemphasized by chance meetings with former acquaintances, so that we are often reminded, as he was, of the point from which he slipped. And we are similarly reminded of the

181

reasons for Hurstwood's fall: chance, material conceit, and his love for Carrie, the three elements which can be symbolically transferred as properties of America. These elements in their larger context would be: problematic changes of fortune, the worship of false values, and the inevitable seduction of the imaginative consciousness by values opposed to a gross materialism, values which might not, in themselves, hold true.

The three chief protagonists, Hurstwood, Drouet, and Carrie have, of course, their own special areas of movement within which are their own patterns of success and failure, and their stories restate Dreiser's belief in the no man's land that existed between the American daydream and the American actuality.

Running underneath the Hurstwood chronicle is the ironic rise of Carrie. Ironic because, while she achieves success in terms of Hurstwood's sense of values, she is never successful or happy by her own implied standards. She has "a mind free of any consideration of the problems or forces of the world and actuated not by greed, but an insatiable love of variable pleasure." And we are reminded at an early stage that she was, in essence, alone, "a lone figure in a tossing, thoughtless sea."

Can Carrie ever be happy, could the Hurstwoods ever be content? Dreiser does not believe in the possibility. Dreiser came to New York roughly the same time as Carrie, and in his book of descriptive pieces on the city (*The Color of a Great City*) we see that the problem of the pointlessness of the struggle, though often showing men at their courageous best, was a constant source of wonder to the young reporter. In one of his sketches, "The Toilers of the Tenements," Dreiser described the pitiful conditions of

those who toiled in their slum rooms at piece work, at the mercy of greedy employers and grafty police. A random few achieved success.

If this basic theme of individual failure were not present in *Sister Carrie*, if Carrie could be viewed as successful, the critics who dismiss Dreiser would have good reason. His details would show no purpose, and the story would remain melodrama. But the work has a specific orientation and proves, as H. L. Mencken once observed, "that accurate representation is not, as the campus critics of Dreiser seem to think, inimical to beauty."

Perhaps Drouet's is the greatest tragedy of all, for he unconsciously assumes all the values of his day without a trace of rebellion. As Carrie's discoverer and as the accidental pivot in Hurstwood's life he is necessary to the plot— as the "drummer" of 1890-1920 he will progress to 1955 where he will become aware of his failure. As Arthur Miller's salesman lies in his grave, the son comments, "He had the wrong dreams. All, all wrong . . . He never knew who he was." Drouet is Willy Loman in a more favorable year.

The price we pay for the Hurstwood of Fitzgerald and Moy's is the Hurstwood of the street-car strike. And as the novel ends Dreiser pictures Carrie at a window in her rocking chair, and he adds ". . . shall you dream such happiness as you may never feel." It is precisely this facet of America that in itself holds a balance—the size of the wish is a measurement of the failure. Or as Dreiser once noted as he watched one of New York City's sandwich men, a member of the army of walking sign-boards who still patrol the streets as a living contrast to whatever they

183

advertise: "to be the antithesis of what life would prefer to be—what could be more degraded than that."

In *Sister Carrie* the theme is the effect, on the individual consciousness, of the misdirection of the American success dream, and eleven years later Dreiser explored in his second novel, *Jennie Gerhardt*, the effects of American materialism on the American family. Though the book ostensibly centers on the almost Pollyanna-like misfortunes of seducible Jennie, the theme that strikes through the work is the disastrous consequences the success psychology has on the American family. Two family groups are presented at opposite social and economic poles, and we see them both as separate entities in their own private worlds and as they are in clash with each other. The novel is probably the most autobiographical of Dreiser's fictional works, and while the Gerhardts are not carbon copies of Dreiser's unhappy family, they do represent, in spirit, the author's impressions of his troubled childhood much in the way that *David Copperfield* or *Little Dorrit* convey Dickens' painful evaluations of his early days. The analogy between the Dreisers and the Gerhardts can be seen by comparing *Jennie Gerhardt* with *Dawn*, the first volume of Dreiser's autobiographical chronicles. In *Dawn* Dreiser speaks of ". . . a particularly nebulous, emotional, unorganized and traditionless character," a tragic group which ". . . had somewhere before my birth taken on the complexion of poverty and failure, or, at least seeming failure."

The other family in *Jennie Gerhardt*, the wealthy, socially prominent Kanes, does not stem, of course, from any personal involvement of Dreiser's, and the picture of this group is often blurred and more often exaggerated, for as F. O. Matthiessen pointed out, there was an element in

184

Dreiser of "the poor boy staring hungrily into the bright windows of the rich." But in spite of some glaring artificialities in descriptions and dialogue, the Kanes are forcefully set up in such a way as to reveal the existence of an underlying fatuous economic motivation which proves the wealthy family to be as bereft as the Gerhardts of the needed essentials of family harmony. Like the Gerhardts they were driven to the position of distorting their lives to fit standards set by the nebulous Joneses and the immediate neighbors, but unlike the Gerhardts the problem had advanced far beyond the stage of worrying about meat and shoes.

Jennie is the prop for the novel; as the chief protagonist she is the moral and financial brace of a flabby, poverty ridden family. We first see her in 1880, a girl of eighteen applying, with her mother, for menial work in a Columbus hotel. They are already stamped. "Poverty was driving them. Together they presented so appealing a picture of honest necessity that even the clerk was affected." The Gerhardt family, a large and uncoordinated affair, is presided over in an economically sloppy but morally straight-jacketed fashion by William Gerhardt, an unemployed glass-blower. Besides Jennie the children include Sebastian (Bass), Genevieve, George, Martha, William, and Veronica. Bass, like his counterpart in the Kane family, is never spiritually united with the others. As David Riesman observes in his study of the relatively new trend towards "outer-direction" in America's lonely crowd, the older children, if any, "are the privileged guests in a rather second-rate hotel, a hotel whose harassed but smiling managers they put under constant pressure for renovation." Self-centered, conniving but for the most part honest, the

185

children struggle between an allegiance to the family and the powerful pull of standards set up by the outside world, standards which are at constant odds with hearthside preachings. The compromise reached is to face family disasters with a "Well, I wouldn't worry about it . . . we'll get along somehow" attitude. Only when he is literally freed from the family can Bass join the crowd in pursuit of the goals set forth by his contemporaries, comrades in a common rootlessness and a common daydream.

The other Gerhardt children play minor roles, important only as they reinforce the theme of the disintegration of the family and the rejection of the father. As they occasionally pop into the novel they become a rather hazy galaxy of ingrates who, it is assumed, will breed more families of the same type.

Jennie is all suffering, almost too fudgey in her passivity. Seduced by Senator Brander, who dies before their child is born, she works as a servant and eventually becomes the mistress of Lester Kane, the "Bass" of the family as rich as the Gerhardts are poor. After much deliberation, societal pressure forces Kane to marry in his own circle, leaving Jennie, who "was never master of her fate," to live a lonely life devoted to others. Jennie was "the product of the fancy, the feeling, the innate affection of the untutored but poetic mind of her mother combined with the gravity and poise which were characteristic of her father." But as Dreiser later points out, "Caged in the world of the material, however, such a nature is almost invariably an anomaly." Meeting misery and insult with a quiet selfishness, she ends her days, appropriately enough, without a real family of her own.

Dreiser is concerned with the family in America which,

186

like Carrie and Hurstwood, is touched and perverted by artificial lures. Thus the children of Dreiser's two families are unsatisfied with any altruistic family orientation and are caught by similar outside forces which swirl them away from the family. It is a profound change in America that Dreiser is cataloguing, for in the break from the family comes confusion. "In place of referring himself against the stars, the other-directed person moves in the midst of a veritable Milky Way of almost but not quite indistinguishable contemporaries." The new generation, the Lester Kanes, the Drouets, and the Gerhardt children seem unresponsive to what Dreiser, in an over-sentimental aside, terms "the few sprigs of green that sometime invade the barrenness of your materialism. . . ." When Dreiser's characters are occasionally forced too close to the green they become ill in a social sense, and according to the unwritten laws which guide and control, they are temporarily quarantined.

The Gerhardt family, nominally headed by an all-suffering mother and a religious father, is shown as it gradually falls apart. The parents, while respected, are never a pivotal force. The role of the parent in the American family structure was shrinking, and this change, while important in altering the values of the children, is devastating in its effects on the parents. "We live," Dreiser notes, "in an age in which the impact of material forces is well-nigh irresistible; the spiritual nature is overwhelmed by the shock." And the shock to the Gerhardt family is severe, especially as reflected by the pathetic father, burdened by his material failure, haunted by his spiritual drive. He is caught in a vise between old and new values. By the standards of either the old or the new he would be considered a

187

failure. Papa Gerhardt, hurt, confused, is one of the memorable character studies in modern fiction.

At first it appears as if his misfortune is simply the result of unemployment due to forces beyond his control or interest. But as the family is forced to disperse we see that Papa Gerhardt's situation is more complex. Alone in a strange city, working and sleeping in a factory, he presents a miserable figure. His stiff religiosity forces him to reject Jennie for an immoral action which was obviously sponsored by her devotion to the family which, by his rules, Gerhardt should have been able to support. For the first time in his life he is forced to question his basic beliefs, the ones which have provided the solace and rationale to his career of want and toil. He receives a letter suggesting that the family reunite in Cleveland and start anew.

> And Gerhardt did take this view of the situation. In answer to his wife's letter he wrote that it was not advisable for him to leave his place, but if Bass saw a way for them, it might be a good thing to go. He was the more ready to acquiesce in the plan for the simple reason that he was half distracted with the worry of supporting the family and of paying the debts already outstanding. Every week he laid by five dollars out of his salary, which he sent in the form of a postal order to Mrs. Gerhardt. Three dollars he paid for board, and fifty cents he kept for spending money, church dues, a little tobacco and occasionally a glass of beer. Every week he put a dollar and a half in a little iron bank against a rainy day. His room was a bare corner in the topmost loft of the doorstep of the mill. To this he would ascend after sitting alone on the doorstep of the mill in this lonely, forsaken neighborhood, until nine o'clock of an evening; and here, amid the odor of machinery wafted up from

the floor below, by the light of a single tallow candle, he would conclude his solitary day, reading his German paper, folding his hands and thinking, kneeling by an open window in the shadow of the night to say his prayers, and silently stretching himself to rest. Long were the days, dreary the prospect. Still he lifted his hands in utmost faith to God, praying that his sins might be forgiven and that he might be vouchsafed a few more years of happy family life.

Dreiser's father had undergone similar separations from his family, and the poignant collection of details which are presented in the paragraph attest to the powerful impression this seclusion must have had on young Theodore. The severe loneliness of the father becomes, for Dreiser, the very worst aspect of the shattered family situation.

Gerhardt's misery increases. Finally, suffering severe injury to his hands, he must return to the family for help. The reunion is a tearful one, the old mill-worker losing control of himself for the moment. He is puzzled by Jennie, admiring her devotion to her child, fearing her apparent relationship with Lester. "Gerhardt went back to his newspaper reading and brooding. His life seemed a complete failure to him and he was only waiting to get well enough to hunt up another job as watchman. He wanted to get out of this mess of deception and dishonesty." When Jennie offers him the hospitality of her home with Lester, Gerhardt rebels. "My whole life comes to nothing." And over and over, querulous and bored, he ponders the value of his life, its apparent purposelessness, its obvious failure.

Ironically Gerhardt's only happiness comes from Vesta, his illegitimate grandchild, the living symbol of Jennie's

189

sin, a sprightly child akin to little Pearl of *The Scarlet Letter*. One day Vesta and Gerhardt go on one of their walks. It is a beautiful spring day.

> Gerhardt took a keen delight in pointing out the wonders of nature to Vesta, and she was quick to respond. Every new sight and sound interested her.
>
> "Oooh! ooh!" exclaimed Vesta, catching sight of a low, flashing touch of red as a robin lighted upon a twig nearby. Her hand was up, and her eyes were wide open.
>
> "Yes," said Gerhardt, as happy as if he himself had but newly discovered this marvelous creature. . . . It is going to look for a worm now. We will see if we cannot find its nest. I think I saw a nest on one of these trees."
>
> He plodded peacefully on, seeking to rediscover an old abandoned nest that he had observed on a former walk. . . . "Here it is," he said at last, coming to a small and leafless tree, in which a winter-beaten remnant of a home was still clinging. "Here, come now, see," and he lifted the baby up at arm's length.

And Gerhardt sadly concludes, "That was a *wren's* nest. They have all gone now. They will not come any more." He trudges back to the house "as if the end of the world had been reached," acutely aware of being, himself, in an alien home. Gerhardt is unhappily comfortable, and without his grandchild life would have been "hard indeed to bear."

Minor insults and major rejections come; one of his daughters marries without notifying him, but Gerhardt stolidly offers no comment. "He had had too many rebuffs." He gives up hoping and sinks into a routine gloom

and once more goes off alone to work and live in "a wee small corner in the topmost loft of a warehouse." His religious views become increasingly bothersome, and he is finally forced to balance Jennie's sinful goodness against the cold correctness of his other children. "And he was getting so old. He shook his head. Mystery of mysteries. Life was truly strange, and dark, and uncertain. Still he did not want to go and live with any of his children. Actually they were not worthy of him—none but Jennie, and she was not good. So he grieved."

During his last years Papa Gerhardt finds a permanent home with Jennie, Lester, and their child. Tolerated by Lester ("The old gentleman oughtn't to be so fussy.") he complains about household problems, worrying about small expenses and petty details. "While not very interesting, Gerhardt was not objectionable to Lester, and if the old man wanted to do odd jobs around a big place, why not?" The day of the patriarchal grandfather at the head of the table was gone, the older folk in the American family had already begun to become obsolete, and in a few years Sunday newspaper supplements and countless Ph. D. theses would be devoted to the "problem" of the aged in our midst.

When Gerhardt is dying Jennie communicates with her brothers and sisters who, characteristically enough, are kept away by other interests. Only Jennie, always kept at a distance by her father as punishment for her great mistake, remains to nurse and comfort him. Finally Gerhardt understands. "You're a good girl. . . . You've been good to me. . . . You forgive me, don't you. . . . I understand a lot of things I didn't. We get wiser as we get older." What Gerhardt was unable to fully comprehend was that beneath

his financial and moral problems hid the primary cause of his failure: that American materialism had passed the pioneer stage, had distorted values, had made a mockery of family life, and had predoomed Gerhardt's honest dream of a happy, secure existence. Dreiser's "comprehensive vision" saw that the evils which brought tragedy to Hurstwood in *Sister Carrie* were inherently antithetical to the continuation of the halcyon days of the American family—if, in truth, the vision of the ideal family organization was ever anything more than a pleasant mirage which was sighted, at a distance, in everyone else's log cabin, in everyone else's Cape Cod cottage.

The universal double standard of preaching morality and practicing materialism could openly wreck an impoverished family, but Dreiser wanted to show that the effects extended beyond the shacks and slums of America and entered the homes of the rich. Lester Kane pities Jennie. "What a family she must have! What queer non-moral natures they must have to have brooked such a combination of affairs." He is oblivious to the parallels with his own family which, in its fashion, is similarly possessed by another form of this "queer non-moral nature."

The Kane family, resting firmly and smugly on the wealth and prestige of a successful first generation business venture, is constantly guided in its private affairs by the paramount concern for the good of the factory. The family is, in fact, a small corporation, guided by the elder Kane in the role of director. There is much surface adherence to an understood mutual admiration, but as in the Gerhardt family, the father never commands more than a half-hearted respect. Lester, returning from a business trip, ". . . knew that his father was around somewhere, but did not bother to

look him up." Kane senior preferred his younger son Lester, but he displays an overt favoritism for another son and daughter who successfully fall into the business pattern. Kane even finds it necessary to alter his will to bring Lester in line. He understands that though Lester is temporarily out of his sphere of control he must eventually return. When he does he can once again assume his place in the family dynasty, providing he remembers the rules. Just as Papa Gerhardt tries to hold his family together with a misplaced religious fanaticism, Kane tries holding his family with a misplaced reliance on position. Neither Gerhardt nor Kane come close to succeeding, and so the failure is not only theirs but that of the American family and the American dream.

The failure of the two families to function as cohesive, loving units is the important theme of the novel. However, there is still the concern for the individuals who, like Hurstwood, attempt to stage one man rebellions. These mavericks are usually torn from their proper position by the attractions of a woman, and in the case of Senator Brander it is Jennie who provides the attraction. Brander is not a fully developed character, a rather sketchy caricature of a middle-aged statesman. "In him there were joined, to a remarkable degree, the wisdom of the opportunist and the sympathetic nature of the true representative of the people." It is the second element in his makeup which brought him close to Jennie.

Lester has the same two qualities. Well aware of his constant life of sham, he still spouts platitudes of the day in an unending stream. "Hew to the line, let the chips fall where they may" was his pet motto. "Keep young or die young" was another, and he admonishes his mistress to

" look facts in the face." All pleasant enough bromides by themselves, all revealing sayings when repeated and believed. Dreiser sums up Lester as being blessed with a fine imagination and considerable insight but lacking " the ruthless, narrow-minded insistence on his individual superiority which is a necessary element in almost every great business success." He is an unsuccessful imitation of Senator Brander, compounded of the same two elements in differing proportions, and for this reason he is less able to cope with his break from the established pattern of behavior. Lester was, above all, " an essentially animal-man, pleasantly veneered by education and environment." His death was from a lesion of a major blood-vessel in his brain and not from the anticipated intestinal trouble; it was not his wealth but the problem it forced that stifled his life. It was not the desire for Jennie but the problems this desire brought forth that smashed his ambition.

The two rebels, Brander and Kane, are both brought back to camp, one by death and one by resignation, and the two families are shown to be ineffective. But there has been a struggle. As Edgar Johnson observed of the novels of Dickens, " It is the wonder but the truth of humanity that it *does* so struggle."

But at what point does the struggle come? For both Hurstwood and Kane it came in middle life.

> There comes a time in every thinking man's life when he pauses and " takes stock " of his condition; when he asks himself how it fares with his individuality as a whole, mental, moral, physical, material. This time comes after the first heedless flights of youth have passed, when the initiative and more powerful efforts have been made, and he be-

gins to feel the uncertainty of results and final values which attaches itself to everything.

Dreiser also saw America as being at middle-age. As Professor Vivas and others have pointed out, he was not an orderly philosopher with a defined system. His announced conversion to Marxism (Communist Party, U. S. A. version) in his last years was a token gesture and not, as he claimed, the logical culmination of his life, or at least not of his life as revealed in his literary works. All that Dreiser does in *Jennie Gerhardt* is caution us to look around, to see what has happened to the individual in America, and specifically, to understand what is happening to the American family. Whether or not Dreiser's insights were accurate for his time is debatable . . . there can be little quarrel about their present application.

WINESBURG, OHIO: THE PURITY AND CUNNING OF SHERWOOD ANDERSON

ANDERSON, 1919

by HERBERT GOLD

A Little Worm in the Fair Apple of Progress

He said it of himself. He saw himself curled up, busily feeding on midwestern America, sheltered, destructive, loving his host, and needed by this age and place in order that they could get some sense of buoyancy and carry within them the richness of growth. He recognized his own childish self-absorption, great event for an artist, a breed accused by everyone of being childishly self-absorbed. Therefore he wrote about death with praise because " it will in any case give us escape from this disease of self." Self-love is surely the beginning of the love of others, but it is only the beginning. Sherwood Anderson, an old child,

suffered a merely erratic love of himself, therefore writhed with a tormented love of others. All his stories are bound up in this sense of the self's isolation, seen as glory and sickness, as sickness and glory. He is one of the purest, most intense poets of loneliness—the loneliness of being an individual and of being buffeted in the current, the loneliness of isolation and that of being swallowed. One type represents the traditional retreat into the self for self-possession; the other, and its adversary at times, arises out of angry resentment of a sensible man in an assembly-line civilization. Anderson's work is a manual of the ways in which loneliness can be used. It was his nourishment and sometimes his poison.

"I pour a dream over it. . . . I want to write beautifully, create beautifully, not outside but in this thing in which I am born, in this place where, in the midst of ugly towns, cities, Fords, moving pictures, I have always lived, must always live." Yet he fled it always. He fled in order to find himself, then prayed to flee that disease of self, to become " beautiful and clear . . . plangent and radiant." He felt that he loved only the midwestern land and people but was still fleeing when he died—in the Panama Canal Zone.

In his photographs he often showed his hair hanging over his eyes. The affectation means a great deal: first mere arty affectation (how he loved the " free spirits " of Greenwich Village and New Orleans!), then something feminine and wanting to be pretty and lovable for prettiness, and then of course the blurring of sight when you try to see through your own hair. What do you see? A world organized by your hair. "I must snap my finger at the world. . . . I have thought of everyone and everything." His sympathy and his oceanic feelings alternate with arrogant despair in

which the arrogance can deceive no one. So desperately hurt he is, trying so hard to convince the "word-fellows" he wanted to admire him. But then his nostalgia gives us the mood he sought to force:

> . . . old fellows in my home town speaking feelingly of an evening spent on the big, empty plains. It has taken the shrillness out of them. They had learned the trick of quiet. It affected their whole lives. It made them significant.

We understand him at last!

And then again the helpless bombast: "At my best, brother, I am like a great mother bird. . . ." He exuded through his pores the ferocious longing of a giant of loneliness. The typical chords from his letters sound under the charging heroes of the stories:

> Youth not given a break—youth licked before it starts.

> Filled with sadness that you weren't there.

> I have a lot I want to tell you if I can. . . . Anyway you know what I mean when we talked of a man working in the small, trying to save a little of the feeling of man for man.

The romantic sentimentalist held up his mirror to look at his world, peered deeply, saw himself instead, of course; wrote painfully about what he saw; and it turned out that he was writing about the world after all, squeezing it by this palpitating midwestern honesty out of his grandiose sorrows and longings. Sometimes, anyway. He was not a pure man; he had a kind of farmer cunning, plus his groaning artiness and pretense, with which he hoped to convince the "word-fellows" and the pretty girls that he was a Poet

although not a young one. What he really wanted was to be alone in that succession of gray furnished rooms he talked about so eloquently, making immortal the quiet noise and gentle terror of his childhood. "I try to believe in beauty and innocence in the midst of the most terrible clutter." But clutter, too, was the truth of his life; he fed on it; how else does a poet take the measure of his need for "beauty and innocence"? He must have remained an optimist, too, amidst all his disillusion. He married four times. To the end of his life he went on believing and marrying.

Anderson the writer arouses a poking curiosity about Anderson the man even in the most resolutely detached reader. The note of confession is always with us: "Here I am, it's good that you know!" he seems to be saying.

His very paragraphs are soaked in his own groping speech. He repeats, he cries out, he harangues, he pleads. All his work, the abysmal failures and the successes which have helped to construct the vision Americans have of themselves, represents an innocent, factitious, improvised, schemed reflection and elaboration of the elements of his own life. He turns the private into the public and then back into the private again. His mystery as a man remains despite his childish longing to reveal himself—the mystery of a man who looks at a man with a beard and a scar in a conference room and sees, instead, a lover fleeing his girl's brothers through the fields. (They had knives and slashed —could this be the same man? he asks himself.) Anderson confounds us with bombast and wit, tenderness and soft-headedness, rant and exquisite delicacy.

199

The best of his work is what matters.

Let us now look more closely at what the worm made of his apple.

My Feet Are Cold and Wet

He loved to create, he loved his fantasy as the lonely boy does. In his best work, as in some of the stories of *Winesburg, Ohio*, the fantasy is most controlled, or if not exactly controlled, simplified, given a single lyrical line. The novels had trouble passing the test of the adult imagination, being wild proliferations of daydream. The simple stories of Kate Swift ("The Teacher") or Wing Biddlebaum ("Hands") join Sherwood Anderson with the reader's sense of wonder and despair at the pathetic in his own past—childish hope of love, failed ambition, weakness and loneliness. As music can do, such stories liberate the fantasies of our secret lives. However, musicians will agree that music is for listening, not to be used as a stimulus for fantasy. We must attend to the song itself, not take advantage of it and make it the passive instrument of our dreaming. In the same way, the great writer hopes to arouse and lead the reader's imagination toward a strong individual perspective on experience. Sherwood Anderson, however, was not of that vividly individualistic company, despite his personal hobby of eccentric Bohemianism. Rather, he was the dreamy, sad, romantic idler within each of us, evoking with nostalgia and grief the bitter moments of recognition which have formed him—formed all of us in our lonely America.

James Joyce used the word "epiphany," which he took from Catholic ritual, to name that moment of revelation when words and acts come together to manifest something new, familiar, timeless, the deep summation of meaning. The experience of epiphany is characteristic of great literature, and the lyric tales of Anderson give this wonderful rapt coming-forth time and time again.

In "The Untold Lie," for example, two men tenderly meet in order to talk about whether one, the younger, should marry the girl he has made pregnant. The older man, unhappy in his own marriage, wants to see the young man's life free and charged with powerful action as his own has never been. But it is revealed to him—revelation is almost always the climax of Anderson's stories—that life without wife and children is impossible and that one man's sorrows cannot be used by him to prevent another man from choosing the same sorrows. It would be a lie to say that the life of conjugal sorrows is merely a life of conjugal sorrows. The story finally breathes the sadness, the beauty, the necessary risks of grownup desire. "Whatever I told him would have been a lie," he decides. Each man has to make his own decisions and live out his chosen failures of ideal freedom.

Many of Anderson's stories take for their realization objective circumstances which have a grandiose folkish quality, and many of both the most impressive and the most mawkish are concerned with an archetypical experience of civilization: the test which, successfully passed, commands manhood. Such a story as "The Man Who Became a Woman" objectifies even in its title the boy's wondering and fearful dreams. The end sought is manliness, that new clean and free life; failure is seen as a process of being made effeminate, or falling into old patterns of feeling and action. At his best in these stories, there is a physical joy in triumph which is fresh, clean, genial—we think of Mark Twain, although a Twain without the robust humor; at his weak moments, we may also think of the sentimental sick Twain, and we find also the maundering moping of a prettified Thomas Wolfe.

The line between the subjects of Anderson's stories

201

and Sherwood Anderson himself is barely drawn. His relation as artist to his material, as shaper of his material, is as intense and personal as that of any modern writer. Unlike most writers dealing with unhappy and frustrated people, Anderson's work is absolutely authentic in the double sense —not merely in communicating the feeling of these people as people but also in giving us the conviction that the author shares both their bitter frustration and their evanescent occasional triumphs. By comparison with Sherwood Anderson, Dostoevsky is a monument of cool detachment. His identification is perfect, sometimes verging on the morbid: "Everyone in the world is Christ and they are all crucified." He has a primitive idealism, a spoiled romanticism like that of Rousseau: we could be all innocent and pure in our crafts if the machines of America and the fates that bring machines did not cripple us.

This romantic idealism can be illustrated again by his treatment of another theme, marriage, in the story "Loneliness," in which he writes of Enoch Robinson: "Two children were born to the woman he married"—just as if they did not happen to Robinson at all, which is indeed the truth about the self-isolated personality he describes. "He dismissed the essence of things," Anderson can write, "and played with realities." Again the romantic Platonist sees a conflict between the deepest meaning and the facts of our lives, between what we do and what we "really" are. With a kind of purity and cunning, Anderson seems to thrive on this curiously boyish notion, the limitations of which most of us quickly learn. We work and love because we know that there is no other way to be ourselves than in relation to the rest of the world. The kind man is the man who performs kind acts; the generous man is a man who behaves

generously; we distrust the "essential" generosity which is sometimes claimed for the soul of a man who watches out only for himself. And yet we can be reminded with a strange force by Anderson's conviction in his boyish dream of isolated personality that there is something totally private, untouchable, beyond appearance and action, in all of us. The observation is a familiar one, but the experience can be emotionally crucial. Cunningly Anderson makes us turn to ourselves again with some of his own purity.

The last sentence of "Departure" says of George Willard: "Winesburg had disappeared and his life there had become but a background on which to paint the dreams of his manhood." Abstracted people, playing out their time in the fragmentary society of Winesburg, these "heroes" are isolated, as Anderson himself was isolated, by art or unfulfilled love or religion—by the unsurmounted challenge of finding the self within relationship with others. It was the deep trouble of Anderson's own life that he saw his self, which could be realized only by that monstrous thing, the Life of Art, as flourishing in opposition to decent connections with others in society. Marriage, work, friendship were beautiful things; but the gray series of furnished slum rooms, in which he wrote, enough rooms to fill a city, were his real home. Writing letters and brooding behind his locked door, he idealized love, he idealized friendship. He withdrew to the company of phantom creatures. He hoped to guard his integrity. He kept himself the sort of child-man he described with such comprehending sympathy in the character of Enoch Robinson.

203

In many writers dealing with the grim facts of our lives, the personal sense of triumph at encompassing the material adds a note of confidence which is at variance with

the story itself. Hemingway is a good example; his heroes go down to defeat, but Papa Hemingway the chronicler springs eternal. In Anderson this external note of confidence and pride in craft is lacking, except in some of the specious, overwilled novels which he wrote under political influences. Generally he does not import his poetry into the work—he allows only the poetry that is *there*—nor does his independent life as a creator come to change the tone of these sad tales. The stories of Winesburg are unself-consciously committed to him as he is sworn true to them; the identification—a variety of loyalty—is torturingly complete; he is related to his material with a love that lacks esthetic detachment and often lacks the control which comes with that detachment. They are practically unique in this among modern storytelling, and it is partially this that gives them their sometimes embarrassing, often tormenting and unforgettable folk quality. Still they are not folktales, but, rather, pseudofolktales. The romantic longing and grieving is not characteristic of the folktale, despite the other elements, a direct matter-of-fact storytelling, colloquial American language (complicated by chivalry and the Bible, but at its best not "literary"), and the authority of Anderson's pious devotion to his lives and people. Later, of course, the romantic judgment culminated in rebellion, sometimes in a kind of esthetic rant against the way things are.

In "The Strength of God," the Reverend Curtis Hartman (as in a parable, Heart-man)

> wondered if the flame of the spirit really burned in him and dreamed of a day when a strong sweet current of power would come like a great wind into his voice and his soul and the people would tremble before the spirit of God made manifest in him. 'I am a poor stick and that will never really

happen to me,' he mused dejectedly, and then a patient smile lit up his features. ' Oh well, I suppose I'm doing well enough,' he added philosophically.

These, as the *New Yorker* would put it, are musings that never got mused and philosophic additions that never got philosophically added. They have a curious archaic directness that amounts to a kind of stylization. The unanalytic simplicity itself is a sophisticated manner. As the officers of the Pharisees said, "Never man spake like this man." It recalls to us the day of the storyteller who suggested the broad line of an action, and allowed us to give our imaginations to it. Nowadays we demand detail upon detail, and the phrase "I am a poor stick" would require a whole book of exposition in the hands of most contemporary novelists.

The pathos of the pious man's temptation by the flesh has a flavor beautifully evocative of adolescence. We no longer think of "carnal temptation" as Anderson did. But we remember our fears and guilts, and are reminded of ourselves as great literature always reminds us. Hartman's silent, secret battle with himself over Kate Swift is given part of its bite by her own story—this pimply, passionate young school teacher who strikes beauty without knowing it and can find no one to speak to her. Her story is told with a brilliant delicacy that reflects Anderson's own strange reticence about women. Enoch Robinson, he says, "tried to have an affair with a woman of the town met on the sidewalk before his lodging house." To have an affair is his strange idiom for a pickup! (The boy got frightened and ran away; the woman roared with laughter and picked up someone else).

205

Except for the poetic schoolteacher and a very few others, women are not women in Anderson's stories. There are the girls who suffer under the kind of sensitivity, passion, and lonely burning which was Anderson's own lot; and then there are the Women. For Anderson women have a strange holy power; they are earth-mothers, ectoplasmic spirits, sometimes succubi, rarely individual living creatures. In "Hands" they are not girls but "maidens," where the word gives a quaint archaic charm to the creature who taunts poor, damned, lonely Wing Biddlebaum. The berry-picking "maidens" gambol while the boys are "boisterous" and the hero flutters in his tormented realm between the sexes.

In somewhere like Wing Biddlebaum's tormented realm, Sherwood Anderson also abode. American cities, as he wrote, are "noisy and terrible," and they fascinated him. He got much of the noise and terror into his writing about big cities, and the quiet noise and gentle terror of little towns into his stories about them. And among the fright of materialistic life, he continually rediscovered the minor beauties which made life possible for him—the moment of love, of friendship, of self-realization. That they were but moments is not entirely the fault of Anderson's own character.

The Air of a Creator

Anderson is shrewd, sometimes just, and has earned the right to even the unjust judgments he makes of other writers. How earned them? He was constantly fighting through both the questions of craft and the deeper risks of imagination. He has won the right to make sweeping pronouncements on his peers. Of Sinclair Lewis, for example, he offers the most damning, most apt criticism: "Wanting

to see beauty descend upon our lives like a rainstorm, he has become blind to the minor beauties our lives hold." Sherwood Anderson wants the same thing, but holds to the good sense which a poet can still have in a difficult time: he clings to the minor beauties which give tenderness to his longing, a hope of something else to his despair. For this reason Anderson's critique of America finally bites more deeply than the novels of the ferocious sentimental satirist who was his contemporary.

Of Henry James, Anderson wrote that he is a man who "never found anyone to love, who did not dare love. . . . Can it be that he is the novelist of the haters? Oh, the thing infinitely refined and carried far into the field of intellectuality, as skillful haters find out how to do." The Jamesian flight from direct fleshly feeling offended Anderson. James objectified, stipulated, laid bare, and then suffused his entire yearning personality over all his work, so that Isabel Archer and Hyacinth Robinson are, really are, Henry James, in all his hopeless longing, and yet spiritualized, that is, without body, epicene as James seems to have made himself in real life. George Santayana believed that by withholding love from a specific object it could be given "in general" to the whole world. This is a curiously commercial, economical notion—the idea that there is a limited amount of love and that we have the choice of spending it on a few selfishly chosen objects or distributing it generally. "In general" we know that this is nonsense; our attachments to individuals are the models for our attachments to humanity as an ideal; but like many sorts of nonsense, it worked for Henry James to the extent that he really loved some spirit of Art which his "puppets," his "fables," as he called them, served.

207

Is Anderson, with all his mid-American distrust of intellectualized love, really so far from Henry James? He is
strikingly the perpetual adolescent in love with love rather
than with a specific girl with changing flesh. One can see
him dreaming after his dreamgirl even as he approached old
age. His romantic chivalry, his lust for the proletariat, his
fantastic correspondence in which the letters seem to be
written to himself, no matter how touching their apparent
candor and earnest reaching out—is he perhaps the other side
of the coin of his accusation against Henry James? To be
the novelist of lovers who did not dare to hate—this, too, is a
limitation. He seems obliged to love others as a function of
his own faulty self-love, and therefore his love of others
seems *voulu*, incomplete, and his moments of hatred a guilty
self-indulgence. He presents an extreme case of the imper-
fections of an artist just because of the disparity between
his intentions and his performance. He wanted to love,
he wanted to sing of love. His failures help to make still
more brilliant his achievements in certain of the stories of
Winesburg, in "The Egg," and in scattered paragraphs,
stories, and sections of novels.

For the fault of bookish derivations for his feelings,
Anderson substituted at his worst the fault of self-indulgent
derivation from gratifications and dreads never altered after
boyhood. He carried his childhood like a hurt warm bird
held to his middle-aged breast as he walked out of his
factory into the life of art. The primitive emotions of
childhood are the raw material of all poetry. Sometimes the
indulgence of them to the exclusion of the mature per-
spectives of adult life prevents Anderson from equalling his
aspiration and own best work.

But this is a vain quibble. Who can do his best work

208

always? What counts is the achievement, not the failures, however exemplary they may seem to a critic. "I have a lot I want to tell you if I can," he wrote in a letter. "I am writing short stories." The faults of unevenness, egotism, lazy acceptance of ideals, and romantic self-glorification are as nothing against the realized works of art which force their way through. Sherwood Anderson "added to the confusion of men," as he said of the great financiers and industrialists, the Morgans, Goulds, Carnegies, Vanderbilts, "by taking on the air of a creator." He has helped to create the image we have of ourselves as Americans. Curtis Hartman, George Willard, Enoch Robinson, all of the people of Winesburg, haunt us as do our neighbors, our friends, our own secret selves which we first met one springtime in childhood.

by JOHN W. ALDRIDGE

It is probably about time we stopped writing essays on *The Great Gatsby*, just at the moment, this is to say, when a really proper criticism seems threatening to begin. Certainly, it has been a saving paradox of criticism up to now that it has taken very little precise note of *Gatsby* while appearing to take vast general note of it. If we are not going to disturb that happy state of affairs, we had perhaps better call a halt before we yield up the book altogether to the dignifying but always transforming fire of criticism, and risk finding, after we have done so, that we are left not with the cleansed bones of the novel itself but with the ashes of one or more of its several meanings. I ask simply that we hold onto the living object in hand: the well-wrought urn

on the mantelpiece can remain empty a while longer. Posterity, if it is to get at *Gatsby* at all, will most assuredly have to breathe back into it the life we take out, and we should take care to see that posterity does not waste its breath on a corpse. For *Gatsby* is above all a novel to be directly experienced and responded to; it is a fragile novel, to be sure, in some ways imperfect, in some ways deeply unsatisfactory, but it is clearly alive because produced by a directly experiencing, living imagination, one which habitually and with great innocence so perfectly confused its own longings, fears, defeats, and chimeras with those of a certain portion of American society, that a certain portion of American society ever since has confused its own image with it and made its plans for itself on the vision of an accessible future which, as a skeptical imagination, it took pains to condemn. *Gatsby*, therefore, is a work of art particularly prone to being confused with its meanings, just as its meanings, if we are not careful, can be made to substitute for its life as a work of art.

Such a cautionary approach to *Gatsby* should count for something with us, although it probably counts for less than it would have at one time. We are accustomed now to having our experience of life abstracted for us by fiction, and our experience of fiction abstracted for us by criticism, both life and literature projected into a construct twice removed from the original and signed, sealed, and delivered over to our captive imaginations. We no longer want to do the imaginative job ourselves: we cannot quite afford the time; the code governing the division of imaginative labor would not permit it, nor do we really believe it can or need be done. Undoubtedly one of the reasons *Gatsby* continues to seem alive to us is that it represents one of the last at-

211

tempts made by an American writer to come directly at the reality of the modern American experience while its outlines were still visible and before the social sciences convinced us that they could do the job and do it better. I assume that those outlines have not since been so visible and that we no longer have the sense of a distinctive American experience or even much of a certainty that there is one. After Fitzgerald, one feels, the door onto the native scene banged shut for American writers; the process of creation ceased to be a matter of opening the eyes and letting the sensibility take moral readings; the forms of social conduct, the traditional modes of action in which the drama of the will in crisis had formerly been displayed, no longer seemed directly accessible to the novel; suddenly no one appeared to know how anyone else behaved. Among the newer writers, certainly, who aspire to something more than journalism, there has been a sort of retreat of consciousness from the nearly insupportable task of dealing creatively with the fluid social situation and with the immense complication of status values and drives which the sociologists have discovered to be typical of the present age, and in comparison with which Fitzgerald's reality seems almost banally primitive. But Fitzgerald came to the novel at a time when the patterns of our present society were just being laid down; he had the inestimable advantage of the primal view, and so we return to him, particularly in *Gatsby*, with the feeling that we are seeing ourselves as we were in the light of an intensity which we are unable to direct upon ourselves as we are. If *Gatsby* is one of the very few books left from the twenties which we are still able to read with any kind of enduring pleasure and without always having to suffer a reminder of emotions we no longer care to feel, I

suspect it is so because it dramatizes for us those basic assumptions and modes of assumption about the nature of American experience which belong to the antique furniture of our minds but which our experience of the present age and its literature has not been able to renew or replace. In this sense *Gatsby* constitutes not only a primal view but, at least to date, a final view; it crystallizes an image of life beyond which neither our books nor our own perceptions seem able to take us; for two generations in fact, in that turgid area of consciousness where life and literature seem interchangeable, it has pretty largely done our perceiving for us. It therefore has about it some of that particular poignancy which we reserve for the lost moments of the past when we felt the emotions we would like still to feel, if we were able to and had again those exactly right opportunities. In this sense too *Gatsby* is mythopoeic: it has created our legend of the twenties, which at the present time is our common legend, and like *Moby Dick* and *Huckleberry Finn* it has helped to create, by endowing with significant form, a national unconscious; its materials are those of the collective American mind at its closest approach to the primary source of native frontier symbols. As a result, we must all feel on reading it a little as Nick Carraway felt on hearing Gatsby's words—"reminded of something—an elusive rhythm, a fragment of lost words, that I had heard somewhere a long time ago." I do not mean that I much hold to the more obvious and popular mythological view of *Gatsby*: carried too far, as it usually is, it threatens always to smother the novel within the strictures of meaning. But I can understand its attraction and its relevance: Fitzgerald's technique of pictorial generalization, along with what Lionel Trilling has called his " ideographic " method of character

213

portrayal, insists on far more than the novel primarily signifies. Yet at this late stage in Fitzgerald criticism one can hope to escape cliché only by refusing to rest content with meaning and by inducing some contemplation of Gatsby's life as fiction.

A prime feature of that life is of course the marvelous style that shows it forth, and while it is now commonplace to say that in *Gatsby* Fitzgerald found, certainly for the first time and probably for the last, his proper form, it is less so to say that he could not have found the form had he not experienced an immense deepening as well as a marked shift of his relation both to himself and to language. The essentially expressive form of the earlier novels had indulged Fitzgerald in all his younger, easier, and more sentimental mannerisms; it encouraged him to describe emotion rather than to embody it, and whenever he could not find emotion, to fake it; it put up no resistance whatever to his habit of seeking, and then descending to, the lowest level of feeling his characters could sustain, or of making use, whenever he thought he could get away with it, of the cheapest rhetorical devices cribbed from Compton Mackenzie and the gothic novel. It is also evident, particularly now, that the subjects of his first novels were not suitable vehicles for his real emotions, and if they were bad, it is partly because they never allowed him to discover what his real emotions were. Fitzgerald never believed with anything like his full heart in the life he was describing; his deeper sensibilities were not only not engaged but offended, and the necessity to appear to believe, to try to pass off childish infatuation as adult devotion only served to make him seem frivolous and girlishly Beardsleyan. In this sense of course Fitzgerald's first subjects kept him young: they arrested him

for the time at a level of emotional development precisely adequate to their capacity for receiving emotion, and they asked nothing more of him than that he disguise the deficiency behind effusion and rhetoric.

It is not clear from his biography exactly what happened in the time between *The Beautiful and Damned* and *Gatsby* to mature Fitzgerald, nor is it very likely that his biography knows. Obviously he found a way of untangling his moral imagination from the gothic bric-a-brac of ghosts, mysterious medieval gentlemen, and wispy lurking presences, among which it had searched for an object through the earlier novels, and under the sponsorship of that imagination he was able to achieve a sufficient penetration of his subject to engage for the first time his real emotions and his best talents. In *This Side of Paradise* " the problem of evil had solidified " for Amory Blaine " into the problem of sex," and one felt that this had behind it some affront to Fitzgerald's romanticism stemming from the discovery that a physical act could be imagined for nice girls beyond the kiss. By the time he wrote *The Beautiful and Damned* the problem appeared to have risen on the anatomical scale and lodged somewhere near the heart, although one could never be certain whether it really belonged there or in Wall Street. But with *Gatsby* there was no longer any doubt: the problem of evil had by then solidified into a problem of responsibility and spiritual condition in those rich enough to be able to choose their morals; Fitzgerald's opposing selves, the giddy, bibulous boy and the morose, hung-over tallier of emotional chits, had struck a bargain and a balance.

215

This deepened understanding of his subject inevitably brought Fitzgerald to an awareness of the need for a narrative form far stricter and at the same time far subtler

than that demanded by his earlier novels. It is doubtful if up to *Gatsby* he had given any serious thought at all to matters of form, and considering the limited conception he had of his subject at the time, he probably felt little necessity to. By Jamesean standards *This Side of Paradise* was abominably constructed, and *The Beautiful and Damned* was only slightly less so. But the loosely episodic, rather spongy form of the juvenile *bildungsroman* borrowed from Mackenzie and Wells was not hopelessly unsuited to the situation of the young man only faintly disenchanted with the life of glamor, particularly so long as in Fitzgerald's mind the difference between the rich and you and me could still be equated with the possession of more money, better looks, looser morals, and greater daring. All that was required was an involved, naïve consciousness capable of moving more or less horizontally through a series of episodes the function of which was slow instruction in a kind of eager irony, and for this the one-dimensional mock-heroes, Amory Blaine and Anthony Patch, were perfectly competent pupils. But with *Gatsby* Fitzgerald's talent took a dramatic turn; his sense of his subject and his involvement with it became too complex and ambivalent to be portrayed through the limited single consciousness; he needed a narrative form at once firm enough to correct his tendency toward emotional bloat and supple enough to allow full range for the development of a set of individual characters who would display his theme and at the same time serve as suitable dramatic equivalents for his contradictory feelings toward it. He had suddenly and without quite knowing it arrived at a point where he was ready to put to use his mature understanding of his material within the framework of his advanced knowledge of the formal art of fiction.

216

The pictorial method of Conrad, James, and Wharton, combining the " single window " technique of the engaged narrator with that of the scenic tableau, made it possible for Fitzgerald to overcome in *Gatsby* the severe limitations of the merely expressive form and to achieve the kind of distance between himself and his subject which must be achieved before the job of true fictional creation can properly begin. In Nick Carraway he found the protagonist of his own most central ambivalence, a median consciousness and conscience vacillating between admiration and judgment, a " first-rate intelligence " able " to hold two opposed ideas in the mind at the same time, and still retain the ability to function." The foil-figures of Gatsby and Tom Buchanan serve him as devices for breaking down into contrasting parts and recombining in even more ambiguous relation his twin senses of the physical glamor of the rich and their spiritual corruption, their force of character and their moral weakness, the ideal nature of romantic vision and the baseness of the methods employed in its service, the essential shabbiness of romantic vision in a society which can measure vision only in money. Daisy Buchanan and Jordan Baker function on a somewhat simpler level to complete the symbolism of identity and contrast, Daisy standing initially as an embodiment of the purity of the vision, finally of the corruption and the baseness of method, Jordan holding up to the world a mask of sophisticated, though precarious self-composure, but concealing behind it, like Nicole Diver, an awful secret of interior derangement. George and Myrtle Wilson alone remain almost untouched by the process of imaginative revision through which Fitzgerald transformed, by immensely complicating, his typical thematic effects in the novel: Wilson carries forward and for the first time

217

fully characterizes Fitzgerald's earlier horror of poverty and illness, while Myrtle dramatizes his formerly incoherent, at moments hysterical aversion to direct sexuality when unaccompanied by beauty and wealth.

Lionel Trilling is undoubtedly right in calling this method of characterization "ideographic" and in applying the term as well to the method of the novel as a whole. Nothing and no one in the course of the narrative is really developed; everything is seen in tableau, in a state of permanent pictorial rest. The characters are little more than a collection of struck attitudes, frieze figures carved on the entablature of a moral abstraction, a greatly generalized intuitive view of the nature of American experience. Their individual identities are subordinated to the central idea they are meant to signify, perfectly embodying the "platonic conception" behind the remark made by Gatsby when he admits the possibility that Daisy may perhaps have once loved her husband: "In any case it was just personal." The secret of the entire technique of the novel may in a sense be said to lie hidden in this remark, for its effect is to divert attention from the personal and particular to the abstract conception, the allegorized whole.

In achieving this effect Fitzgerald carried the pictorial method considerably beyond James; in fact, the closest parallel to its use in *Gatsby* is the Joycean "signature" or "epiphany" technique where character is broken down into its separate parts, and one or two of the parts are made to stand for the whole. The result for Joyce, in both *A Portrait of the Artist* and *Ulysses*, was the establishment of a virtual iconography of character, a system of extravagantly distilled symbolic essences, usually suggested by a gesture or an article of clothing, through which the soul

of being was shown forth. The result for Fitzgerald is not nearly so elaborate, but it is very similar in kind. Nick Carraway is revealed to us through his signature of honesty; Gatsby is identified by his pink suits, Tom Buchanan by his rippling pack of muscle, Daisy by her voice, Jordan by her balancing act, Myrtle by her fleshy vitality, Wilson by his hollow-eyed stare, Wolfsheim by his hairy nostrils, the butler by his nose. In the case of each of the major characters these attributes take on metaphorical significance in the thematic design of the novel. Nick's honesty is called into ironic question by Jordan in an effort to shift the blame for her own dishonesty; Gatsby's pink suits suggest the meretriciousness of his role, Tom's muscle the brutal strength of his; Jordan's balancing act is indicative of her precarious control over herself and her need for a stabilizing moral convention, while Daisy's voice serves as the gauge of her "basic insincerity," which it is the principal business of the novel to penetrate. Initially full of warm excitement and promise it is finally shown to be "full of money," and in the long interval between the two observations the pathetic futility of Gatsby's dream is gradually made clear.

To create an effect of involvement and movement while retaining the advantage of the pictorial method Fitzgerald made constant use of ironic parallelisms of both character and event, still very much in the manner of Joyce. Both Gatsby and Daisy are "insincere," Gatsby about his past, Daisy about her present feelings; Tom's unfaithfulness to Daisy is balanced by Gatsby's faithfulness to her; yet Tom and Daisy belong to a "secret society" of ultimately deeper faithfulness. Nick keeps faith with Gatsby to the end, but not with Jordan. Jordan's dishonesty is revealed in time with the Buchanans' and Gatsby's; Jordan like Daisy is a

219

"careless driver," and the episode in which this fact is first made clear to Nick prefigures the moment when Daisy's carelessness results in Myrtle's death; both, furthermore, are anticipated by the comic accident scene in Gatsby's driveway and are finally commented upon during Nick's last meeting with Jordan when, to conceal her own dishonesty, she insists that she met in Nick another bad driver. Just before the showdown scene with Gatsby in the Plaza Hotel Tom feels that he has lost in one afternoon both his wife and his mistress; during the scene he wins back his wife, and Gatsby loses his mistress and is symbolically murdered by Tom—all to the accompaniment of Mendelssohn's Wedding March being played in the ballroom below. As Gatsby the dreamer dies, Nick remembers that it is his own thirtieth birthday, the time of life when, in his and Fitzgerald's romantically limited chronology, all dreams must end. On the way back to East Egg Daisy kills Tom's mistress, Wilson loses a wife, and a while later Tom arranges through Wilson to murder Gatsby in fact, Wilson believing that Gatsby has been Myrtle's lover as well as her murderer. All the principal male characters lose the women they love, and in each case through some act of faithlessness on the part of one or more of the women.

This system of carefully plotted interior parallels and cross-references serves greatly to enhance the thematic "size" of the novel and to give back to it some of the quality of dramatic specification which the method of static character portrayal takes away. The same can be said for the reflexive relationship of the parts in the narrative design as a whole. Each of the nine chapters is composed of one, or very occasionally more than one, dramatic scene presented pictorially and surrounded by skillfully fore-

shortened panoramic material, and each achieves significance not through the standard depth-wise plumbing of character, but through its contribution of fresh facts to the linearly developing sequence of facts which gradually illuminate Gatsby's central dilemma and mystery. Each functions, furthermore, in reciprocal relation to every other, at times ironically, at times by simple contrast, so that an effect of counterpointed motifs comes ultimately to stand, very much as it does in *The Waste Land*, in place of the more conventional and predictable effect of events arranged chronologically and naturalistically.

The opening and closing pages of the novel frame Gatsby's story within the parentheses of an elegiacally retrospective vision of time, history, and moral conduct. The first two pages state the terms of the ambivalent attitude which Nick is to take toward the subsequent action and which it is to be the task of that action to resolve. Presented initially as a young man taught by his father to "reserve all judgments" in the knowledge that "all the people in this world haven't had the advantages that you've had," Nick describes himself immediately afterward as one who has since been taught better by first-hand contact with some of the people who have had even more of the advantages than he, and who have left him with the feeling of wanting "the world to be in uniform and at a sort of moral attention forever." He then goes on to substitute a new and much more complex ambivalence for the one that, on looking back over his experience, he feels has now been resolved: he has been educated in the power of condemnatory judgment, but he is still unable to condemn Gatsby— "Only Gatsby . . . was exempt from my reaction—Gatsby who represented everything for which I have an unaffected

221

scorn." It is to be Nick's fate in the course of the novel, as unquestionably it was Fitzgerald's, that while he is to learn intolerance and finally moral indignation, he is never to come to terms with his contradictory feelings toward Gatsby: his moral indignation remains to the end the slave of his moral idealism. After Gatsby's death it is simple enough for Nick to recognize the Buchanans as "careless people," for he has accumulated more than sufficient evidence of their irresponsibility to cancel out his earlier admiration of them. But of Gatsby the poseur, racketeer, and liar he can only speak in the name of Gatsby the dreamer, and eulogize him only in the name of the founding of America itself, for Gatsby is one who escapes the monitory conscience of the "spoiled priest" by being himself priest-like, with a priest's passionate and self-sacrificing dedication to an ideal, a religion, of romantic transcendence. Nick's point of view, which we see in the process of gradually becoming reeducated with regard to the Buchanans, is incapable of reeducation with regard to Gatsby, for Gatsby is both a suitable object for the fascination which Nick earlier felt for the Buchanans and an embodiment of the ideal against which he measures and condemns them. It is an inadequate ideal, and Nick—or at least Fitzgerald—is entirely aware of the fact, but within the limits of his given experience it is the only one he has to set against the world of Buchanan values, the only one he has, therefore, to exalt into triumph over those values at the end.

But the image of Nick which dominates the opening chapters is of another, as yet uneducated idealism, the kind indigenous to his Middle West, a rural frontier fascination with the appearance of culture and worldly manners. In fact, the first chapter centered in the scene depicting the

222

dinner party at the Buchanan estate is clearly intended to dramatize Nick in his primal condition of reserved judgment juxtaposed with the gradually emerging facts of spiritual corruption and deceit which finally cause him to arrive at condemnatory judgment and become morally initiated. Firmly established amid the grandeur of his physical setting Tom Buchanan first appears to Nick as an heroic figure, but almost at once Nick is struck by the change in him since their New Haven years.

> Now he was a sturdy straw-haired man of thirty with a rather hard mouth and a supercilious manner. Two shining arrogant eyes had established dominance over his face and gave him the appearance of always leaning aggressively forward. Not even the effeminate swank of his riding clothes could hide the enormous power of that body. . . . It was a body capable of enormous leverage—a cruel body. His speaking voice, a gruff husky tenor, added to the impression of fractiousness he conveyed. There was a touch of paternal contempt in it, even toward people he liked—and there were men at New Haven who had hated his guts.

This swift appraisal of Tom establishes him in the role he is later to play and constitutes the first element in the developing contrast between appearance and reality on which the chapter turns.

223

A moment later Nick is taken in to see Daisy and Jordan, and the picture of glamorous buoyancy and charm which they present temporarily restores his powers of admiration. In fact, the quality of physical inflation, suggested entirely in tableau, which pervades the scene stands as an exact equivalent for the emotion which the sight of the women arouses in him.

> The only completely stationary object in the room was an enormous couch on which two young women were buoyed up as though upon an anchored balloon. They were both in white, and their dresses were rippling and fluttering as if they had just been blown back in after a short flight around the house. . . . Then there was a boom as Tom Buchanan shut the rear windows and the caught wind died out about the room, and the curtains and the rugs and the two young women ballooned slowly to the floor.

But the effect is only temporary. As the scene deflates itself, so subsequent events deflate Nick's illusion and impel him toward condemnatory judgment. At the dinner table he learns that "Tom's got some woman in New York." Gatsby's name is brought into the conversation and hastily dropped. Nick dimly remembers having seen Jordan, or a picture of her, somewhere before. Sitting on the porch with Daisy after dinner and listening to her tell about the birth of her child and her feelings about life in general, he is suddenly struck by "the basic insincerity of what she had to say" and begins to feel that "the whole evening had been a trick of some sort to exact a contributary emotion" from him. A moment later Daisy smirks "as if she had asserted her membership in a rather distinguished secret society to which she and Tom belonged." Nick leaves East Egg that night sufficiently disturbed to want Daisy to "rush out of the house, child in arms," and upon returning home he catches sight of Gatsby standing in the darkness of his lawn and looking across the water to the green light at the end of the Buchanans' dock. Thus, by the end of the first chapter the basic dramatic situation has been established; all the principal characters have been introduced or

alluded to; and the destructive element in the Buchanans has been brought into fatal juxtaposition with both Nick's naïve admiration and Gatsby's naïve aspiration. The contest now will be between the force of the secret society, epitomized by Daisy's insincerity and Tom's cruel selfishness, and the persuasive power of Gatsby's illusion. But we already know the outcome: it has been ordained by the quality and content of the action itself.

The second chapter develops the destructive statement of the first in two ways: through the contextual symbolism of the "valley of ashes" image dominated by the gigantic eyes of the oculist Dr. T. J. Eckleburg, and through the pictorial scene of the drunken party at Tom's New York apartment. The valley of ashes establishes the situation of evil which is conventionally, and in Fitzgerald habitually, associated with hopeless poverty, and it projects that evil into literal contrast with the kind which wealth and privilege induce in the Buchanans. Theirs is at once a more serious and reprehensible kind because it involves the possibility of moral choice and an identical kind because it has behind it an equivalent impoverishment of soul. The eyes of Dr. Eckleburg can be variously and, if one is not careful to preserve a sense of humor, fatuously interpreted. They are reminiscent of some of Fitzgerald's earlier gothic figures of evil—the ghostly apparitions and "somber palls" of *This Side of Paradise* and *The Beautiful and Damned*—but they have the virtue of thematic relevance which these lacked, as well as the dramatic advantage of association with a developed physical milieu. They are of course suggestive of Nick's monitory conscience and are related to the image of "the casual watcher in the darkening streets" which is evoked during the party scene by his sense of being " within

225

and without, simultaneously enchanted and repelled by the inexhaustible variety of life." They are also specifically associated by George Wilson in the eighth chapter with the eyes of God and, since Gatsby is represented as a son of God, we are probably justified in associating them in turn with the holiness of his romantic aspiration. More generally, they operate as an open symbol of transcendence and judgment set down in an opposing environment of defeat and subhuman amorality, or, to put it differently, they serve as a terminal point for the two principal thematic lines of the novel: the evil of the human condition overseen and modified by conscience.

The party episode pictorializes in scenic form the evil implicit in the valley of ashes, and since it stands in ironic contrast with the earlier scene at the Buchanans', it shows up that evil to be merely the nether side of theirs: the moral debasement of the party is the Buchanans' moral hypocrisy with its clothes off, the ugly truth beneath the veneer of social elegance which first charmed Nick, the corruption behind Daisy's enchanting voice and Jordan's delicate balancing act—in effect, the vulgar barroom scene in *The Waste Land* in comparison with the sterile "game of chess" episode.

The third through the sixth chapters perform for Gatsby the same service that the first two chapters performed for the Buchanans: they present him in the alternating conditions of illusion and reality, mystery and fact, successively as genial host, shady character, and romantic visionary. In the third chapter he is dramatized in his public role of host, but like Conrad's Heyst he is seen by various observers in the roles created for him by his legend, and this has the effect of endowing him with the mythic gener-

ality and largeness which his thematic role requires. It also gives concrete endorsement to the premise that he is the product of his "Platonic conception of himself." Nick is himself momentarily taken in by the "Oggsford man" role, but quickly recognizes its absurdity, especially after the luncheon with Wolfsheim when he becomes acquainted with the underworld role. He shortly discovers, however, that the truth about Gatsby, as it is gradually revealed to him, first by Jordan, then by Gatsby himself, is far more remarkable than any of the stories circulated about him, and ultimately far more compelling. By the end of the sixth chapter he has become convinced of the high quality of Gatsby's aspiration, but he has also gathered fresh evidence in the form of the Buchanans' high-handed behavior at one of the parties that that aspiration will eventually be defeated. Daisy has initially been hypnotized by Gatsby's display of wealth and ardor and for the moment is attracted by the prospect of an affair, but during the party she reveals her snobbish inability to participate wholly in any form of life outside herself.

> She was appalled by West Egg, this unprece-
> dented 'place' that Broadway had begotten upon a
> Long Island fishing village—appalled by its raw
> vigor that chafed under the old euphemisms and by
> the too obtrusive fate that herded its inhabitants
> along a short-cut from nothing to nothing. She
> saw something awful in the very simplicity she
> failed to understand.

227

Like Daisy's first show of "basic insincerity," this reaction is proof that she will never finally join Gatsby in his efforts to "repeat the past."

It is interesting to see how these chapters devoted to

Gatsby exactly reverse the revelatory processes of those devoted to the Buchanans. The illusion of sophisticated elegance was penetrated in their case to reveal a basic sickness and poverty of spirit. Gatsby, on the other hand, is seen initially against a veneer of fraudulent finery, is then revealed as actually fraudulent as well as lawless, and finally as morally innocent in the midst of the lawless. Superficially, he is as bad as the Buchanans, but only superficially. Theirs is a fundamental lawlessness of the heart: they are " careless people " in the worst and deepest sense. His is the lawlessness of the merely illegal and is excusable on the ground of the service it renders in enforcing the highest laws of the heart.

The seventh and climactic chapter brings into dramatic conflict the opposing elements of destruction and aspiration, the morally lawless and the morally innocent within the illegal, which have been separately developed in the chapters alternately devoted to the Buchanans and Gatsby. The occasion is a gathering at the Buchanan estate, precisely like that of the first chapter, but the tonal differences between the two are obviously intended to unite them in ironic contrast. Again Daisy and Jordan are seen in tableau, but where formerly they had about them a quality of inflation and buoyancy suggestive of the emotion they first aroused in Nick, they now appear in a state of fatigued deflation, as if the intervening events had drained away their vitality along with their charm. " The room, shadowed well with awnings, was dark and cool. Daisy and Jordan lay upon an enormous couch, like silver idols weighing down their own white dresses against the singing breeze of the fans." The whole situation, furthermore, seems to Nick to be touched with nightmare. He imagines he overhears the

butler replying to a telephone request for "the master's body." Daisy impulsively kisses Gatsby the moment Tom leaves the room. Daisy's child is led in by a nurse and introduced to Gatsby who, Nick is certain, had never "really believed in its existence before." Finally, as the party prepares to leave for New York, Gatsby has his first insight into the quality of Daisy's which is to prevent him from winning her.

> 'Her voice is full of money,' he said suddenly. . . .
> That was it. I'd never understood before. It was
> full of money—that was the inexhaustible charm
> that rose and fell on it, the jingle of it, the cymbal's
> song of it. . . . High in a white palace the king's
> daughter, the golden girl. . . .

This is the quality which indemnifies Daisy's commitment to Tom's world, but it finally involves much more than just money: it is a whole philosophy and tradition of life belonging to those who have always had money and marking them as a separate breed superior to those who have not. And in the chapter's closing scene, following on Gatsby's defeat and Myrtle's death, the difference is epiphanized:

> Daisy and Tom were sitting opposite each other
> at the kitchen table, with a plate of cold fried
> chicken between them, and two bottles of ale. . . .
> They weren't happy, and neither of them had
> touched the chicken or the ale—and yet they weren't
> unhappy either. There was an unmistakable air of
> natural intimacy about the picture, and anybody
> would have said that they were conspiring to-
> gether.

229

The "secret society" has at last won out over romantic illusion, and Gatsby, standing outside in the dark just as he

was at the end of Chapter 1, is now " watching over nothing."

The movement of the novel, then, is from illusion to reality, innocence to knowledge, aspiration to defeat, and of course suffusing them all, tolerance to judgment. It is Gatsby who pays the price for the learning, who functions by turns as the hapless Mme. de Vionnet and the finally unteachable Chad, but it is Nick who does his learning for him and through whose experience—as through Strether's in the case of Chad—it is made dramatically concrete. Gatsby's dream is dramatically unspecific because it is unspecific to him. That is, symbolically, its limitation and meaning: it is based not on things as they are, but on things as they might become. It is real only to the extent that one can imagine for it some successful embodiment in action, and this the logic of the novel never permits. Nick's sensibility, therefore, serves as a surrogate for Gatsby's, making external all that the dream, because it lacks concrete basis in fact and action, cannot make external by itself. In doing this, Nick's sensibility fleshes Gatsby out to very nearly epic size, endowing him with the character of heroism seen against a broadly generalized conception of national life and history.

This is accomplished in the novel in two ways: through Nick's direct participation in the life of the Buchanans, which educates him in the folly of innocence, and through the larger symbolism of place against which Nick measures the meaning of both his own and Gatsby's experience. In practice, however, the two function as one: Nick records the experience as well as the meaning almost entirely in terms of place. Place affords him his basis of vision and evaluation, and the change which occurs in his vision and evaluation results in a change in his evaluation of place.

At the beginning of the novel the East appears to
Nick—as by implication it does to Gatsby—as a land of
wealth and future glittering with the promise of "shining
secrets." But as the action proceeds, the "shining secrets"
tarnish, and it becomes clear that the wealth and quality of
purposeful movement into the future are illusory virtues
imposed upon the East by the innocence of the beholder.
Like Gatsby's isolated dream, the wealth feeds on itself;
the Easterners are imprisoned by it to the point of spiritual
stagnation, the "flow of life" moves in a purposeless circle.
"The rich grow richer" because they have no other way to
grow; "the poor get—children" as well as poorer and end
ultimately in a "valley of ashes." But the Middle West too
is stagnant. There "dwellings are still called through dec-
ades by a family's name"; one is oppressed by the "inter-
minable inquisitions" and by a moral code which demands
that life survive as a tradition rather than flow dynamically
into the future. It follows, therefore, that West Egg, the
Eastern analogy of the Middle West, should also end in a
"valley of ashes," and that *both* East and West Egg should
be imperfect ovals "crushed flat at the contact end,"
equally defective in their reception to life.

Fundamentally *Gatsby* is, as Nick says, "a story of the
West, after all." It begins in the Middle West, makes a
"riotous excursion" into the heart of Eastern promise, and
returns to the Middle West in what at first appears to be
disillusionment. Actually, of course, it is an affirmation of
the true values following on disillusionment: the initial
image of Middle Western stolidity resolves itself into a
closing image of Middle Western solidity. Upon Nick's
return from war the Middle West, "instead of being the
warm centre of the world . . . seemed like the ragged edge

231

of the universe." Coming East to learn the bond business he settles down in West Egg in a "small eyesore" of a house to enjoy "the consoling proximity of millionaires" and to plumb if he can "the shining secrets that only Midas and Morgan and Maecenas knew." Having just left the restrictive environment of the Middle West, he is at first especially aware of the free flow of life in the East, although he is also aware that it is intimately associated with the free flow of wealth. He speaks of Tom and Daisy as drifting "here and there . . . wherever people were rich together." But they "drift unrestfully," and he sees that Tom "would drift on forever seeking, a little wistfully, for the dramatic turbulence of some irrecoverable football game." Like Gatsby's dream, the Buchanans' drifting is an effort to recover in the present some of the lost sensations of the past as well as the sensibilities of youth which, in Americans, alone seem capable of deep response.

But Nick's first impression of the East is one of exciting, restless movement, and throughout the scene of his visit with the Buchanans his enchantment with their kinetic radiance alternates with moments of insight into their superficiality. Their lawn "started at the beach and ran toward the front door for a quarter of a mile, jumping over sundials and brick walks and burning gardens—finally when it reached the house drifting up the side in bright vines as though from the momentum of its run." Tom appears to be "leaning aggressively forward," filling his "glistening boots until he strained the top lacing, and you could see a great pack of muscle shifting when his shoulder moved under his thin coat." Inside the house as well everything seems to be flowing, but only because of a momentary breeze. "A breeze blew through the room, blew curtains in at one end

and out the other like pale flags, twisting them up toward the frosted wedding-cake of the ceiling, and then rippled over the wine-colored rug, making a shadow on it as wind does on the sea." On the "only completely stationary object in the room" Daisy and Jordan appear to be "buoyed up as though upon an anchored balloon." But as soon as Tom shuts the window, the wind dies, and the floating effect proves to have been only an appearance. Nick is charmed and intrigued by the appearances, but soon begins to recognize them for what they are. Tom and Daisy make only a "polite, pleasant effort to entertain and be entertained. They knew that presently dinner would be over and a little later the evening, too, would be over and casually put away." There is little meaning or sincerity in what is going on. Daisy suddenly declares that Nick is an "absolute rose," but he realizes that she is only "extemporizing." Daisy and Jordan converse in language that "was as cool as their white dresses and their impersonal eyes in the absence of all desire." Inevitably Nick compares the scene with similar occasions in the West "where an evening was hurried from phase to phase toward its close, in a continually disappointed anticipation, or else in sheer nervous dread of the moment itself." But here in the East among expatriated Middle Westerners even anticipation has been lost; all desire is dead; the Buchanans are the spent shadows of action. "You make me feel uncivilized, Daisy," Nick says. "Can't you talk about crops or something," and the "or something *substantial*" is implied.

233

In the second chapter culminating in the party at Tom's New York apartment the contrast of place motifs is reinforced by an implicit symbolism relating place to dream and ultimately to Gatsby. The natives of West Egg are

depicted as a race of the living dead, "ash grey men . . . who move dimly and already crumbling through the powdery air." Only Myrtle Wilson is alive: "there was an immediately perceptible vitality about her as if the nerves of her body were continually smouldering." She alone is free of the "white ashen dust" which veiled her husband's "dark suit and pale hair as it veiled everything in the vicinity," and we learn later that she has remained alive and uncontaminated because she is nourished by her dream of an eventually legal life with Tom in the West.

During the party a change occurs in Myrtle which pictorializes a crucial fact about the nature of her own dream and, by implication, Gatsby's. Although the dream has kept her alive, now that she is surrounded by circumstances approaching those of its fulfillment she undergoes an ugly transformation: "the intense vitality that had been so remarkable in the garage was converted into impressive hauteur." She now presents a pathetic, ridiculous figure dressed in expensive clothes that contrast sharply with her commonness and her "violent and obscene language." Apparently the dream, by the very fact of its existence, can be lifegiving, but as it approaches realization it invests life with inconsistency and vulgarity: it is doomed to remain a "Platonic conception," an ideal incapable of embodiment in fact, particularly when the fact can only be material. But Myrtle's dream is a long way from realization. It is confined, as it turns out permanently, to illegality and the East.

For Nick the party represents a vulgarization of what he previously experienced at the Buchanans. The "flow" of the East has become confusion. "People disappeared, reappeared, made plans to go somewhere and then lost each

234

other, searched for each other, found each other a few feet away." There is a photograph on the wall apparently of "a hen sitting on a blurred rock. Looked at from a distance, however, the hen resolved itself into a bonnet, and the countenance of a stout old lady beamed down into the room." It seems to him that there is a "blurred air" to the faces in the room, and in a fatuous effort to restore order he wipes from McKee's cheek "the spot of dried lather that had worried [him] all afternoon." But he is still "simultaneously within and without, simultaneously enchanted and repelled by the inexhaustible variety of life." Tom has told Myrtle that he cannot get a divorce because his wife is a Catholic, and although Nick is "a little shocked at the elaborateness of the lie," he has not yet learned to relate the lie, in all its elaborateness, to the false promise of the East or to the larger lie on which his whole experience rests.

But we cannot help but see the relation, just as we cannot help but see Nick, Myrtle, and the Buchanans as actors in a dumb show caricaturing Gatsby's tragedy. Like Nick, Gatsby is enchanted by the "shining secrets" of the East and mistakes the purposeless movement for the free flow of life into the future; like Myrtle he is given vitality by a dream that is far larger than any possibility of fulfillment; and like the Buchanans he is thwarted in his efforts to "repeat the past." He shares with them all the deficiency which makes them "subtly unadaptable to Eastern life," but he also shares their fate of inhabiting a culture in which dreams along with most demands of the spirit have no place. He aspires to the good life as though it were a thing of the spirit, while the culture can afford him the means only for a life of material achievement—a material woman or a

235

woman corrupted by materialism. In his aloofness from his own material possessions he dramatizes his uncompromising faith that life can and will yield more, if only he can manipulate circumstances properly. And it is no more than the justice of irony that he should finally be thwarted by an utterly faithless, but infinitely more powerful materialism than his own. For the Buchanans' wealth is not a means to the fulfillment of any dream: it is the hard fact of life against which the hard fact of Gatsby's manipulations can have no effect. It is also ironic that the illusions of Gatsby's party guests are seen in conjunction with his cold and aloof factualness, and that this factualness is the product of an illusion far more romantic than theirs. The guests come to his parties in pursuit of some final ecstasy, some ultimate good time which the American Dream has always promised them. Gatsby is the self-appointed agent of that dream, but they can never get close to him or discover his true identity, just as neither he nor they can hope to discover an identity for the dream.

It is dramatically just, therefore, that at the close of the novel Nick should relate Gatsby's aspiration to the feelings aroused in the early Dutch voyagers to America by their first glimpse of the " fresh, green breast of the new world."

236

> For a transitory enchanted moment man must have held his breath in the presence of this continent, compelled into an aesthetic contemplation he neither understood nor desired, face to face for the last time in history with something commensurate to his capacity for wonder. . . . And as I sat there brooding on the old, unknown world, I thought of Gatsby's wonder when he first picked out the green light at the end of Daisy's dock. He had come a long way to this blue lawn, and his

dream must have seemed so close that he could hardly fail to grasp it. He did not know that it was already behind him, somewhere back in that vast obscurity beyond the city, where the dark fields of the republic rolled on under the night.

It is perhaps too much to say, as at least one critic has, that Gatsby is a symbol of America itself. But he is a major figure in the legend created by the complex fate of being American, and he is the hero of the tragic limitations of that fate in a world which, as the eclipsing myth of the twenties recedes, seems more contemporary than we knew.

THE DEATH OF LOVE IN *THE SUN ALSO RISES*

HEMINGWAY, 1926

by MARK SPILKA

> She turns and looks a moment in the glass,
> Hardly aware of her departed lover;
> Her brain allows one half-formed thought to pass:
> "Well now that's done: and I'm glad it's over."
> When lovely woman stoops to folly and
> Paces about her room again, alone,
> She smoothes her hair with automatic hand,
> And puts a record on the gramophone.
>
> T. S. Eliot, *The Waste Land*

One of the most persistent themes of the twenties was the death of love in World War I. All the major writers recorded it, often in piecemeal fashion, as part of the larger postwar scene; but only Hemingway seems to have caught it whole and delivered it in lasting fictional form. His

intellectual grasp of the theme might account for this. Where D. H. Lawrence settles for the shock of war on the Phallic Consciousness, or where Eliot presents assorted glimpses of sterility, Hemingway seems to design an extensive parable. Thus, in *The Sun Also Rises*, his protagonists are deliberately shaped as allegorical figures: Jake Barnes and Brett Ashley are two lovers desexed by the war; Robert Cohn is the false knight who challenges their despair; while Romero, the stalwart bullfighter, personifies the good life which will survive their failure. Of course, these characters are not abstractions in the text; they are realized through the most concrete style in American fiction, and their larger meaning is implied only by their response to immediate situations. But the implications are there, the parable is at work in every scene, and its presence lends unity and depth to the whole novel.

Barnes himself is a fine example of this technique. Cut off from love by a shell wound, he seems to suffer from an undeserved misfortune. But as most readers agree, his condition represents a peculiar form of emotional impotence. It does not involve distaste for the flesh, as with Lawrence's crippled veteran, Clifford Chatterley; instead Barnes lacks the power to control love's strength and durability. His sexual wound, the result of an unpreventable " accident " in the war, points to another realm where accidents can always happen and where Barnes is equally powerless to prevent them. In Book II of the novel he makes this same comparison while describing one of the dinners at Pamplona: " It was like certain dinners I remember from the war. There was much wine, an ignored tension, and a feeling of things coming that you could not prevent happening." This fear of emotional consequences is the key to

239

Barnes' condition. Like so many Hemingway heroes, he has no way to handle subjective complications, and his wound is a token for this kind of impotence.

It serves the same purpose for the expatriate crowd in Paris. In some figurative manner these artists, writers, and derelicts have all been rendered impotent by the war. Thus, as Barnes presents them, they pass before us like a parade of sexual cripples, and we are able to measure them against his own forbearance in the face of a common problem. Whoever bears his sickness well is akin to Barnes; whoever adopts false postures, or willfully hurts others, falls short of his example. This is the organizing principle in Book I, this alignment of characters by their stoic qualities. But stoic or not, they are all incapable of love, and in their sober moments they seem to know it.

For this reason they feel especially upset whenever Robert Cohn appears. Cohn still upholds a romantic view of life, and since he affirms it with stubborn persistence, he acts like a goad upon his wiser contemporaries. As the narrator, Barnes must account for the challenge he presents them and the decisive turn it takes in later chapters. Accordingly, he begins the book with a review of Cohn's boxing career at Princeton. Though he has no taste for it, college boxing means a lot to Cohn. For one thing, it helps to compensate for anti-Semitic treatment from his classmates. More subtly, it turns him into an armed romantic, a man who can damage others in defense of his own beliefs. He also loves the pose of manhood which it affords him and seems strangely pleased when his nose is flattened in the ring. Soon other tokens of virility delight him, and he often confuses them with actual manliness. He likes the idea of a mistress more than he likes his actual mistress; or

he likes the authority of editing and the prestige of writing, though he is a bad editor and a poor novelist. In other words, he always looks for internal strength in outward signs and sources. On leaving Princeton, he marries " on the rebound from the rotten time . . . in college." But in five years the marriage falls through, and he rebounds again to his present mistress, the forceful Frances Clyne. Then, to escape her dominance and his own disquiet, he begins to look for romance in far-off countries. As with most of his views, the source of this idea is an exotic book:

> He had been reading W. H. Hudson. That sounds like an innocent occupation, but Cohn had read and reread " The Purple Land." " The Purple Land " is a very sinister book if read too late in life. It recounts splendid imaginary amorous adventures of a perfect English gentleman in an intensely romantic land, the scenery of which is very well described. For a man to take it at thirty-four as a guidebook to what life holds is about as safe as it would be for a man of the same age to enter Wall Street direct from a French convent, equipped with a complete set of the more practical Alger books. Cohn, I believe, took every word of " The Purple Land " as literally as though it had been an R. G. Dun report.

Cohn's romanticism explains his key position in the parable. He is the last chivalric hero, the last defender of an outworn faith, and his function is to illustrate its present folly—to show us, through the absurdity of his behavior, that romantic love is dead, that one of the great guiding codes of the past no longer operates. " You're getting damned romantic," says Brett to Jake at one point in the novel. " No, bored," he replies, because for this generation

241

boredom has become more plausible than love. As a foil to his contemporaries, Cohn helps to reveal why this is so.

Of course, there is much that is traditional in the satire on Cohn. Like the many victims of romantic literature, from Don Quixote to Tom Sawyer, he lives by what he reads and neglects reality at his own and others' peril. But Barnes and his friends have no alternative to Cohn's beliefs. There is nothing here, for example, like the neat balance between sense and sensibility in Jane Austen's world. Granted that Barnes is sensible enough, that he sees life clearly and that we are meant to contrast his private grief with Cohn's public suffering, his self-restraint with Cohn's deliberate self-exposure. Yet, emasculation aside, Barnes has no way to measure or control the state of love; and though he recognizes this with his mind and tries to act accordingly, he seems no different from Cohn in his deepest feelings. When he is alone with Brett, he wants to live with her in the country, to go with her to San Sebastian, to go up to her room, to keep her in his own room, or to keep on kissing her—though he can never really act upon such sentiments. Nor are they merely the yearnings of a tragically impotent man, for eventually they will lead Barnes to betray his own principles and to abandon self-respect, all for the sake of Lady Ashley. No, at best he is a restrained romantic, a man who carries himself well in the face of love's impossibilities, but who seems to share with Cohn a common (if hidden) weakness.

The sexual parade continues through the early chapters. Besides Cohn and his possessive mistress, there is the prostitute Georgette, whom Barnes picks up one day "because of a vague sentimental idea that it would be nice to eat with some one." Barnes introduces her to his friends as his

242

fiancée, and as his private joke affirms, the two have much in common. Georgette is sick and sterile, having reduced love to a simple monetary exchange; but like Barnes, she manages to be frank and forthright and to keep an even keel among the drifters of Paris. Together they form a pair of honest cripples, in contrast with the various pretenders whom they meet along the Left Bank. Among the latter are Cohn and Frances Clyne, the writer Braddocks and his wife, and Robert Prentiss, a rising young novelist who seems to verbalize their phoniness: "Oh, how charmingly you get angry," he tells Barnes. "I wish I had that faculty." Barnes' honest anger has been aroused by the appearance of a band of homosexuals, accompanied by Brett Ashley. When one of the band spies Georgette, he decides to dance with her; then one by one the rest follow suit, in deliberate parody of normal love. Brett herself provides a key to the dizzy sexual medley. With a man's felt hat on her boyish bob, and with her familiar reference to men as fellow "chaps," she completes the distortion of sexual roles which seems to characterize the period. For the war, which has unmanned Barnes and his contemporaries, has turned Brett into the freewheeling equal of any man. It has taken her first sweetheart's life through dysentery and has sent her present husband home in a dangerous state of shock. For Brett these blows are the equivalent of Jake's emasculation; they seem to release her from her womanly nature and expose her to the male prerogatives of drink and promiscuity. Once she claims these rights as her own, she becomes an early but more honest version of Catherine Barkley, the English nurse in Hemingway's next important novel, *A Farewell to Arms*. Like Catherine, Brett has been a nurse on the Italian front and has lost a sweetheart in the war; but for her

243

there is no saving interlude of love with a wounded patient, no rigged and timely escape through death in childbirth. Instead she survives the colossal violence, the disruption of her personal life, and the exposure to mass promiscuity, to confront a moral and emotional vacuum among her postwar lovers. With this evidence of male default all around her, she steps off the romantic pedestal, moves freely through the bars of Paris, and stands confidently there beside her newfound equals. Ironically, her most recent conquest, Robert Cohn, fails to see the bearing of such changes on romantic love. He still believes that Brett is womanly and therefore deeply serious about intimate matters. After their first meeting, he describes her as "absolutely fine and straight" and nearly strikes Barnes for thinking otherwise; and a bit later, after their brief affair in the country, he remains unconvinced "that it didn't mean anything." But when men no longer command respect, and women replace their natural warmth with masculine freedom and mobility, there can be no serious love.

Brett does have some respect for Barnes, even a little tenderness, though her actions scarcely show abiding love. At best she can affirm his worth and share his standards and perceptions. When in public, she knows how to keep her essential misery to herself; when alone with Barnes, she will express her feelings, admit her faults, and even display good judgment. Thus her friend, Count Mippipopolous, is introduced to Barnes as "one of us." The count qualifies by virtue of his war wounds, his invariable calmness, and his curious system of values. He appreciates good food, good wine, and a quiet place in which to enjoy them. Love also has a place in his system, but since he is "always in love," the place seems rather shaky. Like Jake and Brett

and perhaps Georgette, he simply bears himself well among the postwar ruins.

The count completes the list of cripples who appear in Book I. In a broader sense, they are all disaffiliates, all men and women who have cut themselves off from conventional society and who have made Paris their permanent playground. Jake Barnes has introduced them, and we have been able to test them against his stoic attitudes toward life in a moral wasteland. Yet such life is finally unbearable, as we have also seen whenever Jake and Brett are alone together, or whenever Jake is alone with his thoughts. He needs a healthier code to live by, and for this reason the movement in Book II is away from Paris to the trout stream at Burguete and the bull ring at Pamplona. Here a more vital testing process occurs, and with the appearance of Bill Gorton, we get our first inkling of its nature.

Gorton is a successful writer who shares with Barnes a love for boxing and other sports. In Vienna he has helped to rescue a splendid Negro boxer from an angry and intolerant crowd. The incident has spoiled Vienna for him, and as his reaction suggests, the sports world will provide the terms of moral judgment from this point onward in the novel. Or more accurately, Jake Barnes' feelings about sports will shape the rest of the novel. For with Hemingway, the great outdoors is chiefly a state of mind, a projection of moral and emotional attitudes onto physical arenas, so that a clear account of surface action will reproduce these attitudes in the reader. In " Big Two-Hearted River," for example, he describes Nick Adams' fishing and camping activities along a trout stream in Michigan. His descriptions run to considerable length, and they are all

carefully detailed, almost as if they were meant for a fishing manual. Yet the details themselves have strong emotional connotations for Nick Adams. He thinks of his camp as "the good place," the place where none of his previous troubles can touch him. He has left society behind him, and as the story begins, there is even a burnt town at his back, to signify his disaffiliation. He has also walked miles to reach an arbitrary camp site, and this is one of the ways in which he sets his own conditions for happiness and then lives up to them. He finds extraordinary pleasure, moreover, in the techniques of making coffee and pitching camp, or in his responses to fishing and eating. In fact, his sensations have become so valuable that he doesn't want to rush them: they bring health, pleasure, beauty, and a sense of order which is sorely missing in his civilized experience; they are part of a healing process, a private and imaginative means of wiping out the damages of civilized life. When this process is described with elaborate attention to surface detail, the effect on the reader is decidedly subjective.

The same holds true, of course, for the fishing trip in *The Sun Also Rises*. As Barnes and Gorton approach "the good place," each item in the landscape is singled out and given its own importance. Later the techniques of fishing are treated with the same reverence for detail. For like Nick Adams, these men have left the wasteland for the green plains of health; they have traveled miles, by train and on foot, to reach a particular trout stream. The fishing there is good, the talk free and easy, and even Barnes is able to sleep well after lunch, though he is usually an insomniac. The meal itself is handled like a mock religious ceremony: "Let us rejoice in our blessings," says Gorton. "Let us utilize the fowls of the air. Let us utilize the produce of

the vine. Will you utilize a little, brother? " A few days later, when they visit the old monastery at Roncevalles, this combination of fishing, drinking, and male camaraderie is given an edge over religion itself. With their English friend, Harris, they honor the monastery as a remarkable place, but decide that " it isn't the same as fishing "; then all agree to " utilize " a little pub across the way. At the trout stream, moreover, romantic love is given the same comparative treatment and seems sadly foolish before the immediate joys of fishing:

> It was a little past noon and there was not much shade, but I sat against the trunk of two of the trees that grew together, and read. The book was something by A. E. W. Mason, and I was reading a wonderful story about a man who had been frozen in the Alps and then fallen into a glacier and disappeared, and his bride was going to wait twenty-four years exactly for his body to come out on the moraine, while her true love waited too, and they were still waiting when Bill came up [with four trout in his bag]. . . . His face was sweaty and happy.

As these comparisons show, the fishing trip has been invested with unique importance. By sticking closely to the surface action, Barnes has evoked the deeper attitudes which underly it and which make it a therapeutic process for him. He describes himself now as a " rotten Catholic " and speaks briefly of his thwarted love for Brett; but with religion defunct and love no longer possible, he can at least find happiness through private and imaginative means. Thus he now constructs a more positive code to follow: as with Nick Adams, it brings him health, pleasure, beauty and order, and helps to wipe out the damage of his troubled life in Paris.

Yet somehow the code lacks depth and substance. To gain these advantages, Barnes must move to Pamplona, which stands roughly to Burguete as the swamp in "Big Two-Hearted River" stands to the trout stream. In the latter story, Nick Adams prefers the clear portion of the river to its second and more congested heart:

> In the swamp the banks were bare, the big cedars came together overhead, the sun did not come through, except in patches; in the fast deep water, in the half light, the fishing would be tragic. In the swamp fishing was a tragic adventure. Nick did not want it. . . . There were plenty of days coming when he could fish the swamp.

The fishing is tragic here because it involves the risk of death. Nick is not yet ready for that challenge, but plainly it will test his manhood when he comes to face it. In *The Sun Also Rises* Barnes makes no such demands upon himself; but he is strongly attracted to the young bullfighter, Pedro Romero, whose courage before death lends moral weight to the sportsman's code.*

So Pamplona is an extension of Burguete for Barnes: gayer and more festive on the surface, but essentially more

---

* Hemingway's preoccupation with death has been explained in various ways: by his desire to write about simple, fundamental things; by his "sado-masochism"; or more fairly and accurately, by his need to efface an actual war wound, or to supplant the ugly, senseless violence of war with ordered, graceful violence. Yet chiefly the risk of death lends moral seriousness to a private code which lacks it. The risk is arbitrary; when a man elects to meet it, his beliefs take on subjective weight and he is able to give meaning to his private life. In this sense, he moves forever on a kind of imaginative frontier, where the opposition is always Nature, in some token form, where the stakes are always manliness and self-respect, and where death invests the scene with tragic implications. In *The Sun Also Rises*, Romero lives on such a frontier, and for Barnes and his friends he provides an example of just these values.

serious. The spoilers from Paris have arrived, but (Cohn excepted) they are soon swept up by the fiesta: their mood is jubilant, they are surrounded by dancers, and they sing, drink and shout with the peasant crowd. Barnes himself is among fellow *aficionados*; he gains "real emotion" from the bullfights and feels truly elated afterwards. Even his friends seem like "such nice people," though he begins to feel uneasy when an argument breaks out between them. The tension is created by Brett's fiancé, Mike Campbell, who is aware of her numerous infidelities and who seems to accept them with amoral tolerance. Actually he resents them, so that Cohn (the perennial Jewish scapegoat) provides him with a convenient outlet for his feelings. He begins to bait him for following Brett around like a sick steer.

Mike's description is accurate enough. Cohn is always willing to suffer in public and to absorb insults for the sake of true love. On the other hand, he is also "ready to do battle for his lady," and when the chance finally comes, he knocks his rivals down like a genuine knight-errant. With Jake and Mike he has no trouble, but when he charges into Pedro's room to rescue Brett, the results are disastrous: Brett tells him off, the bullfighter refuses to stay knocked down, and no one will shake hands with him at the end, in accord with prep-school custom. When Brett remains with Pedro, Cohn retires to his room, alone and friendless.

249

This last encounter is the highpoint of the parable, for in the Code Hero, the Romantic Hero has finally met his match. As the clash between them shows, there is a difference between physical and moral victory, between chivalric stubbornness and real self-respect. Thus Pedro fights to repair an affront to his dignity; though he is badly beaten,

his spirit is untouched by his opponent, whereas Cohn's spirit is completely smashed. From the beginning Cohn has based his manhood on skill at boxing, or upon a woman's love, never upon internal strength; but now, when neither skill nor love supports him, he has bludgeoned his way to his own emptiness. Compare his conduct with Romero's, on the following day, as the younger man performs for Brett in the bull ring:

> Everything of which he could control the locality he did in front of her all that afternoon. Never once did he look up. . . . Because he did not look up to ask if it pleased he did it all for himself inside, and it strengthened him, and yet he did it for her, too. But he did not do it for her at any loss to himself. He gained by it all through the afternoon.

Thus, where Cohn expends and degrades himself for his beloved, Romero pays tribute without self-loss. His manhood is a thing independent of women, and for this reason he holds special attractions for Jake Barnes.

By now it seems apparent that Cohn and Pedro are extremes for which Barnes is the unhappy medium. His resemblance to Pedro is clear enough: they share the same code, they both believe that a man's dignity depends on his own resources. His resemblance to Cohn is more subtle, but at this stage of the book it becomes grossly evident. Appropriately enough, the exposure comes through the knockout blow from Cohn, which dredges up a strange pre-war experience:

> Walking across the square to the hotel everything looked new and changed. . . . I felt as I felt once coming home from an out-of-town football game. I was carrying a suitcase with my football

things in it, and I walked up the street from the station in the town I had lived in all my life and it was all new. They were raking the lawns and burning leaves in the road, and I stopped for a long time and watched. It was all strange. Then I went on, and my feet seemed to be a long way off, and everything seemed to come from a long way off, and I could hear my feet walking a great distance away. I had been kicked in the head early in the game. It was like that crossing the square. It was like that going up the stairs in the hotel. Going up the stairs took a long time, and I had the feeling that I was carrying my suitcase.

Barnes seems to have regressed here to his youthful football days. As he moves on up the stairs to see Cohn, who has been asking for him, he still carries his "phantom suitcase" with him; and when he enters Cohn's room, he even sets it down. Cohn himself has just returned from the fight with Romero: "There he was, face down on the bed, crying. He had on a white polo shirt, the kind he'd worn at Princeton." In other words, Cohn has also regressed to his abject college days: they are both emotional adolescents, about the same age as the nineteen-year-old Romero, who is the only real man among them. Of course, these facts are not spelled out for us, except through the polo shirt and the phantom suitcase, which remind us (inadvertently) of one of those dreamlike fantasies by the Czech genius, Franz 251 Kafka, in which trunks and youthful clothes are symbols of arrested development. Yet there has already been some helpful spelling out in Book I, during a curious (and otherwise pointless) exchange between Cohn and another expatriate, the drunkard Harvey Stone. After first calling Cohn a moron, Harvey asks him to say, without thinking about it, what he would rather do if he could do anything he

wanted. Cohn is again urged to say what comes into his head first, and soon replies, " I think I'd rather play football again with what I know about handling myself, now." To which Harvey responds: " I misjudged you. . . . You're not a moron. You're only a case of arrested development."

The first thought to enter Cohn's mind here has been suppressed by Barnes for a long time, but in Book II the knockout blow releases it: more than anything else, he too would like to "play football again," to prevent that kick to his head from happening, or that smash to the jaw from Cohn, or that sexual wound which explains either blow. For the truth about Barnes seems obvious now: he has always been an emotional adolescent. Like Nick Adams, he has grown up in a society which has little use for manliness; as an expression of that society, the war has robbed him of his dignity as a man and has thus exposed him to indignities with women. We must understand here that the war, the early football game, and the fight with Cohn have this in common: they all involve ugly, senseless, or impersonal forms of violence, in which a man has little chance to set the terms of his own integrity. Hence for Hemingway they represent the kinds of degradation which can occur at any point in modern society—and the violence at Pamplona is our current sample of such degradation. Indeed, the whole confluence of events now points to the social meaning of Jake's wound, for just as Cohn has reduced him to a dazed adolescent, so has Brett reduced him to a slavish pimp. When she asks for his help in her affair with Pedro, Barnes has no integrity to rely on; he can only serve her as Cohn has served her, like a sick romantic steer. Thus, for love's sake, he will allow her to use him as a go-between, to disgrace him with his friend, Montoya, to

252

corrupt Romero, and so strip the whole fiesta of significance. In the next book he will even run to her rescue in Madrid, though by then he can at least recognize his folly and supply his own indictment: " That was it. Send a girl off with one man. Introduce her to another to go off with him. Now go and bring her back. And sign the wire with love. That was it all right." It seems plain, then, that Cohn and Brett have given us a peacetime demonstration, postwar style, of the meaning of Jake's shell wound.

At Pamplona the demonstration continues. Brett strolls through the fiesta with her head high, " as though [it] were being staged in her honor, and she found it pleasant and amusing." When Romero presents her with a bull's ear " cut by popular acclamation," she carries it off to her hotel, stuffs it far back in the drawer of the bed-table, and forgets about it. The ear was taken, however, from the same bull which had killed one of the crowd a few days before, during the dangerous bull-run through the streets; later the entire town attended the man's funeral, along with drinking and dancing societies from nearby communities. For the crowd, the death of this bull was a communal triumph and his ear a token of communal strength; for Brett the ear is a private trophy. In effect, she has robbed the community of its triumph, as she will now rob it of its hero. As an *aficionado*, Barnes understands this threat too well. These are decadent times in the bull ring, marred by false aesthetics; Romero alone has " the old thing," the old " purity of line through the maximum of exposure ": his corruption by Brett will complete the decadence. But mainly the young fighter means something more personal to Barnes. In the bull ring he combines grace, control and sincerity with manliness; in the fight with Cohn he proves

253

his integrity where skill is lacking. His values are exactly those of the hunter in "Francis Macomber," or of the fisherman in *The Old Man and the Sea*. As one of these few remaining images of independent manhood, he offers Barnes the comfort of vicarious redemption. Brett seems to smash this as she leaves with Pedro for Madrid. To ward off depression, Barnes can only get drunk and retire to bed; the fiesta goes on outside, but it means nothing now: the "good place" has been ruined.

As Book III begins, Barnes tries to reclaim his dignity and to cleanse himself of the damage at Pamplona. He goes to San Sebastian and sits quietly there in a cafe, listening to band concerts; or he goes swimming there alone, diving deep in the green waters. Then a telegram from Brett arrives, calling him to Madrid to help her out of trouble. At once he is like Cohn again, ready to serve his lady at the expense of self-respect. Yet in Madrid he learns to accept, emotionally, what he has always faintly understood. As he listens to Brett, he begins to drink heavily, as if her story has driven home a painful lesson. Brett herself feels "rather good" about sending Pedro away: she has at least been able to avoid being "one of these bitches that ruins children." This is a moral triumph for her, as Barnes agrees; but he can scarcely ignore its implications for himself. For when Brett refuses to let her hair grow long for Pedro, it means that her role in life is fixed: she can no longer reclaim her lost womanhood; she can no longer live with a fine man without destroying him. This seems to kill the illusion which is behind Jake's suffering throughout the novel: namely, that if he hadn't been wounded, if he had somehow survived the war with his manhood intact, then

he and Brett would have become true lovers. The closing lines confirm his total disillusionment:

> "Oh, Jake," Brett said, "we could have had such a damned good time together."
> Ahead was a mounted policeman in khaki directing traffic. He raised his baton. The car slowed suddenly pressing Brett against me.
> "Yes," I said, "Isn't it pretty to think so?"

"Pretty" is a romantic word which means here "foolish to consider what could *never* have happened," and not "what can't happen now." The signal for this interpretation comes from the policeman who directs traffic between Brett's speech and Barnes' reply. With his khaki clothes and his preventive baton, he stands for the war and the society which made it, for the force which stops the lovers' car, and which robs them of their normal sexual roles. As Barnes now sees, love itself is dead for their generation. Even without his wound, he would still be unmanly, and Brett unable to let her hair grow long.

Yet according to the opening epigraphs, if one generation is lost and another comes, the earth abides forever; and according to Hemingway himself, the abiding earth is the novel's hero. Perhaps he is wrong on this point, or at least misleading. There are no joyous hymns to the seasons in this novel, no celebrations of fertility and change. The scenic descriptions are accurate enough, but rather flat; there is no deep feeling in them, only fondness, for the author takes less delight in nature than in outdoor sports. He is more concerned, that is, with baiting hooks and catching trout than with the Irati River and more pleased with the grace and skill of the bull-fighter than with the bull's magnificence. In fact, it is the bullfighter who seems to

255

abide in the novel, for surely the bulls are dead like the trout before them, having fulfilled their roles as beloved opponents. But Romero is very much alive as the novel ends. When he leaves the hotel in Madrid, he "pays the bill" for his affair with Brett, which means that he has earned all its benefits. He also dominates the final conversation between the lovers, and so dominates the closing section. We learn here that his sexual initiation has been completed and his independence assured. From now on, he can work out his life alone, moving again and again through his passes in the ring, gaining strength, order, and purpose as he meets his own conditions. He provides no literal prescription to follow here, no call to bullfighting as the answer to Barnes' problems; but he does provide an image of integrity, against which Barnes and his generation are weighed and found wanting. In this sense, Pedro is the real hero of the parable, the final moral touchstone, the man whose code gives meaning to a world where love and religion are defunct, where the proofs of manhood are difficult and scarce, and where every man must learn to define his own moral conditions and then live up to them.

THE STILLNESS OF *LIGHT IN AUGUST*

FAULKNER, 1932

by ALFRED KAZIN

Light In August begins unforgettably with a pregnant
young woman from Alabama sitting beside a road in Mississippi, her feet in a ditch, her shoes in her hand, watching
a wagon that is mounting the hill toward her with a noise
that carries for a half mile " across the hot still pinewiney
silence of the August afternoon." She has been on the road
for a month, riding in a long succession of farmwagons or
walking the hot dusty roads with her shoes in her hand,
trying to get to Jefferson. There, she firmly expects, she
will find her lover working in a planing mill and ready to
marry her, and there—that is the big city—she will put
her shoes on at last.

This opening chapter, so dry and loving in its pastoral

humor, centering on the picture of Lena and her precious burden being carried in one wagon or another, by one farmer after another, to her hoped-for destination in a husband, ends sharply on the outskirts of Jefferson, from which she can see smoke going up from a burning house. It is the house of Joanna Burden, who has just been murdered by Joe Christmas. The images that have crowded us—the dust and heat of the unending road; the young woman continually amazed at how far a body can go; the serenity of her face, "calm as a stone, but not hard"; the "sharp and brittle crack and clatter" of identical and anonymous wagons "weathered and ungreased wood and metal"; the mules plodding in a steady and unflagging hypnosis; the drowsy heat of the afternoon; Lena's faded blue dress, her palm leaf fan, her small bundle in which she carries thirty-five cents in nickles and dimes, and the shoes that she takes off and carries in her hand as soon as she feels the dust of the road beneath her feet—all these, we soon discover, provide us with that foundation in the local and the provincial, the earth and the road which man must travel on it, against which are set images of fire and murder, of aimless wandering and of flight, embodied in the figure who soon enters the book and dominates it in his remorseless gray anonymity. Joe Christmas does not even have a name of his own, only a mocking label stuck on him at the orphanage where he was deposited one Christmas Eve. "Joe Christmas" is worse than any real name could be, for it indicates not only that he has no background, no roots, no name of his own, but that he is regarded as a *tabula rasa*, a white sheet of paper on which anyone can write out an identity for him and make him believe it.

It is the contrast of Lena Grove and Joe Christmas, of

258

the country girl and the American wanderer, who is a stranger even to himself, the ultimate personification of modern loneliness, that frames the book—literally so, since Lena Grove begins and ends it, while Joe Christmas's agony and crucifixion are enacted as within a circle round which he runs in an effort to catch up with himself. When he finds that he cannot run out of this circle and stands still at last in order to die, the book comes back to Lena Grove and ends on her ritualistic procession up the road with her baby and Byron Bunch—Faulkner's version of the Holy Family. By the time we have finished *Light In August*, we have come to feel that the real greatness of Faulkner in this book (and indeed of his extraordinary compassion) lies in the amazing depth which he brings to this contrast of which American writers—particularly in the South—are so fond: between the natural and the urban, between Lena Grove's simplicity and the world in which Joe Christmas walks all city pavements with the same isolation and indifference, eats at the coldly smooth wooden counter, and is murdered. Faulkner even leads up to a strange and tortured fantasy of Joe Christmas as Lena Grove's still unnamed son. There is virtually an annunciation to Lena, in the moving last phase of the book when Lena, delivered of her child just as Joe Christmas is running for his life, hears Mrs. Hines, Christmas's grandmother, calling the baby " Joey "— he who is a " nigger " murderer, and whom Lena has never seen. The reader comes to this with a shock, only because of Faulkner's reckless, desperate eagerness to wrest all the possible implications from his material, to think it out interminably, since there is no end to all one's possible meditations round and round the human cycle. One of the conflicts of which the book is made—between life and anti-

259

life, between the spirit of birth and the murderous abstractions and obsessions which drive most of the characters—is in Faulkner himself, in his attempt to will his painful material into a kind of harmony that it does not really possess.

But in any event, it is Lena who opens the book, Lena's world, Lena's patience, that set the ideal behind the book—that world of the permanent and the natural which Joe Christmas seeks all his life without knowing that he does, and seeking it, runs full tilt into the ground. "Light In August" is itself a country saying: light as a mare or a cow is light after delivery. And it is this world of Lena Grove from Doane's Mill—the tiny hamlet too small for any post-office list, though Lena, living in the backwoods, had not seen it until her parents died—with the sound of the wagon wheel taking her away from it, that becomes in the book not merely a world that Faulkner celebrates but a mythic source of strength. As indeed it is. For it is this intense sense of the earth, this superb registering of country sights and sounds as the stillness is broken by the creaking and lumbering wagon coming up the hill, that is the secret of Southern writing. In his attachment to the irretrievable, in his obstinate feeling for the earth, the good Southern writer makes so much writing in America seem as shallow as if it had been composed by a young instructor in English sitting in his study surrounded by manuals on the great novels. Albert Camus, talking appreciatively about Southern novelists, once remarked to a friend of mine that what he liked about their books was "the dust and the heat." And to the man from North Africa, with his memories of the blazing world described in *Noces*, that world into which Paris can never enter, Faulkner's sense of local color must be especially

moving. But after all, it is this sense of place that is the great thing about American writing. It is the " mossy scabs of the worm fence, heap'd stones, elder, mullein and poke-weed " in *Song Of Myself*; the landscape that in *Walden* seems always to be reflected in water; the strong native sense of the here and now that is the basis of Emerson's esthetic; the edge of the world seen from Hemingway's Michigan woods; " reading the river " in *Life On The Mississippi* and *Huckleberry Finn*; the " snow, the real snow " seen only beyond Chicago that Scott Fitzgerald described so rapturously in his memories of Midwesterners in Eastern colleges going home for Christmas. And if we ask what is so remarkable about that sense of place which is, after all, essential to imaginative writing, the answer is that we Americans are in fact just the opposite of the homogeneous mass we are always trying to be, and that what distinguishes American writing is exactly the fact that we are strangers to each other and that each writer describes his own world to strangers living in the same land with himself.

Now of all parts of the United States the South is certainly the strangest to the others; it is, in fact—or used to be—a separate nation. And almost all the good Southern writers have this sense of local color to an extreme, for to the degree that the South is what it is because of its rural background, its " backwardness," its isolation, its comparatively homogeneous white population—to that degree does the American's need to value and venerate his own region or place as the only escape from American bigness, American smoothness, American abstractness, American slogans, the juggernaut of American progress, find (at least it used to find) its deepest expression in the South. Even poverty, which in America certainly is a disgrace, becomes

261

in Southern writing a sign of the natural man (Huckleberry Finn) or the earth-mother (Lena Grove). And, as so often happens in Southern writing—for sensitive Southerners are likely to feel that they are lost in the modern industrial world and, in mourning their traditional homeland, to see the immediate world around them as damned—Faulkner's pictures of the impersonal modern world, the opposite of Lena's sacred grove, are lurid. As Lena is all fertility, so the others are all barrenness. Destruction, fire, obsession, inhumanity, anonymity, the "frictionsmooth" wooden counter at which Joe Christmas eats, the hard cold eyes of Bobbie the prostitute and Mame the madam and Max the pimp—these against the images of locality, the farmers in their faded and patched but clean overalls, and of time, the wagon along the road and the "heelgnawed porch" of the country store around which the farmers sit. As soon as we get to Jefferson, we catch the typical dialectic of life and anti-life, the contrast of birth and destruction on which the book is built, in the fact that the slow patient rhythms of Lena, the wagon, the road, are immediately followed by the whine of the saw in the planing mill, the reiteration of *smooth*. The world is narrowing down to the contest between the good Christian laborer, Byron Bunch, the very essence of the common ordinary good man, and those who, like Lena's seducer, have either taken on a name which is not their own, "Brown," a name too conventional even to be *his* name, or who, like Joe Christmas, have no name to begin with.

This contrast is familiar enough in Southern opinion, and one can find the same horror of miscegenation, of uprooting, of the city man's anonymity, in any expression of Southern agrarianism. But Faulkner does not stop at the abstraction of the alien: he carries it on, he carries it out

to astonishing lengths. And it is this intensity of conception that makes the portrait of Joe Christmas so compelling rather than believable, that makes him a source of wonder, of horror, yet above all of pity, rather than of pleasure in the creation of a real human being. For Joe Christmas remains, as he is born, an abstraction; from the moment he appears, " there was something definitely rootless about him, as though no town nor city was his, no street, no walls, no square of earth his home." He comes to work in the only clothes he has, a serge suit and a white shirt; and Byron Bunch, watching him, knows that Joe Christmas " carried his knowledge with him always as though it were a banner, with a quality ruthless, lonely, and almost proud." So from the moment Joe Christmas appears, he is seen as what others say about him, he is only a thought in other people's minds. More than this, he is looked at always from a distance, as if he were not quite human, which in many ways he is not.

We see Joe Christmas from a distance, and this distance is the actual space between him and his fellows. It is also the distance between the name " Joe Christmas," which is clownish, and the actual suffering of someone who has to live up to the non-humanity of his name, to the obsession (founded on hearsay, not on actual evidence) that his father had " some " Negro blood in him. Joe Christmas, then, is really " man " trying to discover the particular kind of man he is. He is an abstraction created by the racist mania of his grandfather, a former preacher whose tormented life is spent insisting that Negroes are guilty in the eyes of God and must serve white men. When his daughter ran away with a " Mexican " circus hand, Doc Hines not only killed the man, and after his daughter died in childbirth on Christmas Eve, left the baby on the steps of an orphanage, but

263

later took a job as a janitor in the orphanage in order to make sure that his "nigger" grandson would never be allowed to contaminate anyone. This obsession about race goes hand in hand with a Calvinist obsession of the elect and of the hopeless sinfulness of others, an obsession which is found both in Joe Christmas's rigidly doctrinaire foster-father, Calvin MacEachern, and in his future mistress, Joanna Burden, a descendant of New Hampshire Puritans who remains in the South though she is the sworn enemy of its ways. All these obsessions about purity and guilt are, Faulkner indicates, the remnants of an inhuman religion that has added bigotry and arrogance to the curse of slavery. They are the symbols of a church that has lost its spiritual function and that has been deserted by the Reverend Gail Hightower, who spends his days in endless reveries of the South's irretrievable glory. The obsessions are all summed up in the fate of Joe Christmas, who is trying to become *someone*, a human being, to find the integrity that is so ripely present in Lena Grove. Lena does not have to try; her symbol is the wheel on the road. Joe Christmas's is flight: flight on the same road, but flight toward himself, which he cannot reach, and away from hatred of himself, which he cannot escape. Only his pursuers catch up with him, to murder and to castrate him.

Joe Christmas is an abstraction seeking to become a human being. In the race-mad South, many a Negro—and Mexican, and Jew—is turned into an abstraction. But this man is *born* an abstraction and is seeking to become a person. He is an orphan, brought up in a foundling home, who in earliest childhood is watched by his own grandfather as if he were a caged beast. He is then bribed by the dietitian, whom he has heard making love with the interne, as

if he knew enough to betray her. He is adopted by a farmer who re-names him, lectures him, starves him, beats him for not learning the catechism. He is robbed and beaten by the pimp of the prostitute with whom he has fallen in love. He is constantly treated by his Negrophile mistress, Joanna Burden, as if his own personality were of no account and is beseeched in her sexual transports as "Negro." And finally, after being starved, betrayed, flogged, beaten, pursued by bloodhounds, he is castrated. The essential picture behind Joe Christmas is his grandfather's carrying him to the orphanage and then from it in a savage parody of loving care. Joe Christmas is nothing but the man things are done to, the man who has no free will of his own, who is constantly seeking a moment of rest ("When have I ever eaten in peace?") and who looks for an identity by deliberately provoking responses that will let him be *someone*, if only as a white man among Negroes, or as someone calling himself a Negro in an effort to shock the white prostitute he has just slept with. His passivity, his ability to lend himself to situations and to people who will "carry" him for a while, is immense and pitiful.

Joe Christmas is the most solitary character in American fiction, the most extreme phase conceivable of American loneliness. He is never seen full face, but always as a silhouette, a dark shadow haunting others, a shadow upon the road he constantly runs—a foreshadowing of his crucifixion, which, so terrible and concentrated is his suffering, already haunts the lives of others like a black shadow. For, almost *because* he does not look it, he becomes the "Negro," or the thought of, the obsession with, Negroes in the minds of those who, looking at Joe Christmas, can think of nothing else. And Joanna Burden, whose abolitionist grandfather

265

was murdered in the South, whose whole life has been an obstinate carrying on, deep inside Mississippi, of her family's coldly abstract espousal of Negroes, shows us how much of an abstraction Joe Christmas is when she makes love crying to him " Negro! Negro! " Whether the " Negro " represent the white man's guilt or the white man's fear, he is always a thought in the white's mind, and—in the South— an obsession. So Joanna Burden, who befriends him, and Doc Hines, who hates him, come to see in him the cause of guilt that is finally the image of guilt. " I thought," Joanna says to her lover,

> of all the children coming forever and ever into the world, white, with the black shadow already falling upon them before they drew breath. And I seemed to see the black shadow in the shape of a cross. And it seemed like the white babies were struggling, even before they drew breath, to escape from the shadow that was not only upon them but beneath them, too, flung out like their arms were flung out, as if they were nailed to the cross.

> And she quotes her father:

> " In order to rise, you must raise the shadow with you. But you can never lift it to your level. I see that now, which I did not see until I came down here. But escape it you cannot. The curse of the black race is God's curse. But the curse of the white race is the black man who will be forever God's chosen own because He once cursed Him."

266

The grounds of this obsession, then, can be a compassion for the Negro that is as profound as hatred, and equally removed from brotherhood. This compassion seems to me the essence of Faulkner's approach to Joe Christmas, and the triumph of the book is Faulkner's ability to keep his

leading character a shadow, and yet to make us feel all his suffering. Compare Joe Christmas with the types of the Northerner, the city man, the "stranger" in Southern writing, to say nothing of the Negro, and you realize that where so many neo-orthodox Southern literary critics are hysterically fearful of the "stranger," Faulkner, by a tremendous and moving act of imagination, has found in Joe Christmas the incarnation of "man"—that is, of modern man, reduced entirely to his unsupported and inexplicable human feelings. There are no gods in Faulkner's world; there are only men—some entirely subject to circumstances, some protesting against them, and some even moved to change them. The hero of *A Fable* is of the last; Joe Christmas is of the first. He is human to us because of the experiences he undergoes, but his passivity is so great that he is finally a body castrated, a mere corpse on a dissection table—or someone whose body has been turned into the host, material for a ritual, so that his last agony will earn him the respect he never earned while he was alive. He is not, like the Christ of *A Fable*, a man who gives new meaning to life; like Benjy in *The Sound And The Fury*, he is an incarnation of human suffering, unable to speak—except in the tremendous action near the end of the book when he stops running from his pursuers and waits for them, and attains in this first moment of selfhood, the martyrdom that ends it.

267

We see Joe Christmas always from a distance. This distance from ourselves to him seems to me the key to the book, for it explains why Joe exists for us principally as a man who is described, not seen. He is so far away that we cannot see him; he is reported to us. And this distance is filled with the stillness of a continuous meditation. *Light*

In August tells a story of violence, but the book itself is curiously soundless, for it is full of people thinking to themselves about events past. As soon as Lena Grove arrives in Jefferson, at the end of the first chapter, the story of Joe Christmas comes to us through flashbacks, through talk by the other men at the planing mill, through a whole chapter of summary biography, Chapter VI, through rumors and gossip of the townspeople, and at the very end, when Joe Christmas's whole story is put together for us, by Gavin Stevens's telling a stranger about the grandparents. Almost everything we learn about Joe Christmas comes to us in the form of hearsay, accusation, the tortured memories of others; even his death is told as an incident in the life of his murderer, Percy Grimm. All these reports about the stranger sufficiently suggest his alienation. But in themselves they also create that stillness, that depth of meditation into which all the characters are plunged.

This meditation begins in Joe Christmas himself, who in his distance from other men is constantly trying to think himself back to life, and who, without knowing exactly how his ordeal began—and certainly not why—finds himself like a caged animal going over and over the same ground. We hear him talking to himself, and we follow his slow and puzzled efforts to understand the effect of his actions upon others. We see him as a child in the orphanage, eating the toothpaste, frightening the dietitian out of her wits because he is staring straight at her trying to understand what she is accusing him of. We watch him walking the path between his cabin and Joanna Burden's house for his meals, thinking out everything he finds between the four walls of her kitchen. Finally we watch him running, and thinking deliriously in his flight, until, in that magnificent and piercing

scene near the end of his flight, he falls asleep as he runs. The pressure of thought, the torture of thought, is over-whelming—and useless—since Joe Christmas does not know who he is and so cannot locate the first cause of his misery. But still he thinks, he broods, he watches, he waits. And it is this brooding silence in him, fixed in attention over he knows not what, that explains why he is so often described in the book as looking like a man in prayer—even like a "monk." There is a strange and disturbing stillness about him that eases him, more swiftly than most men, into the stillness of non-being.

The stillness of the book has, of course, an immense reverberation within it. Describing Doc Hines, Faulkner notes about him "a quality of outworn violence like a scent, an odor," and the actual violence of Joe Christmas is always felt about him even when he sits rigidly still at counters like a man in prayer. When Joe's past history is run off in the rapid newsreel style of Dos Passos, one feels not only his personal insignificance, but the just leashed violence of American life of which Joe is, in his way, completely the creature:

> He stepped from the dark porch, into the moonlight, and with his bloody head and his empty stomach hot, savage, and courageous with whiskey, he entered the street which was to run for fifteen years.

269

> The whiskey died away in time and was re-newed and died again, but the street ran on. From that night the thousand streets ran as one street, with imperceptible corners and changes of scene, broken by intervals of begged and stolen rides, on trains and trucks, and on country wagons with he at twenty and twenty-five and thirty sitting on the seat with his still, hard face and the clothes

(even when soiled and worn) of a city man and
the driver of the wagon not knowing who or what
the passenger was and not daring to ask.

Yet it is a stillness of thought that generally pervades the
book, in the form of enormous meditations by which
Faulkner tries to lift his material into place. The stillness
is interrupted by shooting, burning, beating, the barking of
blood-hounds and Percy Grimm's mutilation of Joe Christmas, which interrupts the pervading stillness like the sound
which nails must make when they are driven into wood
through human flesh. Yet, just behind this obvious figure of
the Roman soldier torturing Christ, there is a pastoral world.
As Irving Howe has noted, the arrangement of the book
" resembles an early Renaissance painting—in the foreground
a bleeding martyr, far to the rear a scene of bucolic peace-
fulness, with women quietly working in the fields." Despite
its violence, *Light In August* is one of the few American
novels that remind one of the humanized and tranquil landscape in European novels. Its stillness is rooted in the
peaceful and timeless world which Lena Grove personifies
and in which she has her being. It is the stillness of the
personal darkness inside which Joe Christmas lives. But his
stillness is also the sickly, after-dark silence of the Reverend
Gail Hightower sitting in his study, with his stale clothes
and stale thoughts, going over and over the tragedy of his
life, his grandfather's " glorious " death, his wife's desertion
and suicide—and finally and typically summing it all up into
a stale round of human illusion and defeat. Faulkner wishes
us to understand that Hightower finally cuts the gordian
knot of his thoughts when he delivers Lena's baby and is
struck down by Percy Grimm as he stands between him
and Joe Christmas. But Hightower, whether brooding out

upon the street, or sitting behind the green lamp in his parlor when he receives Byron Bunch, his only visitor, enlarges the stillness, increases its weight, by personifying what is immediately present in the book, and throughout Faulkner's novels—the Southern effort to explain, to justify, and through some consummation in violent physical action even to lighten, the burden of this obsession with the past.

Hightower, by general consent, is one of the failures of the book: he is too vague, too drooping, too formless, in a word too much the creature of defeat and of obsession, to compel our interest or our belief. But this is so partly because Hightower is both a surrogate figure for Faulkner's meditations and a kind of scapegoat on whom Faulkner can discharge his exasperation with Southern nostalgia and the endless searching in the labyrinths of the past for the explanation of the Southern defeat and of the hold it keeps on the descendants of the Confederate aristocracy. Hightower is a failure because Faulkner both uses and parodies him. Because of the absurdly literal symbolism of his name, his constant watchful position behind the green lamp, his useless reveries, he is never on the same scale with the other characters, who are equally obsessed by the past, but who function on the plane of some positive action. Hightower not only lives by his thoughts; he has no life but his thoughts. We miss in him the life-like element of violence (the only possible end to characters so entirely formed of reverie) that we find in Joanna Burden's degeneration, in Joe Christmas's hatred, in Percy Grimm's fanaticism, in Doc Hines's mania. Hightower, acting in various sections of the book as a foreground observer, brings to them not merely a stillness but a deadness which intervenes between us and the other characters. This shapeless, ghostly body of

271

thought has its symbolic place in the mind of Hightower. For just as his life is over, and he has no function but to brood, so Faulkner has signified in Hightower that wholly retrospective, watchful concern, not with the past but with their bondage to the past, that seems to be the essence of what Faulkner's characters are always thinking about.

Joe Christmas, Joanna Burden, Gail Hightower—each of these is the prisoner of his own history, and is trying to come to terms with this servitude in his own mind. None of them can ever lift themselves out of the labyrinth by taking thought. But in this effort to think man's life out of the circumstances that enclose it, Faulkner sees the condition of man. Man is engulfed in events that are always too much for him. Hightower, listening to Byron Bunch make plans for Lena's confinement, thinks: " It is because so much happens. Too much happens. That's it. Man performs, engenders, so much more than he can or should have to bear. That's how he finds out that he can bear anything. That's it. That's what is so terrible. That he can bear anything, anything." Endurance, as we know, is the key-word in Faulkner's system of values. At least this was so up to *A Fable*. There, as Faulkner himself has told us, the highest value is represented not by the young Jewish pilot officer who says, " This is terrible. I refuse to accept it, even if I must refuse life to do so "; not by the old French quartermaster general who says, " This is terrible, but we can weep and bear it," but by the English battalion runner who says, " This is terrible, I'm going to do something about it." *Light In August* does not arrive at this step. Man never thinks of changing the world; it is all he can do to get a grip on it, to understand some part of what has happened to him and to endure all of it. Any release that occurs is a

purely individual one, as when Hightower finally frees himself, in the one profoundly unselfish act of his life, by delivering Lena's baby. In the freshness of the early morning, after Lena has given birth, Hightower feels that he is in touch with the earth again—the symbol throughout the book of rightness, authenticity, peace. But the earth is not his life, as it is Lena Grove's. Man's highest aim in this book is to meet his destiny without everlasting self-concern. Yet this profoundly tragic cast to *Light In August*, so much like a Hardy novel in the implacable pattern that unrolls against a country background and the inarticulate stillness of its leading characters, is matched by Faulkner's ironic awareness that man, in his endless brooding over events, can never stop, that the event is nothing compared with the speculation that follows and in a sense replaces it. One of the most revealing phrases in Faulkner's rhetoric is: "not that"—it is not peace, not an end, that his people ever want. The violence may be "outworn," but it is the human passion. He describes his chorus, the townspeople, scurrying around Joanna Burden's house after her murder, looking "for someone to crucify":

> But there wasn't anybody. She had lived such a quiet life, attended so to her own affairs, that she bequeathed to the town in which she had been born and lived and died a foreigner, an outlander, a kind of heritage of astonishment and outrage, for which, even though she had supplied them at last with an emotional barbecue, a Roman holiday almost, they would never forgive her and let her be dead in peace and quiet. Not that. Peace is not that often. So they moiled and clotted, believing that the flames, the blood, the body that had died three years ago and had just now begun to live

again, cried out for vengeance, not believing that
the rapt infury of the flames and the immobility of
the body were both affirmations of an attained
bourne beyond the hurt and harm of man. Not
that.

We can never let the event go, for that would mean an
end to the human history that is lived in retrospection. Just
as Faulkner's language is full of words, like "avatar" and
"outrage," which are really private symbols left over from
his unceasing meditation, and just as his style is formed
from the fierce inner pressure of problems which give no
solution, so the actual texture of *Light In August* suggests,
in the tension and repetition of certain verbal motifs, that
man can never quite say what the event originally meant,
or what he is to think of it now. Language never quite
comes up to the meaning of events. To adapt Faulkner's
phrase, it is not that, or that. The townspeople exist in
Light In August, as in so many Faulkner novels, to ask
questions whose very function is to deny the possibility of
an answer. Faulkner's grim sarcastic asides show that he
views language as in some basic sense unavailing. The
astounding repetition of certain key phrases and verbal
rhythms in his work signifies his return back and back on
the question.

Call the event history, call it the Fall: man is forever
engaged in meditating, not the past itself, for that would
bring knowledge, but man's guilt, for that may bring freedom. Guilt, not history, is the nightmare from which all of
Faulkner's deepest characters are trying to escape. The
guilt arises from man's endless complicity in his own history,
as when the innocent, gravely staring child that Joe Christmas was, ate toothpaste and listened to the dietitian making
love. Hightower is guilty because his sickly, foolish nos-

274

talgia for his grandfather's one day of glory made him un-available to his own wife, who committed suicide; Joanna Burden feels so guilty that she has remained an alien in the Southern town in which she was born, accepting her isola-tion as the price of her identification both with her Aboli-tionist forbears, who were shot down in the South, and with the Negroes, on whom a curse must have been laid. Even Doc Hines and Percy Grimm murder in order to " clean " life of the stain that Negroes have put on it, for as the Negroes were cursed by God, so they have cursed life, and the maniac " saviors " of Southern racial purity have to save their hallowed country from contagion. But just as no one of them can really distinguish the hate they feel for others from self-accusation, so no one can say with whom guilt began, where the ultimate human crime was committed. The paths which lead back to the human past are endless through the human brain, and sitting at his study window after he has gained new self-respect by delivering Lena's baby and by standing up to Percy Grimm, the dying Hightower still ruminates, goes over and over the past, as " the final copper light of afternoon fades " and " the world hangs in a green suspension in color and texture like through colored glass." The everlasting reverie begins again, but now the wheel of life that brought Lena Grove to Jefferson begins to slow down, runs into sand, " the axle, the vehicle, the power which propels it not yet aware." These memories are endless, and the style in which they are described is over-colored in a way that shows how static action often becomes in Faulkner's work, how much it serves as the raw material for reflection, which is why he can lavish so many Joycean compound words on objects which do not seem to move of their own accord, but to be rallying points in Faulkner's tortured concern with guilt.

275

Guilt is endless; in the labyrinths of the mind, there is turning, but no deliverance. Like T. S. Eliot, Faulkner is a favorite today because he takes his stand on human guilt; this is the side of ourselves that we can recognize, and, curiously, stand by; for in this alone, as we feel, is the possibility of our freedom. When men feel so wretchedly small before their own past, they must be guilty. So runs the legend. This is the argument behind Faulkner's novels: of the God who made Yoknapatawpha County. In the beginning, life was free and good and natural; but something inexplicable, a curse, was put on it. Perhaps the curse is nothing more than man's effort to get the better of events that are "too much for us"; the evil lies in arrogance. Doc Hines hears God addressing him personally, ordering him to act for Him. Calvin MacEachern, Joe Christmas's adopted father, starves and beats him because he cannot memorize portions of the catechism on order. "He asked that the child's stubborn heart be softened and that the sin of disobedience be forgiven him also, through the advocacy of the man whom he had flouted and disobeyed, requesting that the Almighty be as magnanimous as himself, and by and through and because of conscious grace." Even Joanna Burden tries to play God to her Negro charges. *Light In August* is one of the sharpest criticisms of Calvinism ever written, but unlike so many Southern writers on Puritanism, Faulkner knows that the same religion is found in Doc Hines and Joanna Burden. The guilt that is the mainstay of their faith is embodied in the assumption of excessive authority by fathers, law-givers, teachers, ministers. Everyone wants to play God to the orphan Joe Christmas. In Faulkner's eyes, life is an ironic and tragic affair that is beyond human rule and mis-rule; but Calvinists

like Doc Hines and Calvin MacEachern, the children of Calvinists like Joanna Burden, even murdering simon-pure "patriots" like Percy Grimm, take life in their hands, they dominate and they murder. Joe Christmas is their favorite pupil; he is the man "things are done to." His final ignominy comes when his mistress, Joanna Burden, regarding him in her new phase as a Negro charge to be "brought up," tells him that she wants him to go to school so that he can become a lawyer. And it is at this point that he breaks. It is this point that has always been the signature of the everlasting victim. Other men are the law-givers; the law is passed out to him, through him, inflicted on him. And so finally he murders and dies, a pure victim, shot, castrated, treated like a thing. It is the final ignominy. But in the very unattainability of his suffering, in its inexpressibility, is the key to his healing power over others. For where life exists so much in the relation of master to man, of the elect to the sinner, the only possible consummation man can ever reach, for Joe Christmas as for Uncle Tom, is in the final consistency of his suffering, in a fate so extreme that it becomes a single human word which men can read. This is what Faulkner means in that exalted passage after Joe Christmas's immolation:

> . . . when they saw what Grimm was doing one of the men gave a choked cry and stumbled back into the wall and began to vomit. Then Grimm too sprang back, flinging behind him the bloody butcher knife. "Now you'll let white women alone, even in hell," he said. But the man on the floor had not moved. He just lay there, with his eyes open and empty of everything save consciousness, and with something, a shadow, about his mouth. For a long moment he looked up at

277

them with peaceful and unfathomable and unbearable eyes. Then his face, body, all, seemed to collapse, to fall in upon itself, and from out the slashed garments about his hips and loins the pent black blood seemed to rush like a released breath. It seemed to rush out of his pale body like the rush of sparks from a rising rocket; upon that black blast the man seemed to rise soaring into their memories forever and ever. They are not to lose it, in whatever peaceful valleys, beside whatever placid and reassuring streams of old age, in the mirroring faces of whatever children they will contemplate old disasters and newer hopes. It will be there, musing, quiet, steadfast, not fading and not particularly threatful, but of itself alone serene, of itself alone triumphant.

Joe Christmas has attained the stillness that will finally allow us to see him. Of sufferings alone is he made, and in this sense, and in this sense alone, is he a figure whose condition is so total that he reminds us of Christ in the sense of Christ's integrality. That tortured and would-be Christian philosopher, Simone Weil, understood this when she found that *malheur*, affliction, could become so much in itself that she felt riven to the universe by bonds of pain. The arch-victim may not be a "martyr," as students of totalitarianism have noticed; but there is a kind of suffering in our time which is so extreme that it becomes an integral *fact* of the human condition. Father Zossima bowed down to Dmitri Karamazov because of all the affliction he would undergo. So marvellous is Faulkner's compassion, he can visualize in the man who was nothing but a victim, the shadow thrown from the Cross of Christ, who was nothing, as it were, but Himself. Men are men because events are always "too much" for them; Joe Christmas became one

with his life in that extreme moment when even he had no longer to search out the past. The figure on the Cross is the most tremendous interventive symbol in history; the castrated man on the floor has only one free power in his life—to stop running at last and to face his murderer. Faulkner intends no parody; he is moved by the likeness of totality to totality. But neither is he a Christian. There is no redemption; there is not even in *A Fable*—but there man has the courage to redeem circumstances by denying their fatality. In *Light In August*, the past is not merely exigent; it is malicious, the spirit of pure bad luck, a godlike force that confronts man at every turn with everything he has been, and so seems to mock and to oppose him. This spirit is called "The Player": Lena's seducer, "Brown," still running away from her at the last, sends a Negro boy to the sheriff for the reward money he has earned in informing on Joe Christmas, but knows despairingly that he will never see the money.

> 'He wont do it. He cant do it. I know he cant find him, cant get it, bring it back.' He called no names, thought no names. It seemed to him now that they were all just shapes like chessmen—the negro, the sheriff, the money, all—unpredictable and without reason moved here and there by an Opponent who could read his moves before he made them and who created spontaneous rules which he and not the Opponent, must follow.

279

This is the Opponent that Joe Christmas decides finally not to elude again, the "Player" who moves Percy Grimm unerringly from position to position:

> He was beside the ditch now. He stopped, motionless in midstride. Above the blunt, cold rake

of the automatic his face had that serene, unearthly luminousness of angels in church windows.
He was moving again almost before he had stopped,
with that lean, swift, blind obedience to whatever
Player moved him on the Board. He ran to the
ditch.

All things are fated; man is in any place because the
Player moved him there. Our past sets up the positions
into which we fall. This is why Joe Christmas's grandmother, Mrs. Hines, utters the most significant lines in the
book when, at the end, she pitifully cries:

> "I am not saying that he never did what they
> say he did. Ought not to suffer for it like he made
> them that loved and lost suffer. But if folks could
> maybe just let him for one day. Like it hadn't
> happened yet. Like the world never had anything
> against him yet. Then it could be like he had just
> went on a trip and grew man grown and come
> back. If it could be like that for just one day."

And it is in these terms that we come to understand why
Joe Christmas, in running away from a past that he cannot
escape, seems constantly to be looking back as he runs.
Not only is no one free of his past; he even has, at the most
critical moments, the sense of not moving at all, but of
being silently lifted from position to position. It is because
of this curious effect of immobility in Faulkner's characters
as they run (as if they were held up in the air by wires)
that Faulkner can lavish such idle poetic largesse upon
them: can see in a Percy Grimm that "serene, unearthly
luminousness of angels in church windows," and at various
points throughout the book emphasize Joe Christmas's rigid
likeness to a man in prayer. Even the countrymen in overalls move at one point "with almost the air of monks in a

280

cloister." The reason is that all these characters are lost in contemplation as they are moved here and there by the Player. There is no free action for anyone; everyone is carried, as Lena Grove was carried to Jefferson in a whole succession of farmwagons, by the fate that was and so shall be.

Faulkner's world is grim—a world in which the past exerts an irresistible force, but against which there is no supernatural sanction, no redeeming belief. He believes in original sin, but not in divine love, and he is endlessly bemused by the human effort to read fate or to avoid it. The highest reach of his belief is the effort to become "a saint without God" (Albert Camus), but this is a point not yet tried for in *Light In August*. Correspondingly, there is great power in his work, but little color, and *Light In August*, for all its brilliance, somehow wears the lack-lustre look of the year in which it was published, 1932. It is a grim book, and the countryside described in it already has the pinched, rotted look that one sees in so many depression novels about the South. The greatest fault of the book is its over-schematic, intellectualized past. Although Faulkner himself has lived more like Joe Christmas than like the Sartorises, he is socially far from the world of Joe Christmas and Lena Grove, and there are tell-tale signs in the novel that it is written *down*—for Faulkner, too much from his head down, and about people whom he tends to generalize and to over-praise, as if he saw them only as symbols rather than as entirely complex beings. And it is a simple fact that the opening of *Light In August* is so beautiful that nothing after quite comes up to it.

On the other hand, it is one of Faulkner's greatest

books, and although it does not have the blazing directness of *The Sound And The Fury* (a book written more directly out of Faulkner's own experience), it has much of the creative audacity which is Faulkner's highest ideal in art. With this book, published in 1932, Faulkner completed a period of extraordinary fertility. He was only thirty-five; since 1929, he had published, in rapid order, *Sartoris*, *The Sound And The Fury*, *As I Lay Dying*, *Sanctuary*, and *Light In August*. It was a period of tremendous creative power. When he was recently in Japan, Faulkner said of this period:

> I think there's a period in a writer's life when he, well, simply for lack of any other word, is fertile and he just produces. Later on, his blood slows, his bones get a little more brittle, his muscles get a little stiff, he gets perhaps other interests, but I think there's one time in his life when he writes at the top of his talent plus his speed, too. Later the speed slows; the talent doesn't necessarily have to fade at the same time. But there's a time in his life, one matchless time, when they are matched completely. The speed, and the power and the talent, they're all there and then he is . . . 'hot.' "

Light In August comes out of that "one matchless time." The only possible objection one can have to the book is the number of implications which Faulkner tries to bring out of his material—for just as the characters' own lives are "set" for them to mull over, so Faulkner constantly mulls over them, wringing a poetry that has grandeur but also an intensity of contemplation that is sometimes more furious in expression than meaningful in content. If we see Faulkner's narrative method as essentially recollective, in the form of individual meditation over past

events, we can recognize the advantage he has over most "naturalistic" writers and we understand why Faulkner refers to himself as a "poet." For what makes the portrait of Joe Christmas so astonishing is the energy of imagination lavished upon it, the consistency of texture that derives from the poet's sense that he has not only to *show*, in the modern realistic sense, but to *say*—that is, to tell a story which follows from his contemplation of the world, and which preserves, in the nobility of its style and in the serene independence of its technique, the human victory over circumstances.

It is this that makes us hear Faulkner's own voice throughout the book, that allows him to pull off the tremendous feat of making us believe in a character who in many ways is not a human being at all—but struggling to become one. And this, after all, is the great problem of the novelist today. Joe Christmas is an incarnation not only of the "race problem" in America, but of the condition of man. More and more, not merely the American novel, but all serious contemporary novels, are concerned with men who are not real enough to themselves to be seriously in conflict with other men. Their conflicts, as we say, are "internal"; for they are seeking to become *someone*. Joe Christmas lives a life that is not only solitary but detached. He lives in society physically, but actually he is concerned only with the process of self-discovery, or of self-naming, even of self-legalization. This is a fate which, as we know, can be as arduous and deadly as that of the classic heroes. But in Joe Christmas's case, there is no conflict from positions of strength, no engagement between man and man— only the search of the "stranger," *l'étranger*, to become man.

283

NOTES ON THE CONTRIBUTORS

JOHN W. ALDRIDGE, a devoted and controversial critic of contemporary fiction, was co-founder of *Discovery* magazine and has contributed to such periodicals as *Partisan Review*, *The Nation*, and *Harpers*. He is the author of *After the Lost Generation* (1951) and *In Search of Heresy* (1956), as well as the editor of *Critiques and Essays on Modern Fiction* (1952). He has taught at Sarah Lawrence College, New York University, and The New School For Social Research.

RICHARD CHASE, Associate Professor of English at Columbia University, is a Fellow of the Indiana University School of Letters. His books include *Quest for Myth* (1949), *Herman Melville* (1949), and *Emily Dickinson* (1951). Dr. Chase's critical essays have appeared in many of our leading literary magazines. Doubleday recently published his *The American Novel and Its Tradition*.

One of America's most distinguished men of letters, MALCOLM COWLEY is perhaps best known for his *Exile's Return* (1934), a saga of the post World War I expatriate writers. His publications include essays, poetry, and translations. Mr. Cowley has edited works of Hemingway, Hawthorne, Whitman, and Fitzgerald. His latest book is *The Literary Situation* (1951). An editor for Viking Press, he has been honored with the presidency of the National Institute of Arts and Letters.

DAVID BRION DAVIS' first book, *Homicide in American Fiction, 1798-1860*, was published last fall. His essays on American fiction and American history have appeared in *American Quarterly*, *The New England Quarterly*, and *The Western Humanities Review*. Dr. Davis is Assistant Professor of History at Cornell University.

GEORGE P. ELLIOTT, currently on a *Hudson Review* Fellowship in fiction, has over thirty published short stories to his credit. His first novel is scheduled for publication this winter, and he recently edited *Fifteen Modern American Poets* (1956). He has taught at Cornell University, Barnard College, and St. Mary's College (California).

HERBERT GOLD, novelist—*Birth of a Hero* (1951), *The Prospect Before Us* (1954), and *The Man Who Was Not With It* (1956)—critic, and short story writer, has taught at Wayne State University, the State University of Iowa, and Brandeis University. He has been awarded a Guggenheim fellowship and is working on a new novel.

GRANVILLE HICKS, literary consultant for *The New Leader*, is the author of eleven books, among them *The Great Tradition* (1933), *Small Town* (1946), and *Where We Came Out* (1954). He co-edited *Proletarian Literature in the United States* (1935) and *The Letters of Lincoln Steffens* (1938).

ALFRED KAZIN, author of *On Native Grounds* (1942), a survey and interpretation of modern American prose

literature, is a steady contributor to the literary journals. He has written and edited works on Blake, Dostoevsky, Dreiser, Fitzgerald, and Melville. The first volume of his autobiography, *A Walker in the City*, appeared in 1951, and a collection of his essays, *The Inmost Leaf*, came out in 1955. Mr. KAZIN is now teaching at Amherst.

WALTER B. RIDEOUT has taught at Harvard and Northwestern. He worked with Howard Mumford Jones in editing the letters of Sherwood Anderson, and 1956 saw the publication of his important study, *The Radical Novel in The United States, 1900-1954: Some Interrelations of Literature and Society*. Dr. Rideout has been a holder of a Newberry Library Fellowship in Midwestern Studies.

CHARLES SHAPIRO teaches English and humanities at Wayne State University. He is co-editor of *The Stature of Theodore Dreiser* (1955) and has written for *Folio*, *The Nation*, *The New Republic*, and other periodicals. A regular book reviewer for The Louisville *Courier-Journal*, Mr. SHAPIRO has taught at Indiana University, New Mexico A. and M. College, and Occidental College.

MARK SPILKA's critical study, *The Love Ethic of D. H. Lawrence*, appeared in 1955. His essays have been published in *Accent*, *Folio*, and *19th Century Fiction*. He is a member of the University of Michigan English Department and has taught at Indiana University. He has recently completed a book on Dickens, Dostoevsky, and Kafka.

BERNARD WEISBERGER, who has taught at Swarthmore and Antioch, is now Assistant Professor of History at Wayne State University. He is the author of *Reporters for the Union* (1953) and the forthcoming *They Gathered at the River*. Dr. Weisberger is a contributor to *American Heritage*, *The Mississippi Valley Historical Review* and other journals in the field of American history.

The following are available editions of the twelve novels discussed in this book. Publisher is given. Paperback editions are indicated by an asterisk (*).

The Deerslayer: L. C. Page and Co.

The Scarlet Letter: Dodd, Mead and Co.; E. P. Dutton and Co.; Harper and Brothers; Houghton Mifflin Co.; Macmillan Co.; Modern Library; Thomas Nelson and Sons; Pocket Books;* World Publishing Co.; Ronald Press Co., edited by E. E. Leisy; Hendricks House, edited by Gordon Roper; Henry Holt and Co. in *Four Great American Novels,* edited by R. W. Short; Rinehart and Co.,* edited by A. Warren.

Moby Dick: Wm. Collins Sons; Coward-McCann; E. P. Dutton and Co.; Grosset and Dunlap; Harper and Brothers; Heritage Press; Modern Library; New American Library;* Rinehart and Co.,* edited by N. Arvin; Pocket Books,* edited by M. Geismar; Houghton Mifflin and Co.;* Simon and Schuster,* edited by E. G. Sterne; Grosset and Dunlap, edited by F. Sutton; Oxford U. Press; Hendricks House, edited by L. Mansfield and H. Vincent; Dodd, Mead and Co.; L. C. Page and Co.

Huckleberry Finn: Wm. Collins Sons; E. P. Dutton and Co.; Modern Library; Thomas Nelson and Sons; Henry Holt and Co. in *Four Great American Novels,* edited by R. W. Short; Dodd, Mead and Co.; Doubleday and Co.; Grosset and Dunlap; Harper and Brothers; Heritage Press; Pocket Books;* World Publishing Co.; Rinehart and Co.,* edited by L. Trilling.

Red Badge of Courage: Dodd, Mead and Co.; Grosset and Dunlap; Heritage Press; Modern Library; Peter Pauper Press; Pocket Books;* World Publishing Co.; Appleton-Century-Crofts, edited by M. Herzberg; Harper and Brothers; Rinehart and Co.,* edited by W. Gibson.

The Ambassadors: Harper and Brothers.

The House of Mirth: Charles Scribner's Sons.

Jennie Gerhardt: World Publishing Co.

Winesburg, Ohio: Modern Library; New American Library.*

The Great Gatsby: Charles Scribner's Sons * (hardback and paperback).

The Sun Also Rises: Charles Scribner's Sons * (hardback and paperback).

Light in August: Modern Library * (hardback and paperback).

45916

Designed by Richard Kinney
Text in Janson; Display in
Futura Bold and Futura Medium
Printed on Warren's Old Style Antique
Bound in Holliston Roxite Class C
Manufactured in the United States of America

R-400